Other Titles in the
People Who Made History Series

PEOPLE
WHO MADE
HISTORY

GALILEO

Clarice Swisher, *Book Editor*

Bonnie Szumski, *Editorial Director*
Scott Barbour, *Managing Editor*
David M. Haugen, *Series Editor*

Greenhaven Press, Inc., San Diego, CA

Every effort has been made to trace the owners of copyrighted material. The articles in this volume may have been edited for content, length, and/or reading level. The titles have been changed to enhance the editorial purpose. Those interested in locating the original source will find the complete citation on the first page of each article.

Library of Congress Cataloging-in-Publication Data

Galileo / Clarice Swisher, book editor.
        p.   cm. — (People who made history)
    Includes bibliographical references and index.
    ISBN 0-7377-0670-8 (pbk. : alk. paper) —
ISBN 0-7377-0671-6 (lib. : alk. paper)
    1. Galilei, Galileo, 1564–1642. 2. Astronomers—Italy—
Biography. I. Swisher, Clarice, 1933–   II. Series.

QB36 .G2 S93   2001
520'.92—dc21   00-051864
                                                CIP

Copyright © 2001 by Greenhaven Press, Inc.
PO Box 289009
San Diego, CA 92198-9009
Printed in the U.S.A.

CONTENTS

Chapter 1: The Major Influences on Galileo's Development

Galileo's family had been part of the upper class in Florence for many generations, a status that afforded privileges and education but carried with it duties and responsibilities. Because the culture of Florence was changing during Galileo's time, he adhered to old traditions but secretly embraced some new ideas on the horizon.

Galileo combined his classical and humanistic studies with his own zest for language to develop a new literary style that transformed Italian literature. He employed his ideas by writing critical works of poetry and gained recognition among literary scholars.

At age twenty, Galileo first studied geometry and devoted himself to mastering the works of Archimedes. Though Galileo wrote literary criticism, experimented, and invented instruments, he used these projects to prove mathematical reasoning.

Chapter 2: Galileo's Contribution to Physics

Galileo formulated a method to study events in nature. He stated a problem, defined terms, formed a hypothesis, and carried out experiments until his hypothesis could be accepted as true. Much of scientific research is still conducted in this manner.

In his meetings with the pontiff, he realized the Pope misunderstood his ideas, but he decided to go ahead with his book anyway.

Chapter 5: Galileo Lives Under House Arrest

he wrote many letters explaining his experiments and ideas. When the book was written, Galileo made secret investigations until he found a company in Holland that published it without the church's knowledge.

Chapter 6: Evaluation of Galileo's Place in History

FOREWORD

In the vast and colorful pageant of human history, a handful of individuals stand out. They are the men and women who have come variously to be called "great," "leading," "brilliant," "pivotal," or "infamous" because they and their deeds forever changed their own society or the world as a whole. Some were political or military leaders—kings, queens, presidents, generals, and the like—whose policies, conquests, or innovations reshaped the maps and futures of countries and entire continents. Among those falling into this category were the formidable Roman statesman/general Julius Caesar, who extended Rome's power into Gaul (what is now France); Caesar's lover and ally, the notorious Egyptian queen Cleopatra, who challenged the strongest male rulers of her day; and England's stalwart Queen Elizabeth I, whose defeat of the mighty Spanish Armada saved England from subjugation.

Some of history's other movers and shakers were scientists or other thinkers whose ideas and discoveries altered the way people conduct their everyday lives or view themselves and their place in nature. The electric light and other remarkable inventions of Thomas Edison, for example, revolutionized almost every aspect of home-life and the workplace; and the theories of naturalist Charles Darwin lit the way for biologists and other scientists in their ongoing efforts to understand the origins of living things, including human beings.

Still other people who made history were religious leaders and social reformers. The struggles of the Arabic prophet Muhammad more than a thousand years ago led to the establishment of one of the world's great religions—Islam; and the efforts and personal sacrifices of an American reverend named Martin Luther King Jr. brought about major improvements in race relations and the justice system in the United States.

Each anthology in the People Who Made History series begins with an introductory essay that provides a general overview of the individual's life, times, and contributions. The group of essays that follow are chosen for their accessibility to a young adult audience and carefully edited in consideration of the reading and comprehension levels of that audience. Some of the essays are by noted historians, professors, and other experts. Others are excerpts from contemporary writings by or about the pivotal individual in question. To aid the reader in choosing the material of immediate interest or need, an annotated table of contents summarizes the article's main themes and insights.

Each volume also contains extensive research tools, including a collection of excerpts from primary source documents pertaining to the individual under discussion. The volumes are rounded out with an extensive bibliography and a comprehensive index.

Plutarch, the renowned first-century Greek biographer and moralist, crystallized the idea behind Greenhaven's People Who Made History when he said, "To be ignorant of the lives of the most celebrated men of past ages is to continue in a state of childhood all our days." Indeed, since it is people who make history, every modern nation, organization, institution, invention, artifact, and idea is the result of the diligent efforts of one or more individuals, living or dead; and it is therefore impossible to understand how the world we live in came to be without examining the contributions of these individuals.

INTRODUCTION

"If friction with air becomes an unwanted nuisance, just imagine the weight in a vacuum. Much of science, in fact, is built on these pure pictures of the mind. And the equations themselves are beautiful. The equations have a precision and elegance, a magnificent serenity, an indisputable rightness." Astrophysicist Alan Lightman wrote these words for an article published in the *New York Times* on May 9, 2000, but they could have been written by Galileo Galilei in 1602. It was while teaching at the University of Padua that Galileo confirmed in his mind that observation and experiment, often mind experiments, expressed in mathematics formed the foundation of science. Moreover, he was so convinced of the "indisputable rightness" of his belief that he offended leading philosophers and theologians of his time. Before Galileo, scientists, who were still considered philosophers, focused their attention on the use of reason to search for causes of events in nature. Because of Galileo's courageous campaign to change the methods of doing science, physicist Albert Einstein called him "the father of modern physics—indeed, of modern science altogether."

A new scientific method was not Galileo's only campaign for which he fought a courageous battle. As a devoted Catholic, he worked tirelessly to persuade the church authorities to stop insisting that the earth stood still at the center of the universe with the sun revolving around it. The evidence pointed otherwise, Galileo said. If the church failed to pay attention, its authority and wisdom would soon be compromised. Galileo kept drumming the point until the Inquisition tried him for heresy and sentenced him in 1633.

Today, space ships photograph Mars and signals explore matter at the outer limits of the universe, only 370 years after Galileo was imprisoned for saying that the earth turns and revolves around the sun. Galileo's struggles remind the modern reader just how much knowledge has been gathered in a relatively short time in humankind's history. Galileo's story is a fascinating and complex web woven with his science, his genius, his humor, his determination, and the obstacles he found before him.

GALILEO GALILEI: A LIFELONG STRUGGLE FOR A NEW SCIENCE

Italian scientist Galileo Galilei used his curiosity, charm, intelligence, and unyielding determination to forge new attitudes toward science and new methods of conducting it. His enthusiastic cause for scientific changes, however, led him into controversy with philosophers and theologians, who, he discovered, had the power to silence him, at least temporarily. But the changes he advocated prevailed throughout the Western world in the centuries that followed his life. From the time of his youth, Galileo's biography is a story of rebellion, strategic planning, miscalculation, defeat, and resurgent effort.

GALILEO'S EARLY LIFE AND EDUCATION

Galileo was born in Pisa, Italy, on February 15, 1564, the first of seven children born to Giula and Vincenzio Galilei. Little is known about Giula Galilei, who came from the cloth-merchant Ammannati family. Vincenzio came from a wealthy family that had for generations been part of the ruling class. A highly cultured man, Vincenzio composed music, did research in music theory (considered then a branch of mathematics) and taught his son to sing, to play the organ and the lute, and to study the physics of sound.

In 1574, when Galileo was ten, his family moved to Florence. There Galileo attended grammar school until he was thirteen, at which time his father placed him in the Camaldolese monastery at Vallombroso for instruction in Greek, Latin, and logic. Galileo liked the quiet life and serious study at the monastery and hoped to become a monk, but his father disapproved and took his son home, where Galileo continued his education with a tutor.

In 1581, when he was seventeen years old, Galileo entered the University of Pisa, intending to study medicine according to his father's wish. He soon gained a reputation for contradicting professors who taught Aristotelian ideas concerning physics. In 1583 while attending an off-campus lecture given by the mathematician serving the grand duke of Tuscany (the region in northwest Italy in which the city of Florence lies), Galileo learned of Euclid's geometry. On his own he studied Euclid's *Elements* and took his questions to Ostile Ricci, the court mathematician, who recognized Galileo's talent and requested that Vincenzio allow his son to study mathematics instead of medicine. Vincenzio insisted on the original plan, but Galileo neglected his father's wish and switched his studies to mathematics and philosophy. In 1585, after four years at the university, Galileo left without taking a degree. He continued to study mathematics with private tutors at Florence and Siena.

In his private study, Galileo blended his passion for mathematics with observation, measurement, and design. In 1583 he observed a swinging lamp in the cathedral at Pisa and associated it with the human pulse rate as a source for measuring time. In 1586 he made his scientific debut with *The Little Balance,* detailing an "invention of hydrostatic balance for the determination of the specific gravity of bodies,"[1] a work circulated among scientists but unpublished until after Galileo's death. In 1588 he was invited to address the Florentine Academy "on the location, size, and arrangement of Hell as described in the *Inferno,*"[2] a segment of Dante's long poem *The Divine Comedy.* Galileo turned Dante's topography into a series of geometrical problems. During this period Galileo also wrote a treatise on motion, marking the beginning of his major contribution to physics, and he discovered a new, practical approach to determine the center of gravity of specified solids, a discovery that brought him recognition beyond Florence.

GALILEO TEACHES AT THE UNIVERSITY OF PISA

On the basis of this discovery, Galileo obtained the chair of mathematics (a teaching position) at the University of Pisa in 1589 with a salary of sixty scudi a year, or about three hundred dollars. Though it paid poorly, this position established Galileo as a professor. At this time, Galileo was still grappling with traditional scientific beliefs. For example, he still accepted the ancient astronomer Ptolemy's view that the earth was the center of the universe. While he was at the university, however, he was exposed to many new scientific theories. Many historians believe it was there that Galileo became acquainted with the theory of the sun-centered universe advocated by Polish astronomer Nicolaus Copernicus, and quickly became a convert. Historian Alexandre Koyré "assumes that Galileo's conversion to Copernicanism dates from these years, and closely connects this with his first studies of motion initiated at Pisa."[3]

Although the exact date of Galileo's adoption of Copernican ideas may be the subject of debate, his rejection of Aristotle at the time is not. While at the university Galileo provoked professors by arguing against the physics conclusions of Aristotle. For example, Galileo disagreed with Aristotle's statement that heavy objects fall proportionately much faster than lighter ones; Galileo thought that objects of unequal weight fall at about the same rate. "'Try, if you can,' Galileo exhorted one of his many opponents, 'to picture in your mind the large ball striking the ground while the small one is less than a yard from the top of the tower.'"[4] There developed the legendary story that Galileo dropped balls from the top of the Leaning Tower of Pisa to prove his theory. Though this story has little validity, he apparently did drop balls of varying weights from some tower in the area. These studies of motion led to his treatise, *De motu* (On Motion), in which he also speculated about reconciling Aristotle's philosophical ideas––not his scientific conclusions—with Greek mathematician Archimede's mathematical ideas. Galileo was firm in his beliefs, but he was unsure of some of his findings. Therefore, he did not publish *De motu* at the time because he felt that his conclusions needed further investigation.

Galileo did, however, publish his literary works: his criticism of two Italian poets and a satirical poem. In "Considerations on Tasso" and "Notes to Ariosto," Galileo records his annotations of the two poets' major works. In his poem "Against Wearing the Toga" Galileo lampoons the attitudes of his colleagues and the academic costume they wear in their classes. This three-hundred-line poem says that the long black robe "hid the true merits of character under a cloak of social standing . . . [and] even impeded walking, to say nothing of working."[5] It is best to go naked, he says, although he had resigned himself to wearing clothes. He did not, however, wear the toga, and at the end of the year Galileo was fined for not wearing proper academic garb.

Galileo continued to antagonize many professors and irritate those close to the court who paid his salary. After three years as a teacher, he did not expect his contract at the university to be renewed.

The news of his release from the university came at a bad time. In 1591, Galileo's father Vincenzio died, leaving Galileo, the oldest son, responsible for the expenses of the family. He paid a handsome dowry for his sister Virginia, supported his mother and brother Michelangelo, and maintained his sister Livia in a convent and later paid for her dowry when she left the convent to be married. His finances were drained. Even if his contract at the University of Pisa had been renewed, his meager salary would have been insufficient to cover his new family expenses.

Galileo Lives and Works in Padua

In 1592 the head of the Literary Academy in Florence helped Galileo obtain a position to teach geometry, mechanics, and astronomy at the University of Padua, earning him a salary three times higher than his salary at Pisa. Located twenty miles from Venice, Padua shared its rich cultural climate and atmosphere for freedom of thought, qualities appealing to Galileo. Though Galileo enjoyed his teaching and social life in Padua and Venice, he had to supplement his salary to cover family expenses. He gave "private instruction in military architecture, fortification, surveying, mechanics, and related subjects not included in the university curriculum" to "young foreign noblemen destined for military careers."[6] His most famous private pupil was Cosimo de' Medici, who became the grand duke of Tuscany and later hired Galileo as court mathematician.

Galileo further augmented his salary by making and selling scientific instruments. He established a small shop in his house and employed a skilled workman, Marcantonio Mazzoleni, whose entire family resided in Galileo's house in exchange for part of Mazzoleni's salary. The shop produced surveying instruments, compasses, magnets, thermometers, and, later, telescopes. His geometric and military compass became one of his most important inventions. "By 1599, after various modifications, the device functioned as an early pocket calculator that could compute compound interest or monetary exchange rates, extract square roots for arranging armies on the battlefield, and determine the proper charge for any size cannon."[7] Galileo made little profit on each instrument, but he charged twenty scudi for instruction on how to use it. At first he issued handwritten instructions, but finally he published a booklet to be sold with each instrument, a treatise titled *Operations of the Geometric and Military Compass of Galileo Galilei, Florentine Patrician and Teacher of Mathematics in the University of Padua.* Galileo dedicated the manual to Cosimo de' Medici.

In the late 1590s Galileo met Marina Gamba, with whom he shared his private life for twelve years but never married. Though they kept separate residences, the couple had three children: Virginia, registered in the parish of San Lorenzo in Padua as "born of fornication"; Livia Antonia, "daughter of Marina Gamba and of ____"; and Vincenzio Andrea, "son of Madonna Marina, daughter of Andrea Gamba, and an unknown father."[8] Galileo, who recognized Marina as his mate and his children as heirs to his lineage, named the girls after his sisters and his son after the boy's two grandfathers. Some historians suggest that costly family expenses left Galileo with too little money to establish a family of his own. Others suggest that Galileo never married because it was then the tradition for scholars to remain single.

GALILEO REFINES THE EXPERIMENTAL METHOD

While living and teaching at Padua, Galileo confirmed his belief that observation and experimentation form the foundation of science. In *The Turning Point*, Fritjof Capra explains the importance of this belief:

> Galileo was the first to combine scientific experimentation with the use of mathematical language to formulate the laws of nature he discovered, and is therefore considered the father of modern science. "Philosophy [science]," he believed, "is written in that great book which ever lies before our eyes [nature]; but we cannot understand it if we do not first learn the language and characters in which it is written. This language is mathematics, and the characters are triangles, circles, and other geometrical figures." The two aspects of Galileo's pioneering work—his empirical approach and his use of a mathematical description of nature—became the dominant features of science in the seventeenth century and have remained important criteria of scientific theories up to the present day.[9]

His approach to science, however, was more than a pragmatic method; it offered hope to uncover a world not seen before. As Stephen Hawking says in *A Brief History of Time*, "Galileo was one of the first to argue that man could hope to understand how the world works, and, moreover, that we could do this by observing the real world."[10]

Galileo's most important research into the way the world works involved his search for laws of motion. Between 1602 and 1609 his investigations expanded the work begun in *De motu* and included theorems on acceleration, horizontal and falling motion, projectile motion, and the parabolic curve. Galileo was fascinated by the motion of the pendulum, for example:

> not just that it swung back and forth in equal times, but that the time of the swing remained the same whether the arc through which it swung was large or small ... that the pendulum could adjust its speed so that it took the same time to return through smaller and smaller distances as its motion died down.[11]

While studying acceleration in downward motion, Galileo discovered that he could roll a ball down an inclined plane and measure the time of the rolling ball in each of the intervals he had set up along the plane. Hawking explains,

> No one until Galileo bothered to see whether bodies of different weight did in fact fall at different speeds. ... [H]e rolled balls of different weights down a smooth slope. The situation is similar to that of heavy bodies falling vertically, but it is easier to observe because the speeds are smaller. ... Galileo's measurements were used by Newton as the basis of his laws of motion.[12]

Galileo worked on problems of motion throughout his life; shortly before his death, he elaborated on them and published them in *Two New Sciences*, motion and mechanics.

Galileo's Astronomy Refutes Aristotle

In the early 1600s Galileo turned his attention from motion to astronomy. In October 1604 a supernova (an exploding star that appears very bright for a time before it burns out) was confirmed, a new star similar to the one seen in 1572 by Danish astronomer Tycho Brahe. The appearance of new stars was significant to Galileo because they refuted Aristotle's view that, in the universe, "no change could take place in the heavens, because everything in them was made of a perfect and unalterable substance called 'quintessence.'"[13] Galileo reasoned that if new stars appeared, there had indeed been changes in the heavens, and thus Aristotle's view was incorrect. For the first time he stated publicly that he favored the Copernican view of the solar system and intended to refute the earth-centered theory and oppose the philosophers who taught it. Galileo gave three lectures on the supernova. A ranking philosophy professor, Cesare Cremonini, defended Aristotle, and a feud broke out between them, with each answering the other in published letters. When Galileo published a short dialogue, written in dialect, between two Paduan peasants and the peasants reasoned better than the professor, Cremonini was furious.

In July 1609 Galileo by chance heard that a Dutch inventor had made an "eyeglass" that magnified objects and made them appear closer than they are. By August Galileo had figured out how to make one as powerful as field glasses. His strategy was to promote the "eyeglass" to Venetian merchants, letting them see ships out at sea carrying their goods two hours earlier than the naked eye could see them from shore, and to senators, allowing them to watch for enemy ships approaching their port. After a demonstration, impressed senators doubled Galileo's salary and gave him lifetime tenure at the University of Padua. Within a few weeks, "eyeglasses" from Holland were being sold on the streets of Venice for a few scudi, and the senators were smarting from the deal they had made. By December Galileo had made a twenty-power eyeglass, which he used to study the heavens at night.

With his powerful eyeglass, Galileo made several astonishing discoveries. ("Eyeglass" would be replaced by the term "telescope" in 1611 at a banquet given in Galileo's honor at the Lyncean Academy in Rome.) He first discovered that the moon's surface was covered with mountains and craters, that it was not the smooth, perfect sphere proclaimed by Aristotle. Early in January 1610, Galileo discovered that four satellites revolved around the planet Jupiter, contradicting the philosopher's claim that the earth was the center of *all* heavenly motions. (He named the satellites after the Medici family who, he hoped, would grant him a royal position.) Galileo also charted new stars in constellations that had never been charted and found that the Milky Way consisted of millions of separate stars, more evidence that contradicted Aristotle's view. In March 1610 Galileo published his findings in *Starry Messenger* and dedicated it to Grand Duke Cosimo. The discoveries caused immediate and violent reactions.

GALILEO'S NEW DISCOVERIES AROUSE CONTROVERSY

Starry Messenger evoked great praise and excitement among the public. Copies sold out in six weeks. Galileo sent a copy to Cosimo along with a superior telescope. Cosimo thanked Galileo by appointing him chief court mathematician and philosopher and by providing him a position at the University of Pisa with no teaching obligations so that Galileo could study and publish full-time. Galileo gave three public lectures on *Starry Messenger* at Padua and reported:

> The whole university turned out, and I so convinced and satisfied everyone that in the end those very leaders who at first were my sharpest critics and most stubborn opponents of the things I had written, seeing their case to be desperate and in fact lost, stated publicly that they are not only persuaded but are ready to defend and support my teachings against any philosopher who dares to attack them.[14]

Within a few months Galileo had become famous throughout Europe.

The Italian philosophers' reaction to *Starry Messenger* was indeed very different. Many declared that Galileo was seeing an illusion in his lenses. Others insisted that only direct vision could grasp actual reality. In response, Galileo wrote,

> Are we to make our eyes the measure of the expansion of all lights, so that wherever the images of luminous objects do not make themselves sensible to us, it should be affirmed that light does not arrive from them? Perhaps such stars, that remain hidden from our weak vision, are seen by eagles or lynxes.[15]

Others ridiculed Galileo and accused him of fraud. Cesare Cremonini and Giulio Libri, professors of philosophy at the University of Pisa, refused even to look through the telescope. The mountains of the moon were too objectionable to Jesuit philosophers, who said that a complete theory of optics was necessary before the telescope could be trusted. All of these philosophers, who believed and taught Aristotelian ideas, were particularly vulnerable because Aristotelian philosophy, as it was taught, was an interlocking system: If one part fails, all fails. Consequently, an acceptance of Galileo's findings that cast doubt on one element of Aristotle's philosophy endangered their whole system.

GALILEO BECOMES THE COURT MATHEMATICIAN

The furor had not died down when Galileo moved to Florence in September 1610 to assume his position as court mathematician for Grand Duke Cosimo. Galileo's daughters, Virginia and Livia, moved with him, but his son, Vincenzio, still a toddler, stayed with his mother for the time being. In Florence he and the girls stayed temporarily with

Galileo's mother, but since her unpleasant disposition made an inappropriate home for the girls and since Galileo was often sick, he put his daughters in the Convent of San Matteo in Arcetri near Florence in 1613. Moreover, since both girls were illegitimate, Galileo thought they had no chance of marriage at the social level of the Galileis. Virginia took the name Sister Maria Celeste when she took her vows in 1616, and Livia became Sister Arcangela the following year. Placing his daughters in the convent relieved him of future responsibilities, but the decision was arbitrary, and "if not unquestionably cruel, it certainly disregarded their wishes." While Virginia "accepted in a spirit of resignation the life imposed upon her by her father, and indeed revealed a true religious vocation, the younger daughter suffered much from it, and developed a complaining and unpleasant character."[16]

Despite demands that had been placed on him as a single parent, Galileo continued his work as soon as he arrived in Florence. Just before he left Padua, he had observed the planet Saturn with what he thought were two small adjoining stars and also had noticed spots on the sun, for which he at that time had no explanation. In Florence he charted the phases of the planet Venus and began charting the motions of the satellites surrounding Jupiter. As he gathered more and more evidence, he became ever more convinced that the Copernican theory was true. In March 1611 Galileo went to Rome to publicize his discoveries with authorities of the Catholic Church. He was welcomed by the cardinals; endorsed by the College Romano, the central Jesuit institution; given an audience with Pope Paul V; and introduced to Cardinal Maffeo Barberini, the man in line to be the next pope. All of them were committed to Aristotle's philosophy, but none denied Galileo's findings as long as he interpreted all conclusions he drew from them as hypotheses.

GALILEO'S MISSION TO CHANGE THE CHURCH'S VIEW

Galileo was on the verge of shifting from a scientist to a propagandist for science, a cause he thought he could accomplish because he was famous and because he was protected by the powerful Medicis in Tuscany. He strategically planned to persuade intellectuals and theologians to accept the science of observation and experimentation and, once they had accepted that notion, to persuade them that the evidence pointed to the Copernican view that the earth moved and rotated around the sun. He also planned to mobilize public opinion by writing in the language of the people and sharing with them his findings about the universe. He approached his cause as a dedicated Catholic who thought that church authorities would lose face if they rigidly adhered to the Aristotelian idea of the earth-centered universe when the evidence indicated otherwise. Author Stillman Drake says,

> With this background we can see why Galileo felt compelled to do all he could to prevent a mistake by the Church that would eventually tend to discredit its wisdom. The difficulty in this was that even persons expert in astronomy did not yet understand the weight of the evidence known to Galileo. It was impossible to explain that to theologians expert not in astronomy and physics but only in their erroneous Aristotelian counterparts.[17]

Ludovico Geymonat, on the other hand, thought that Galileo, while recognizing the power of the church, was more concerned with science. "Thence arose Galileo's conviction that he must try by every means to convert the Church to the cause of science, in order to prevent any rupture between the two that might dangerously retard the development of scientific research."[18] Galileo floated his ideas on the compatibility of theology and science in two letters intended for circulation—*Letter to Castelli* and *Letter to Christina.* In them he argued that the Bible was a book about spiritual life, not about science, and that God had given humans the intelligence and skills to tell the truth about nature. He recalled the words of Cardinal Baronius whom he had met in Padua: "The Bible tells us how to go to heaven, not how the heavens go."[19]

Galileo miscalculated the difficulty of converting philosophers and theologians and often seemed baffled by the animosity shown him. He seemed unable to grasp the effect of his style in which he closely followed an opponent's argument and then demolished it, making his opponent look foolish. Moreover, his facility with the language gave a sarcastic spin when he criticized faulty reasoning. For example, on October 2, 1611, at a dinner the grand duke gave for a visiting cardinal, Galileo, responsible for after-dinner entertainment, staged a debate with a philosophy professor from Pisa, Ludovico delle Colombe, on floating objects, which Galileo had been studying. Galileo, following the professor, who argued that ice is heavier than water but floats anyway because the flat-bottomed pieces cannot pierce the water's surface, listened and then observed that a piece of ice of any shape when pushed to the bottom of a container of water, pops right back to the surface. If shape were all that kept the ice from sinking, he argued, then shape would also keep the ice from rising to the surface, and especially so if ice were heavier than water. His conclusion was obviously right, and the professor was humiliated. Colombe was so angry that he started an anti-Galileo movement in response to Galileo's anti-Aristotelian stand. Dava Sobel reports, "Supporters of Galileo, in turn, took up the title of 'Galileists' and further deflated Colombe's flimsy philosophy by playing derisively on his name. Since *colombe* means 'doves' in Italian, they dubbed Galileo's critics 'the pigeon league.'"[20]

Criticism of Galileo Becomes Serious

Galileo became alarmed, however, when rumors circulated that he was guilty of heresy, a crime he considered abhorrent. The rumors took a serious turn on December 21, 1614, when Tommaso Caccini, a Dominican priest with ties to the "pigeon league," denounced Galileo from the pulpit of the Church of Santa Maria Novella in Florence. He "began his attack, taking as his text an excellent pun, *Veri Galilei, quid statis aspicientes in coelum?*—'Ye men of Galilee, why stand ye gazing up into the heavens?' (Acts I:11)—and proceeding to show that the Copernican theory was in irresoluble conflict with the Bible."[21] He then turned to a text from the Old Testament, in which Joshua commands the sun, "Sun, stand thou still" (Joshua 10:12); Caccini intended the text to prove that the sun normally moves around the earth except during miracles. Sobel reports, "Caccini wound up branding Galileo, Galileo's followers, and all mathematicians in general 'practitioners of diabolical arts . . . enemies of true religion.'"[22] Even though the priest's Dominican superior apologized to Galileo for the attack, suspicion of Galileo had been aroused.

Further suspicion grew when another Florentine Dominican, Niccolò Lorini, sent a copy of Galileo's letter to Castelli to the inquisitor general in Rome for investigation and when Caccini lodged a formal complaint against Galileo with the Congregation of the Holy Office (the Inquisition). Fearing the Castelli letter had been modified, Galileo sent a copy of the original to Rome to be reviewed by Cardinal Bellarmine, who was noted for his respect for Galileo. The Inquisition report had no objection to Galileo, but he was warned: If he referred to Copernicanism as *hypothesis*, he would not be bothered.

Toward the end of 1615, Galileo sought permission from the grand duke to go to Rome to argue Copernicanism and his loyalty to the church. The Tuscan ambassador in Rome warned that because Pope Paul V was hostile to intellectuals and because the Dominicans and Jesuits were fighting, this "was no time to come to Rome and argue about the moon."[23] Galileo went in spite of the warning, and his presence there set off a series of events in 1616. First, on February 23, the Holy Office ordered theologians to vote on two propositions regarding the truth of Copernicanism, concluding that both were "absurd" and "foolish" contradictions of Holy Scriptures. Second, the pope directed Bellarmine to order Galileo not to "hold, defend, or teach" Copernicanism. On February 26, Bellarmine reported this to Galileo, but the minutes of this meeting were never signed and, therefore, not official. Third, as a result of the theologians' vote, on March 5, the Holy Office banned all books teaching Copernicanism, though none of Galileo's publications were listed. Fourth, since Galileo had no record of the February 26 meeting, he asked Bellarmine for a report in writing; Bellarmine responded with a letter on May 26 saying that Copernicanism was contradictory to the scriptures, but he omitted the words that Galileo could not "hold, defend, or teach" Copernicanism. Galileo went back to Florence believing that he could discuss Copernicanism as long as he admitted there was no proof of its truth.

GALILEO TEMPORARILY GIVES UP HIS CAUSE

Back in Florence Galileo attended to personal matters. Since he was often sick in Florence and periodically spent weeks in bed, he took a villa in Bellosguardo, a few miles from Florence, to recuperate. He now had full custody of his son, Vincenzio, who at the age of seven had come to live with him in 1612. In 1616 and 1617 Galileo was present when his daughters took their vows at the convent. In 1619 he persuaded the Grand Duke Cosimo to legitimize Vincenzio's birth. Four important people in Galileo's life died in succeeding years: Marina Gamba in 1619, Galileo's mother in 1620, and Cardinal Bellarmine and the Grand Duke Cosimo in 1621. Cosimo's eight-year-old son Ferdinando II became the grand duke of Tuscany, and Galileo continued as his chief mathematician.

The pope's order of 1616 convinced Galileo that public silence constituted his best strategy for the time being, at least until he regained his composure and serenity after his defeat. He focused again on science. He finished the chart that used accurate tables of Jupiter's satellites as a navigation tool for identifying longitude. Though Italian sailors never used his scheme, the Dutch government paid him a handsome sum for it. He was about to take up motion problems again when three comets appeared in 1618, an event that initiated a series of statements and replies between Galileo and Jesuit Horatio Grassi. Grassi took the view of Tycho Brahe, who "had declared them to be bodies located beyond the lunar heaven, and hence far above the sphere of fire."[24] Galileo attacked Grassi's view and his method of argumentation. Thinking he was on safe ground discussing a topic not even addressed by Copernicus, Galileo broke his silence and treated the topic of comets in the larger context of science. Over the next two years he wrote the *Assayer*, composed as a letter to the pope's Lord Chamberlain Virginio Cesarini. It began superficially with the topic of comets, but in reality it was a propaganda piece promoting scientific reasoning, as contrasted with "the tiresome logical quibbles that satisfied natural philosophers."[25]

Galileo's hopes had been raised in August 1623 when his Florentine friend and admirer Cardinal Maffeo Barberini was elected Pope Urban VIII, his friend Castelli appointed as the pope's mathematician, and his pupil Father Niccolò Riccardi appointed as chief censor of the press. The *Assayer* was dedicated to the new pope, who directed Cesarini to read it aloud to him over lunch; apparently the pope enjoyed the work because it expressed his own philosophy of science.

GALILEO AGAIN TRIES TO INFLUENCE THE CHURCH

Given the improved intellectual climate, Galileo went to Rome in April 1624 to sound out the pope's position and try to get the decree banning Copernicanism lifted. During his month and a half there, Galileo had six audiences with the pope and obtained for his son a scholarly position that included a pension, but the pope's opinion on Copernicus seemed ambiguous to Galileo. Back in Florence in June, he again tested the waters by sending a letter to Monsignor Francesco Ingoli. In this letter, intended for the eyes of the pope, Galileo used all the diplomacy and tact he could muster to argue that science and religion should be separate and that Copernicanism should be discussed. Such openness, he contended, would show that Italian Catholics were informed and not closeminded. Hearing no objection to the Ingoli letter, Galileo began working on the book he really wanted to write, the work that became *Dialogue Concerning the Two Chief World Systems: Ptolemaic and Copernican.*

Galileo began *Dialogue* in the fall of 1624 and finished it six years later in April 1630. Sobel describes its form: "His book took the form of an animated encounter, spread over four days' time, like a play in four acts, among three acquaintances who breathed their own personalities into the theories they entertained."[26] Based on Galileo's friend from Florence, the character of Salviati represented Galileo's beliefs; Sagredo, based on Galileo's Venetian friend, usually took Salviati's side; and Simplicio, whose name recalled the sixth-century Greek philosopher Simplicius, presented the Aristotelian point of view. The setting was Venice, and the topics covered questions of the earth's motion, the organization of heavenly bodies, and the ebb and flow of the tides. The five-hundred-page book was written in Italian. According to Sobel, Galileo used "grand gorgeous language, by turns poetic, didactic, reverent, combative, and funny. He illustrated the text, too, but only sparsely, by having his characters create simple line drawings for each other as the need arose."[27]

During the six years Galileo wrote *Dialogue*, he also attended to family issues. He grew much closer to his daughter Maria Celeste, who favored her father with handmade lace collars and cuffs. Sobel writes, "Ever a source of love and financial aid to Suor Maria Celeste, as well as the grateful recipient of her labors, he now began to do favors for her that required the skilled work of his own hands."[28] In 1626 Galileo's son, Vincenzio, received his doctorate degree in law from the University of Pisa and became engaged to Sestilia Bocchineri. She came from a prestigious family in Prato, near Florence; they provided her with a dowry of seven hundred scudi, but Galileo helped the couple finance their house. Vincenzio and Sestilia later had two sons, Galileo and Carlo. In 1627 Galileo's brother, Michelangelo, in Germany asked Galileo if he could send his wife Anna Chiara and eight children to stay with him, since the Thirty Years' War made living in Germany unsafe. Galileo supported Anna, the children, and a nurse in his home for a year and gave his nephew a grant to study music in Rome, an opportunity the nephew squandered. Michelangelo later died as a result of the plague.

GALILEO'S *DIALOGUE* BRINGS PRAISE AND ANGER

When Galileo had finished *Dialogue*, Maria Celeste recopied the manuscript in perfect handwriting to prepare it for publication. Then in April 1630 Galileo left for Rome to submit the manuscript to the pope's censor, Father Riccardi, for permission to publish. On June 16 Galileo learned that *Dialogue* had passed Riccardi's inspection, with two requests—a new title (not *Dialogue on the Tides,* as Galileo had originally called it) and changes in the preface and ending. Galileo returned to Florence to make the changes. New problems, however, complicated the process of publication. The plague hit Italy and interrupted travel. A new publisher had to be found because Prince Federico Cesi of the Lyncean Academy, who was responsible for publishing *Dialogue,* died suddenly in August. Furthermore, Riccardi asked Galileo to return the manuscript to Rome for further revisions as a result of pressure from Galileo's enemies. Galileo objected. Since travel during the plague was almost impossible, he proposed that the text be reexamined by a theologian in Florence and then published there. Riccardi compromised and required only the preface and conclusion to be sent to Rome; the rest of the manuscript could be reviewed by Dominican Father Giacinto Stefani at Florence. Finally, all revisions had been completed and permission to publish had been granted. The book was published in Florence on February 21, 1632, with the title *Dialogues of Galileo Galilei, Lincean . . . wherein, in the meetings of four days, are discussed the two chief systems of the world, Ptolemaic and Copernican.*

The book was immensely successful, and it quickly sold out in Florence bookshops. Galileo sent copies to friends in Bologna and Rome and heard words of praise from them. Trouble began, however, when Father Christopher Scheiner, who had argued with Galileo over sunspots and lost, urged Riccardi to have Galileo's book banned. Scheiner's request came at a time when the pope was frustrated by the revolt of the Protestants in Germany, by infighting among factions within the Catholic Church, and by accusations that he had unfairly appointed relatives to high positions in the church hierarchy. Angry theologians convinced the pope that

Galileo was making "sport" of the pope in the character of Simplicio and mocking him when Simplicio speaks words almost identical to the pope's doctrines. Then the pope saw the unsigned 1616 memorandum, rumored to have been dug up by Scheiner, and felt that Galileo had deliberately deceived him by hiding its existence. In August 1632 he ordered a three-man commission to reexamine *Dialogue;* in their September report, they said that Galileo had overstepped his 1616 instructions. The pope was furious and moved against both the book and the author. He ordered all bookstores to stop selling *Dialogue* (they were already sold out) and ordered Galileo to appear before the Holy Office of the Inquisition in October. Galileo protested that he was ill, that the plague made travel dangerous, and, moreoever, that he had followed all of the church's rules. After the pope rejected a doctor's report explaining Galileo's bad health, he threatened to arrest Galileo and drag him to Rome in irons. Galileo knew the problem was serious and as a precaution made out a will.

GALILEO BROUGHT TO TRIAL

Galileo left for Rome on January 20, 1633, and after twenty-five days of travel and quarantine because of the plague, he arrived in Rome on February 13. Rather than relegating Galileo to jail, the grand duke allowed him to stay in safety at the Tuscan embassy, where ambassador Francesco Niccolini and his wife Caterina treated him as a guest. When Monsignor Lodovico Serristoti, consultant to the Holy Office, came to see Galileo, Niccolini suspected he came just to evaluate Galileo's attitude so that the officials could plan their best strategy for the trial. Geymonat suggests that the trial

> became nothing more than a dark succession of maneuvers by means of which his prosecutor, the Dominican Vencenzio Maculano [of Firenzuola], sought to trap Galileo in a net ably woven beforehand, and of the much less able countermaneuvers by which Galileo tried to escape from his adversary.[29]

On April 12, 1633, after two months in the embassy, Galileo was brought to the Holy Office of the Inquisition for the first of four days of interrogation. He gave testimony to two officials and a secretary in a series of formally stated questions, after which he was placed in the officials' dormitory located in the Palace of the Holy Office. He could not leave, and he was ordered to remain silent. Meanwhile three theologians analyzed his *Dialogue* and concluded that Galileo had indeed defended and taught Copernicanism. On April 28 the commissary general of the Inquisition negotiated with Galileo, offering him lenient treatment for the admission of wrongdoing. Even though Galileo had a stronger case than the church, he "could not be acquitted without damage to the reputation and authority of the Roman Inquisition."[30] On the second day of interrogation, April 30, Galileo signed a statement admitting wrongdoing, but without malicious intent, and offered to add a refutation to the *Dialogue*. After this session Galileo was allowed to return to the embassy, but was warned not to discuss the case with anybody. On the third day of the trial, May 10, Galileo gave his formal, written defense; it was based primarily on the fact that the letter from Bellarmine, which Galileo had saved as evidence, omitted the part forbidding him to "defend or teach" Copernicanism; Galileo argued that the document stating such was never signed nor had Bellarmine ever shown it to him. Since Bellarmine had died in 1621, there was no way to verify Galileo's testimony. On the fourth day of interrogation, June 21, the Inquisition, by the pope's direction, examined Galileo's intentions and used the formal threat of torture. Galileo complied with their wishes, claiming, "I do not hold this opinion of Copernicus, and I have not held it after being ordered by injunction to abandon it. For the rest, I am here in your hands; do with me what you please." And when he was told to tell the truth, otherwise the court would have recourse to torture, Galileo responded, "I am here to obey, but I have not held this opinion after the determination was made, as I said."[31] The court, however, did not find Galileo's plea satisfactory.

GALILEO FOUND GUILTY AND SENTENCED

On June 22, Galileo was sentenced at the Church of Santa Maria Sopra Minerva, where he was convicted of heinous crimes. His sentence, signed by seven of the ten cardinals, required him to give up Copernican thought, to recite seven penitential psalms once a week for three years, and to remain imprisoned at the will of the Holy Office. In addition, the Holy Office placed *Dialogue* on the Index of Prohibited Books, where it remained until 1835. Dressed in the white robe of the penitent, Galileo knelt as ordered and read the abjuration prepared for him. A century later the story appeared that at some point, perhaps as he left the church, Galileo muttered defiantly, *"Eppur se muove!"* (And yet it does move!)

While Galileo waited in the embassy for further instructions, Niccolini begged the pope to pardon Galileo, as he did several times, but the pope refused every time. Galileo spent three days in prison before the pope allowed more lenient facilities. Galileo was placed in the custody of his friend Archbishop Ascanio Piccolomini in Siena, with whom he stayed for five months. The trial and sentencing broke Galileo's spirit to the point that he could not sleep and his conversation rambled in distraction. He wrote to his daughter Maria "that he felt as if his name had been stricken from the roll call of the living."[52] Piccolomini, a humane and understanding man, did much to save Galileo's life and sanity; he gathered intellectuals for conversations, made Galileo the guest of honor, and raised topics on which Galileo was an authority. He got Galileo interested again in science and writing, and Galileo began a new book on motion and mechanics, writing again in dialogue using the same three characters he had used in his banned book.

GALILEO AT HOME UNDER HOUSE ARREST

While Galileo was enduring the trial and the imprisonment that followed, his daughter Maria Celeste was one of his main sources of support. Her letters from this period express her concern and love and report daily happenings at his villa at Arcetri, where Galileo had moved in 1631, a villa adjoining the Convent of San Matteo. Maria saw that the gardens and vineyards were tended, the wine made, and Galileo's bills paid. Finally, in November 1633 Pope Urban VIII agreed to let Galileo be imprisoned at Arcetri; he saw a chance to punish Galileo with greater isolation, since his life at Siena had become comfortable and productive. Under house arrest, Galileo was allowed no visitors interested in scientific ideas and he was forbidden to go anywhere except to the convent next door. When Galileo arrived in December, Grand Duke Ferdinand came in person to welcome him home. From then on Galileo datelined all of his letters "From my prison in Arcetri."[53]

Galileo experienced another tragic blow when Maria Celeste died on April 2, 1634, at the age of thirty-three, just four months after Galileo returned home. His letter to a friend in late April suggests that he had little energy to try to recover from his grief. He had problems with a hernia and heart palpitations. He said,

> Immense sorrow and melancholy [accompany] loss of appetite; hateful to myself, I continually hear calls from my beloved daughter; . . . in addition to which I am not a little frightened by constant wakefulness. . . . I have at present no heart for writing, being quite beside myself so that I neglect even replying to the personal letters of friends.[34]

As he had done earlier, however, Galileo conquered grief by immersing himself in his science and writing.

He lived several years of solitude sprinkled with only a few visitors. British poet John Milton visited him, after which he made reference to Galileo in one of his poems. His daughter-in-law's family visited and comforted him. Sestilia's brother Geri Bocchineri, who worked for the grand duke, visited often, and her sister Alessandra Castelli developed a special relationship with Galileo. She was beautiful and intelligent and able to draw out his spirit in conversations and letters. In response to her request that he visit, he wrote, "I can never tell you sufficiently the pleasure I should take in uninterrupted leisure to enjoy your conversation, elevated above usual feminine talk." He regretted being unable to accept "because I am held in prison for reasons well known to my lord your husband."[35] His last letter was to her.

As Galileo's health faltered, authorities in Rome softened enough to allow a young scholar to live with him. Vincenzio Viviani admired Galileo and had an insatiable interest in the same scientific problems that interested Galileo. He helped Galileo focus on his research, wrote out his proofs, and drew his diagrams. In 1641 Evangelista Torricelli joined Viviani as a pupil and provided the same kind of stimulation and help. These two young scholars stayed with Galileo until his death.

GALILEO'S LAST BOOK

With the help of the two scholars, Galileo made progress on his book on motion and began searching for a publisher outside of Italy. After possibilities in Germany and France failed, Galileo's Parisian friend Elia Diodati found a Dutch publisher, Louis Elzevir, who visited Galileo in May 1636 to settle the agreement. Fra Fulgenzio Micanzio, theologian to the Venetian republic and still loyal to Galileo, knew the publisher and volunteered to serve as conduit between Arcetri and Holland; "this gave the old theologian the pleasure of reading *Two New Sciences* in installments as each finished part reached him."[36] Galileo sent the last pages of the manuscript in June 1637 and printing began in Leiden, Holland, in the fall. Galileo dedicated the book to François de Noailles, the French ambassador in Rome, who had campaigned on Galileo's behalf. In the preface dated March 6, 1638, Galileo pretended to be surprised that the manuscript reached a foreign printer and expressed his appreciation to the ambassador for finding his work important enough to have it printed. *Two New Sciences* was published in June 1638 and sold very well, but Galileo never saw the published book. In his declining years, his eyesight failed. He had become completely blind by the time his copy arrived.

GALILEO'S FINAL YEARS

When Galileo's health was failing, he appealed to the Holy Office to be allowed to see a doctor in Florence, but the authorities still insisted on tight control over him. Antonio Cardinal Sant' Onofrio sternly doubted the sincerity of his ailments and denied his request, saying, "Galileo's return to the city would give him the opportunity of having meetings, conversations, and discussions in which he might once again let his condemned opinions on the motion of the Earth come to light."[37] After making a second request and submitting to the inquisitor's physical examination, he was allowed to stay at his son's house and see a doctor, but he was not allowed to go into the city or have public or private conversations. While in Florence, Galileo also asked to attend Easter mass at the neighborhood church and was given permission as long as he had no personal contacts.

In his final years Galileo reflected on his blindness and his long-suffering imprisonment. On his blindness he said,

> Alas, your friend and servant Galileo has for the last month been irremediably blind, so that this heaven, this earth, this universe which I, by my remarkable discoveries and clear demonstrations had enlarged a hundred times beyond what has been believed by wise men of past ages, for me is from this time forth shrunk into so small a space as to be filled by my own sensations.[38]

Though his world had shrunk and he was a prisoner to the end, he was still vehement about his innocence, that he had

committed no crime. The severity of his punishment resulted, he said, because the judges needed to cover up their
wrong application of the law. His conscience was clear: He
had not been irreverent toward the church, and no one had
spoken with more piety than he.

Galileo died on January 8, 1642. A few days after his
death, Luke Holste, of the household of Cardinal Barberini,
the most important cardinal to withhold his signature from
Galileo's sentence, wrote to a friend in Florence:

> Today news has come of the loss of Signor Galileo, which
> touches not just Florence but the whole world, and our whole
> century which from this divine man has received more
> splendour than from almost all of the other ordinary philoso-
> phers. Now, envy ceasing, the sublimity of that intellect will
> begin to be known which will serve all posterity as guide in
> the search for truth.[39]

NOTES

1. Quoted in Ludovico Geymonat, *Galileo Galilei: A Biography and Inquiry into His Philosophy of Science.* New York: McGraw-Hill, 1957, p. 10.

2. Stillman Drake, *Galileo.* Oxford, England: Oxford University Press, 1980, p. 24.

3. Quoted in Geymonat, *Galileo Galilei,* pp. 11–12.

4. Quoted in Dava Sobel, *Galileo's Daughter.* New York: Walker, 1999, p. 19.

5. Quoted in Sobel, *Galileo's Daughter,* p. 19.

6. Drake, *Galileo,* p. 29.

7. Sobel, *Galileo's Daughter,* p. 26.

8. Quoted in Sobel, *Galileo's Daughter,* pp. 23–24.

9. Fritjof Capra, *The Turning Point: Science, Society, and the Rising Culture.* New York: Bantam, 1983, pp. 54–55.

10. Stephen W. Hawking, *A Brief History of Time: From the Big Bang to Black Holes.* New York: Bantam, 1988, p. 179.

11. Drake, *Galileo,* p. 32.

12. Hawking, *A Brief History of Time,* pp. 15–16.

13. Drake, *Galileo,* p. 38.

14. Quoted in Drake, *Galileo,* p. 44.

15. Quoted in Geymonat, *Galileo Galilei,* p. 45.

16. Geymonat, *Galileo Galilei,* p. 55.

17. Drake, *Galileo,* p. 56.

18. Geymonat, *Galileo Galilei,* p. 62.

19. Quoted in Drake, *Galileo,* p. 29.

20. Sobel, *Galileo's Daughter*, p. 48.

21. Will and Ariel Durant, *The Age of Reason Begins: A History of European Civilization in the Period of Shakespeare, Bacon, Montaigne, Rembrandt, Galileo, and Descartes: 1558–1648*. New York: Simon and Schuster, 1961, p. 606.

22. Sobel, *Galileo's Daughter*, p. 66.

23. Quoted in Drake, *Galileo*, p. 63.

24. Geymonat, *Galileo Galilei*, p. 98.

25. Quoted in Drake, *Galileo*, p. 70.

26. Sobel, *Galileo's Daughter*, p. 144.

27. Sobel, *Galileo's Daughter*, p. 146.

28. Sobel, *Galileo's Daughter*, p. 187.

29. Geymonat, *Galileo Galilei*, p. 148.

30. Drake, *Galileo*, p. 78.

31. Quoted in Sobel, *Galileo's Daughter*, p. 272.

32. Sobel, *Galileo's Daughter*, p. 316.

33. Quoted in Sobel, *Galileo's Daughter*, p. 344.

34. Quoted in Drake, *Galileo*, p. 79.

35. Quoted in Geymonat, *Galileo Galilei*, p. 192.

36. Sobel, *Galileo's Daughter*, p. 351.

37. Quoted in Sobel, *Galileo's Daughter*, p. 353.

38. Quoted in Drake, *Galileo*, p. 85.

39. Quoted in Drake, *Galileo*, p. 93.

CHAPTER 1

The Major Influences on Galileo's Development

A Product of Florentine Culture

Georgio Spini

Georgio Spini analyzes the role of Florence's ruling class—the cittadini—and the privileges and duties the families of this class passed on from one generation to the next. According to Spini, the Galilei family provided Galileo with an education traditional of the ruling class, but by his generation the old traditions were breaking up. Consequently, Spini explains, Galileo followed the old ways in his public life, but forged a new private life for himself. Georgio Spini taught history at Magistero, University of Florence, Italy, and he lectured in the United States on several occasions. He has published extensively on the intellectual and religious history of Italy and on the history of Colonial America.

Our information is exasperatingly scarce on Galileo's experience and thought on religion before 1612. His biographers, such as Vincenzio Galilei, [Vincenzio] Viviani, and [Niccolo] Gherardini are silent on this topic; his works and correspondence give us but scant or uncertain data; the documents that the modern erudites have gathered about him are not much richer. We are compelled to resort to conjectures, however reluctant one can be to advance on so slippery a ground.

THE SIGNIFICANCE OF THE GALILEI FAMILY

Perhaps one of the few sure pieces of data we can rely upon is the fact that Galileo was a child of the Galilei family of Florence. That is not a joke, nor a Lapalissian [self-evident] truth by any means. A Galilei, in sixteenth-century Florence, was not unlike a Norton or a Prescott, if not a Winthrop or an Adams, in later centuries in New England.

A Bostonian Brahmin belonged to a well-defined social, cultural, and even religious environment by birth. A Renaissance Florentine was not less conditioned by his birth, if he was the scion of a family of *cittadini*. From this point of view, the fact that Galileo was actually born in Pisa and resided there or in Padua for many years was irrelevant. Not all the people who were born or dwelled within the city walls were citizens of Florence, but only those whose families had given members to the city government in the past. Practically speaking, that was the same as being members of the Arti, and possibly of the Arti Maggiori, which controlled the most lucrative trades and professions. Inversely, all the scions of these families were cittadini, regardless of their place of birth and of their residence. In her golden age, Florence was not unlike a modern corporation, whose cittadini were the shareholders by hereditary right. And that had a deciding influence not only in social status, but also in professional orientation. A striking evidence of that is offered by Galileo's own family. Its fortune was made mostly by a Galileo Galilei (1370?–1450?) who served a term as *gonfaloniere di giustizia* [administrator of justice] and was a successful physician, that is, a member of the Arte dei Medici e Speziali, one of the Arti Maggiori to which Dante belonged in his time. When our Galileo was born, the old gonfaloniere had been in his grave for more than a century and Florence had ceased to be a republic since 1530. By that time, many a family of cittadini, including the Galilei, felt sorely the effects of the economic crisis brought about by the wars and the inflation of the American silver. However, Galileo's father Vincenzio was still a merchant, as was becoming to a descendant of cittadini, although he was prominent also as a musician. He gave his son the same name as the gonfaloniere and tried to put him in the same medical profession, after a first vain attempt—if we are to believe the doubtful witness of Gherardini—to make a wool-trader out of him. Probably Galileo was a bit of a rebel, when he put aside medicine for mathematics. But he clung to family traditions enough to call his own son Vincenzio; this son tried to find a living in a bureaucratic career but finally became a chancellor of the Arte dei Mercatanti. Incidentally, in his time, Galileo the gonfaloniere owned a villa in the Arcetri Hill, where Galileo the scientist was to put his daughters in a convent and spend the last years of his life.

THE PRIVILEGES AND DUTIES OF FAMILY TRADITION

Family tradition was influential also in ethics, religion, and intellectual life. A cittadino felt that he had a hereditary share in Florence's moral, intellectual, and artistic treasure, as well as in her wealth. He paid homage to the great Trecento writers, Dante [Alighieri], [Francesco] Petrarch, and [Giovanni] Boccaccio, as to a kind of household god; in particular he worshiped the "altissimo poeta," [the greatest poet Dante] whose *Divine Comedy* was supposed to be full of high moral and philosophical truth, along with its superhuman beauty. He considered as part of his heritage the masterpieces with which Florence had been filled by an uninterrupted chain of geniuses from [painter and sculptor] Giotto to [sculptor and painter] Michelangelo. But, here again, beauty and truth coincided, since the Florence cittadino was convinced that the works of the great artists had a lofty philosophical and religious message for those spirits who could go beyond exterior appearances. The "divino Michelangelo," in particular, was not less great as a "moral philosopher" and a Christian than he was as an artist. Many a cittadino had a spiritual share also in the treasure of the sanctity and martyrdom of [Fra Girolano] Savonarola[1] or in that of the idealism of the Neoplatonic philosophers;[2] many more had a share in the treasure of classical learning accumulated by the Florentine humanists.[3] But each cittadino was sure that he had at least a share in the *volgare* [the language of the people], the most perfect jewel of Florence's spiritual crown, which the other Italians could only labor to imitate, but could never possess.

Each of these privileges had its counterpart in a duty. A cittadino was aware that he was given so many gifts not so much as an individual, part of the city community, but rather as a part of a series of communities such as Florence, and possibily a determined quarter of the city; or a well-determined social group; or a family group. He felt himself belonging to these communities in the fullest sense of the word. He was expected to serve in the various public offices when his turn came; he was to embrace a profession

1. a Dominican monk who was tried and executed as a heretic after his political activities angered the Pope 2. philosophers that had rediscovered Plato 3. participants in a cultural and intellectual movement of the Renaissance that emphasized secular concerns as a result of the rediscovery and study of the literature, art, and civilization of ancient Greece and Rome

or a trade becoming to his status; he was to lead the kind of active, useful, and responsible life that the Florence Humanists had described in their treatises; he was to live up to his artistic, intellectual, and moral heritage. Above all, he was to be a dedicated member of his family, ready to sacrifice his own tastes or interests to the family's honor, wealth, and continuity. He was to respect in his father the visible symbol of the family and to obey him even as an adult. All these duties were not so much prescribed by men's written laws as imposed on the cittadino's conscience by God's own law: Christianity was the same with family and city, with morals and art, with father Dante and one's own father, with Michelangelo's *David* and the duty of caring for the poor and the hospitals. All this was the cornerstone of the solid moral universe of the Florence cittadino.

In fact, the cittadini's God was not unlike a solid businessman: he paid everyone his due in this life or after, and expected to be given sound facts of charity and righteousness and not to be cheated by empty words. Therefore, conscience did not play a lesser role in old Florence than it was to play in a later age among the Puritans. After all, much of the Puritan doctrine was drawn from the teaching of a Florentine, Peter Martys Vermigli. But that did not imply a sheepish attitude toward God's ministers: on the contrary, priests and friars were not held particularly high in the cittadini's opinion. A Florence cittadino knew too well the mocking stories about faked miracles and impudent friars circulated by Boccaccio or the strong words used by Dante and Petrarch to brand the vices of the clergy. In a sense, a bit of anticlericalism was as necessary as a sound amount of the fear of God to a really respectable cittadino and a good Christian.

OLD TRADITIONS DISINTEGRATE IN GALILEO'S TIME

However, when Galileo was born, the formerly coherent and solid Florentine moral universe was disintegrating. Florence was no more a republic, and the Medici *signoria* [lordship] was now a *principato* [manager], whose grand dukes modeled themselves on the pattern of the absolute kings of their times. As bureaucracy replaced the formerly honorary offices, so a dull conformity to the will of the *superiori* [authority] replaced the old sense of public responsibility. But a king of Spain or of France was clearly such by divine right, while

God could hardly be invoked to justify a Medici's rule. The members of the former ruling class called themselves *nobili* [noble] instead of cittadini and addressed each other as *signore*, instead of *messere* [mister], as their more austere ancestors did. But it was not a matter of words only. The economic crisis discouraged the traditional business activities, as it encouraged an idler and more lavish way of life. It was not so sure anymore that God required an active, conscientious, and relatively parsimonious life. Artists and poets were no more supposed to have lofty messages of religious and human idealism; they were to offer a purely aesthetic delight or to be the instruments of Church and state propaganda. A frightened silence replaced the traditional Florentine taste for political and ideological discussion. Apparently religion was untouched by the crisis of the old political, social, and economic ways of life. Articles of faith and acts of worship were more or less the same as in the days of Dante and Savonarola, although they had lost much of their former meaning. Christianity had been too tightly associated with the old order of things to survive as more than an empty shell.

The shell was even harder than it used to be. The Counter-Reformation had stressed the institutional aspects of the Church and increased its power of repression. The clergy could impose its influence far more effectively than before, and obtained by terror what it had never obtained previously by consent. Few if any dared to defy this overwhelming machinery of power, and those who did paid dearly for it. As in all totalitarian regimes, propaganda and brain-washing could get spectacular effects; they could stampede the mobs into near-frenzied emotions and give all the appearances of an impressive unanimity of consent. But in several instances compulsory unanimity hardly masked the creeping skepticism. At any rate, the old unity was lost; a layman knew he had to leave religious policy to the care of the Church's superiori just as a citizen knew he had to leave politics to the care of the state's superiori. Equally, an artist knew he had to content himself with being an expert on beautiful form, and a scholar knew he had to let certain sleeping dogs lie, if he did not want to get himself into trouble.

We have significant evidence of the spiritual crisis the late sixteenth-century Florentines underwent, which ranges from Michelangelo's madness in his last works of art and poems to [Antonio] Doni's nervous restlessness. Another interesting, if less known, item of evidence of the same thing is Bastiano Arditi's diary, the journal of an old and pious cittadino, who wrote when Galileo was a boy, under Grand Duke Francesco I. Arditi was as saddened by Florence's economic decadence as by Francesco's ruthless absolutism and dissipated way of life, and he still considered that politics, morals, and economics were one with Christianity, so much so that the decadence of the one appeared to him as the decadence also of the other. Galileo was born too late to feel the same pangs of conscience; however, the Galilei were close friends of the Buonarroti.[4] Moreover, his tremendous vitality and joie de vivre made him temperamentally impenetrable to melancholy. But he was enough a man of his times to bear the marks of the disintegration of the old unity.

GALILEO'S PERSONALITY FORMED BY THE FLORENTINE CITTADINO

It is almost superfluous to emphasize how much in Galileo's personality corresponded still to the portrait of the Florence cittadino: his manly realism, his love of an active life, and of anything useful and concretely practical; his typically Florentine irony and his high opinion and masterly use of the volgare; his enthusiasm for poetry, music, fine arts in general, and for Dante and Michelangelo in particular; his strong humanistic background, his fondness for Plato, and his exalted conception of man's intellectual dignity, so near to that of the fifteenth-century Florentine Neoplatonists. Galileo's dedication to his family was not less typical. A respectful child of his father, Vincenzio, as long as the latter lived, Galileo underwent the heaviest financial sacrifices after his father's death to supply his sisters with appropriate dowries and to help his irresponsible and luckless brother Michelangelo. (Incidentally, it is interesting to note how, in his letters to Galileo, Michelangelo insisted on couching his requests for help in religious terms: God in person requested that Galileo support his unpecunious brother.) And Galileo eventually let himself be plundered by his not-always-deserving or grateful family all through his life. Perhaps his celibacy was also an effect of his sense of family responsibility. He spent so much to marry off his sis-

---

4. Michelangelo Buonarotti was a nephew of the great artist, a friend of Galileo, and author of a play which mirrored the morals of the time.

ters that he did not have enough money for himself, to set
up a home, when the time was opportune.

GALILEO DEPARTS FROM THE OLD WAYS

But, on the other hand, Galileo's private life had little in
common with the parsimonious austerity of the former generations' cittadini. One has but to compare the ribald verses
of Galileo's poem "Contro il portare la toga" ["The Pros and
Cons Associated with the Academic Gown"] with Michelangelo's love poetry, so filled with lofty Neoplatonic idealism,
or Michelangelo's thrifty investments of his earnings with
Galileo's endless struggles against debt and casual handling
of money to grasp the difference between the two ages. It is
possible that Galileo left his Venetian mistress, Marina
Gamba, when he decided to move back from Padua to Florence, in deference to the morals of his native environment.
The Florence cittadini not infrequently had natural children
with a house servant or with a *contadina* [peasant], but public opinion frowned upon Cosimo I and Francesco I when
they had steady relations with a kind of official mistress. But
Galileo's private life did not become more puritanical for
that, if we are to judge from the fact that he could be exhorted to set aside his "disorders" even in his old age, and
even by so worldly a friend as Sagredo. Anyhow, the important fact is that love did not exist for him except in the physical sense of the word. There was no Beatrice, Laura, or Vit-
toria Colonna to give love the same idealistic meaning that it
had for Dante, Petrarch, and Michelangelo. Physical love
was in a compartment of its own, without relation to the rest
of Galileo's life.

Even as a fervent lover of music and the fine arts, Galileo
never tried to draw a moral, philosophical, or religious
message from them. In his notes on Ariosto and Tasso[5] he
showed himself to be a penetrating and gifted literary critic,
but his criticism was exclusively literary. It did not allow
any room for ideological issues. In his youth, he paid his
tribute to Dante's worship in the form of an essay, on the
topography of the *Inferno,* which is a little masterpiece of
logic, technical skill, and volgare prose. But it does not reveal any particular commitment to Dante's ideals. The

---

5. Galileo wrote critical commentary on the poetry of Lodovico Ariosto, his favorite
poet, and Tasso, whom he criticized as too sentimental.

reader cannot even detect whether Galileo was convinced that an "Inferno" existed. . . .

GALILEO SHUNNED POLITICS AND MADE HIS OWN WAY

According to all evidence, there was still a strong vein of Florentine patriotism in Galileo. Since the "nazione e città di Firenze" [people of the city of Florence] was now identified with the house of the Medici, it is probable that he was reasonably sincere when he professed his loyalty to the grand dukes. But Galileo's letters are silent on anything concerning politics. A reader could go through all of them without realizing that he lived in an age of terrific European convulsions, corresponding to most of the Thirty Years War. Politics and government were no longer integral parts of the general problem of man's destiny upon this earth, as they had been for Dante and Savonarola, Machiavelli[6] and Michelangelo. They were a technical department of their own, to be left to the care of authorized experts. Whether Galileo was happy or unhappy with that is anyone's guess. The fact is that he did not let himself become entangled in problems of that kind, either by willful choice or by sheer prudence. In a hopelessly fragmented world each man was to choose his compartment to live in and his goal to live for. Galileo had no doubt that his life's raison d'être [reason for being] was in his activities as a "mathematician" and as a "natural philosopher," to put it in the words of his times. The rest was relatively unimportant to him; or, rather, it could only be instrumental to the achievement of his goal—*all* the rest, including madonna Marina, of course.

On the other hand, the historical environment in which Galileo lived did not provide him with a foundation upon which to build anew. As we will see later, in his investigation of the natural universe a religious element was not foreign. But his fight for truth had little in common with the conflicts that his contemporaries considered religious: Catholicism versus Protestantism; curialism versus anticurialism;[7] orthodoxy versus hereticism—or "libertinism," as [monk and philosopher Tommasa] Campanella called it in his *Atheismus triumphatus*. In his adolescence, Galileo was the pupil of a Vallombrosa monk and probably was also a novice in a

6. Politician and statesman Niccoli Machiavelli is best known for his *The Prince*.   7. for or against the central administration of the Roman Catholic Church

convent of that order. (From Vincenzio Galilei's correspondence with his friend Muzio Tedaldi, Antonio Favaro deduced that the latter congratulated himself, along with Galileo's father, when the adolescent came back from the Vallombrosa friars. Evidently, although a man of rigid morality, Vincenzio was not an enthusiast of having a male child distracted from active life by the monks' influence. And that is well in line with a typical attitude of the old Florence cittadini; they seldom considered a call to monastic life as a blessing, except for women, and then only to save the family the expense of paying dowries. Anyhow, Galileo's experience among the monks was short and negative. If we are to believe in Viviani's witness, it left him but a sense of boredom for the dry formalism of the scholastics he had been introduced to.

A Classical and Humanistic Education

Leonardo Olschki

As a young man, Galileo had already earned a reputation for his literary scholarship and talents. Leonardo Olschki analyzes the Italian literary traditions and humanist education that provided Galileo with the background to achieve a new prose style. Leonardo Olschki taught romance languages at the University of Heidelberg in Germany and oriental languages at the University of California at Berkeley. He published several books in German and *The Genius of Italy* in English.

In the period between Machiavelli and Manzoni,[1] Galileo is the master of Italian prose as well as the creator of its classic style; to discover the roots of subsequent Italian prose one must seek them in Galileo's writings. That perfection of prose as an art form should be achieved in the field of natural science is a unique, almost paradoxical phenomenon in the history of world literature because, while science and prose ordinarily developed separately, significant advancements in both areas are nevertheless evident in the works of Galileo. His writings not only put an end to a basically erroneous method of scientific thought, but also rejected strained style in artistic language. Conventionality in content and expression gave way to the adventure of creative thought, and a personal confrontation between nature and man. The beauty of Galileo's prose lies in the harmonious relationships of objective knowledge and subjective realization, of mathematics and literature, of abstraction and reality. The interplay of these factors explains the complexity and intrinsic difficul-

1. Niccolo Machiavelli (1469–1527), Italian statesman and political theorist is best known for his *Prince;* Alessandro Manzoni (1785–1873) was an Italian novelist, dramatist, and poet.

From "Galileo's Literary Formation," by Leonardo Olschki, translated by Thomas Green and Maria Charlesworth, in *Galileo: Man of Science*, edited by Ernan McMullin (New York: BasicBooks, 1967). Reprinted with permission.

ties of his writings. In this essay, we shall examine the formative elements of his style, its development from instinct to consciousness, and finally to mature art.

GALILEO EVOLVES A NEW LITERARY STYLE

Galileo, like all the other molders of Italian prose, was a humanist.[2] In his scientific research, he linked empirical knowledge with a rediscovered and thoroughly comprehended blend of Platonic thought and Archimedean method,[3] to their mutual refinement and enrichment. Similarly, he combined in a literary way the norms of national prose with the vital natural forms of his mother tongue, again to their mutual advantage and enrichment. Before Galileo's time, Italian prose had never attained so uniform a harmony in tone and structure. One would search in vain in the rich variety of Renaissance literature to find such a perfect balance between artistic will and natural inclination, between respect for established canons and driving originality, of the sort that pictorial art from [Italian painters] Masaccio to Michelangelo manifests in such diverse and delicate nuances. In [Italian writer and humanist Giovanni] Boccaccio, the literary design, determined by Latin rhythm and syntax, stifled the natural evolution of a living style of speech. The resulting tension between artistic language-formation and ordinary language-usage, which had been confirmed and emphasized by the literary and cultural predominance of humanism, survived for centuries until resolved by Galileo.

This act of liberation for which he was acclaimed by his contemporaries, although not itself an explicitly literary accomplishment, was nevertheless his greatest contribution to literary history. The extent of this achievement becomes clear when one notes the stylistic inconsistency of those of his predecessors who, like Machiavelli and [Italian philosopher Giordano] Bruno, oscillated between realistic and artistic expression; they were often driven by the demands of the latter to employ a style alien to reality, a compromise which in turn affected both their thinking and their power of imagination. Even the most original thinkers of the Renaissance saw the objects of their contemplation from a double per-

2. a participant in the cultural and intellectual movement of the Renaissance that emphasized secular concerns as a result of the rediscovery and study of the literature, art, and civilization of ancient Greece and Rome.   3. the logic of Plato and the mathematics of Archimedes, both Greeks.

spective: from their own standpoint and from that of antiquity. As these two points of view did not always coincide, inner tensions resulted which not only reflected on their style, but also gave rise to varied interpretations of their assertions. Just as during the Quattrocento[4] the predominance of Latin as the artistic language prevented the rise of any other language, so also in the following centuries the notion of Boccaccio's style as an unattainable ideal led to the "academizing" of all literary expression. The direct, unaffected naturalness of [Italian sculptor and biographer Benvenuto] Cellini has scarcely anything in common with the verbose and empty bombast of other writers of his time. Even scientific literature, as several examples attest, was wavering between these two extremes.

The idea that a writer of prose must have something to say was still unfamiliar to the authors of that day, so that they continued to view prose in terms of fixed, constantly recurring and academically enforced concepts. Thus, without real necessity, language changed over the years from a bare skeleton for thought into a brilliantly colorful theatrical dress. Fiction, history and moral philosophy were all equally an excuse for rhetorical exercise, so that there was no room for personal style or individual opinion. Throughout the full range of his accomplishments, however, Galileo adapted this art-language to his own difficult, compact and multileveled world of thought. He infused literary prose with positive and personal content, and transformed it into a language both monumental and practical, both literary and scientific, a language at once expressive and highly polished. He effected this not only by a new and concrete richness of content, but also by adhering to definitive norms of style. Sometimes these agreed with academic prescriptions, but they were subject to a conscious modification arising from a new and personal interpretation of their purpose. What made this possible was his lifelong interest in literary matters—a concern which went hand in hand with his researches in natural science and whose fruits matured just as slowly as did the results of his scientific work. Galileo was as intent to express the latter in a precise, purposeful formulation as to bring together science and literary style in a richly articulated formal relationship; he thereby satisfied his aesthetic sense as well

4. the fifteenth-century period of Italian art and literature.

as his desire for scientific clarity. Although these qualities were not unknown to his contemporaries, it was from him that they received form and purpose. By bringing out the distinctiveness of his educational background and the general direction of his criticism, the story of his literary formation will reveal the process whereby his artistic and scientific ideals—in short, his taste—were gradually refined.

GALILEO'S LITERARY BACKGROUND

Disregarding the conventional, elementary literary instruction which every boy of good family received in Galileo's day, we will direct our attention especially to his humanistic education, which laid the foundation for his later literary and critical activity. The writings and interests of his father, who showed great concern for Galileo's education, reveal the humanistic milieu in which the boy was reared. [Galileo's first biographer Vincenzio] Viviani tells of Galileo's thorough and profound knowledge of Latin poetry, his favorites being Virgil, Ovid, Horace and Seneca, a large part of whose poetry he knew by heart. This predilection is not remarkable, however, for it betokens simply an ordinary humanistic education rather than a personal preference; but taken as such, it is an indication of the principal area of his literary interests. The few quotations from, and allusions to, these authors' works appearing in Galileo's writings show that he, unlike contemporary thinkers such as Bruno and [monk and philosopher Tommaso] Campanella, liked them not because of their philosophical content but solely for their poetic quality. The fact that [Roman poet] Lucretius is never mentioned confirms the impression that Galileo held poetry and science to be fields distinct from one another.[5] As he separated poetic attitudes and language from philosophical concepts, each to prosper or languish in its own proper sphere, he brought to completion the slow development of what we would call today the "aesthetic approach" to ancient poetry.

In the Middle Ages, this aesthetic approach was less significant than that of the moralizing allegory, and in the Renaissance it was less influential than were mystical and philosophical interpretations drawn from antiquity. Galileo's aversion to allegory and mysticism, and his striving for clarity and exactitude in scientific and philosophical questions,

5. Lucretius wrote a long poem attempting to explain the universe in scientific terms.

resulted in his seeing the art of poetry in its purity. He sought in it no hidden reality; for him, it was not a source of secrets or revelations. The aesthetic consciousness that led him to break with the traditional canons of judging poetry that had influenced all the humanistic thinkers, manifested itself in his categorical condemnations of complex poetry, in his criticism of any intentional combining of ethical and aesthetic goals, or of mystical and sensual motifs, in a single work of art:

> Poetic fables and fiction should be taken allegorically only when no slightest shadow of strain can be detected in such an interpretation; otherwise they will seem weak, forced, irrelevant and absurd. It is like a work of art in which perspective is emphasized and which, if viewed from the wrong angle, will appear ridiculous and distorted.

GALILEO AS A LITERARY CRITIC

Before Galileo, no one had recognized so clearly nor expressed so precisely the absolute and symbolic value of art. This was Galileo's yardstick in appraising all poetry. The feeling for limits which led him to circumscribe the provinces of knowledge and their respective purposes, to separate rigorously science from theology, to isolate the phenomena and to grasp the problems of each discipline separately—this feeling was also at work for him in the spheres of literature and of aesthetics in general. The aesthetic value of poetic art, for Galileo, is characterized by the victory over philosophically or philologically oriented humanism, for he considered poetry to be a self-contained creation in the endless yet bounded world of artistic imagination. Galileo's classical understanding of art was, therefore, different from that of both the humanist and the classicist. The former regarded ancient poetry as a model for imitation, while the latter saw in it didactic beauty in the highest sense. At the height of the Baroque period, classical poetry was, for the greatest thinkers, a world of beauty freed from all intermediaries, a world in which the spirit submitted only to its own laws.

Galileo arrived at his views in the more mature years of his young manhood, but his active life prevented these feelings from degenerating into a purely sensual aesthetic. His classical sense made him not a poet but a critic, especially in the context of Latin poetry, the knowledge of which he

shared with all educated men of his time. No less notewor-
thy is his attitude toward the Greek world, one which makes
understandable both his later choice of reading material and
his personal assimilation of certain decisive ideas. Some of
his papers are testimony even today of his youthful preoccu-
pation with the Greeks; on one side they contain notes for his
early treatise, *De motu,* and on the other, are the young scientist's translation exercises, corrected by an unknown hand.
This remarkable coincidence, however, does not give a real
clue to the time of his interest in the Greeks, although we
can conclude that the technical-scientific and philological-
humanistic aspects of his formation went on simultaneously,
at least insofar as the latter extended to the usually more remote field of Greek thought. Galileo did not allow his knowledge of Greek to remain unused, for in 1604 he began a verse
translation in Italian of the *Batrachomyomachia*[6] about
which, unfortunately, we possess no further information.
While this undertaking shows his particular fondness for
light verse, his general attitude toward Greek poetry is the
same as that toward Latin. The extent of his concern with its
formal peculiarities, in contrast to that of Bruno, is shown by
a striking characterization of [Greek lyric poet] Pindar's poetry in a letter on a scientific topic written shortly before his
death. It reveals Galileo's continuing interest in Greek poetry
in his old age, despite the fact that his remark reflects no
more than a standard attitude, and that he makes but few allusions elsewhere to the other great poets of Greece.

Galileo's relationship to classical poetry was more intense
than that of any other mathematician or natural philosopher
of the Renaissance. It was not of the objective, or expository
type, but rather of a sensual nature, that of a dilettante of
good taste. His interest nevertheless became livelier when-
ever the art-forms of a style offered an appealing theory and
dialectic. Of all the ancient authors, for Galileo as for all humanists, Plato was the master and the model of every combination of beauty and truth. There is no trace in Galileo's
writings of the usual custom of playing Plato against Aristotle, or of the dialectical reconciliation of the two which was
so often attempted, even in his day. Nor did he ever use specific Platonic ideas in order to verify his own; he never, for
example, adopted any of the Platonic maxims as a starting

6. a mock-heroic poem, *The Battle of the Frogs and the Mice*

point for his own deductions. Since he always spoke of Plato with words of esteem, however, commenting on Plato's thoughts with respectful criticism, we realize that his relationship to Plato was more emotional than scientific and scholarly; it rested on a feeling of spiritual kinship rather than on any consciousness of a similarity of view. His general intellectual orientation was Platonic, but he was more attracted by Plato's literary characteristics than by his philosophical theories. The fruit of his intensive study of the Platonic dialogues can be seen in the structure and organization of his own dialogues.

For the most part, Galileo's literary training can be inferred only indirectly from his specifically critical writings and from his attempts at poetry. The humanistic custom was to quote and interweave poetical passages into scientific and scholarly contexts, but he was careful not to allow such considerations of form to outweigh the demands of realism. His classical education, his readings in poetry and literature, were his very element, and not a mere treasure chest of rhetorical or aesthetic riches. His world was one of cheerful outlook, linguistic music and absolute integrity of expression, and in it he fashioned his own sense of form. In doing this, he chose the features which answered to his own everyday need for beauty. One would never gather from his writings that he knew [Italian poet Francesco] Petrarch's poems from memory, nor ever suspect that he owed the clarity of his own works to his complete knowledge of his favorite poet, [Ludovico] Ariosto. This last statement will appear less strange if we realize that his literary activities were for him both linguistic training and intellectual pleasure, a lifelong engagement for his vivid imagination as well as for his sense of criticism. To his literary interests we owe his early philological writings, whose aesthetic canons suggested that perfection of literary form should be blended with scientific objectivity. From these writings, we can discover something of his literary formation and in particular, of the development of his critical standards in the field of Italian poetry.

Young Galileo Recognized by Scholars

Shortly before he assumed the position of lecturer in mathematics at Pisa, and therefore long before his originality as a scientist and author had clearly manifested itself, Galileo was invited by the Florentine Academy to solve once and for all an argument about the topography of the Dantean hell, a problem with which the interpreters of the *Divina commedia* had long struggled without success. He had to appear solemnly in the role of judge before the entire Academy and its guests; this would suggest that even at the age of twenty-four he was already a member of this institution, whose concern was "the cultivation and enrichment of the vernacular". So that his linguistic talents and literary interests must already have been acknowledged among those who were concerned professionally with the diffusion of knowledge and the refinement of language. Since the executive board of the Academy specifically entrusted this young scholar with the Dantean problem, the choice must have been made in view of the conjunction of literary and mathematical interests which distinguished him even at so youthful an age. One can see that these academicians, who are usually blamed for the decline of Italian poetry, were not lacking in knowledge of human character, and that Galileo's expression of gratitude at the end of his lectures is not mere rhetoric. More than thirty years later, he was chosen as their chairman "in recognition of his admirable services to Florentine letters". On this occasion, the younger [poet] Michelangelo Buonarotti delivered the address.

A Passion for Mathematics

William R. Shea

William R. Shea argues that Galileo's early study of Greek mathematician Archimedes sustained his interest in mathematics throughout his career. According to Shea, Galileo periodically turned his attention to literature, experimentation, or technology, but while attending to these studies, he still found the underlying issues of geometry more alluring. William R. Shea has taught philosophy at the University of Ottawa in Canada. He is the author of *Revolutions in Science: Their Meaning and Relevance* and *Contemporary Issues in Political Philosophy;* he is the editor with Trevor H. Levere of *Nature, Experiment, and the Sciences: Essays on Galileo and the History of Science.*

Galileo was born in Pisa on 15 February 1564, and in 1581 he entered the University of his native city where he was enrolled as a student in the faculty of arts. During the summer vacation of 1584, he met [mathematics tutor] Ostilio Ricci, a former pupil of [Galileo's predecessor] Niccolò Tartaglia, and an exponent of the 'new' mathematics in the Florentine *Accademia del Disegno* [Academy of Design]. Galileo was immediately drawn to the subject and he gave himself to the study of geometry. He developed several theorems on the centre of gravity of solids, and it is largely on the strength of this work that he was appointed to the chair of mathematics in Pisa in 1589. As is evidenced by his early writings, Galileo's interest in mathematics was sustained, and he devoted himself to mastering the works of Archimedes. His first extant work in Italian, *The Little Balance*, dates from 1586, and was inspired by the hope of finding the method Archimedes used to solve the problem of a crown fashioned for King Hiero by a smith of rare skill but doubtful honesty,

Excerpted from *Galileo's Intellectual Revolution: Middle Period, 1610–1632*, by William Shea (New York: Neale Watson, 1972). Reprinted by permission of the author.

whom the King suspected of having used an alloy instead of pure gold. Galileo prided himself that the hydrostatic[1] balance he had invented was actually the one Archimedes had devised. Along with contemporary mathematicians, he believed that there could be no greater achievement than to walk in the footsteps of the great Syracusan. 'Those who read his works', he wrote with youthful admiration, 'realise only too clearly how inferior are all other minds compared with Archimedes', and what small hope is left of ever discovering things similar to the ones he discovered'.

GALILEO APPLIES MATHEMATICS TO DANTE'S HELL

Steeped in the Florentine tradition, Galileo also produced literary works. These include *Two Lectures to the Florentine Academy on the Shape, Place, and Size of Dante's Inferno, Considerations on Tasso, Postils to Ariosto*[2] and a satirical poem entitled *Against Wearing the Gown*. In the first of these Galileo attempted to determine certain physical characteristics of Dante's *Inferno*, but his approach was mathematical rather than experiential or observational.

> It is an admirable and difficult thing ... that men should have been able by long observations, continuous vigils, and perilous navigations, to measure and determine the intervals of the heavens, the ratios of their fast and slow motions, the size of the neighbouring and the distant stars, and the place of earth and sea, things that completely, or for the greater part, *fall under the senses.* How more wonderful should we consider the study and the description of the place and size of hell which lies in the bowels of the earth, *hidden from all the senses, and by experience known to no-one.*

Here again, it is to Archimedes that he turned for guidance and inspiration: 'We shall reckon according to the things demonstrated by Archimedes in his books *On the Sphere* and *On the Cylinder*'. In an illuminating essay, [scientist] Charles B. Schmitt comments: 'Whereas we might expect the analysis to contain some elements of the technology and craftsmanship so vividly and graphically portrayed by Dante himself in the description of the *Inferno,* they are wholly absent. The whole approach to this problem is mathematical and one might observe that, not only is "the book of nature" written in mathematical terms, but, in this

---

1. Hydrostatics is the branch of physics that deals with fluids at rest and under pressure.   2. Italian poets Dante Alighieri, Torquato Tasso, and Ludovico Ariosto, Galileo's favorite

case at least, the "book of the supernatural" is as well'.

Although Archimedes was not completely unknown in the Middle Ages, it was not until the sixteenth century that his works received serious and scholarly attention. Their rediscovery opened a new and fresh vista on the world, and they exerted the fascination of novelty on a young man who had been subjected to the tedium of the spent force of Aristotelianism. All of Galileo's extant letters which do not concern personal matters are addressed to the mathematicians Christopher Clavius, Guidobaldo del Monte and Michel Coignet. To these we may add an anonymous letter praising one of his geometrical theorems, and attestations of the originality of his *Theoremata circa centrum gravitatis solidorum* [*Theory about the Solid Center of Gravity*] by Guiseppe Moletti, the professor of mathematics at Padua, and other notabilities.

GALILEO IS NOT DRAWN TO TECHNOLOGY

During this period, Galileo does not seem to have been interested in problems of technology. The first documentary evidence of any direct concern with applied science occurs in his description of the hydrostatic balance where he notes possible difficulties:

> Since the wires are very fine, as is needed for precision, it is not possible to count them visually, because the eye is dazzled by such small spaces. To count them easily, therefore, take a very sharp stiletto and pass it very slowly over the wires. Thus, partly through our hearing, partly through our hand feeling an obstacle at each turn of wire, we shall easily count the number of turns.

One does not find such practical indications in the two versions of Archimedes' method that have been handed down to us. An incipient experimentalism is also manifested in the table of specific gravities[3] which Galileo derived from the hydrostatic balance. This represents his closest approximation during this period to what was later to become known as 'experimental science'.

Professor Stillman Drake has recently drawn attention to another possible source of Galileo's subsequent interest in experimental verification of mathematical laws. Between

---

3. the ratio of the mass of a solid or liquid to the mass of an equal volume of distilled water at 39˚F or of a gas to an equal volume of air or hydrogen under prescribed conditions of temperature and pressure

1585, when he left the University of Pisa without a degree, and 1589, when he obtained the chair of mathematics in Pisa, Galileo lived mainly in Florence, giving private instruction in mathematics. It was precisely during these years that his father, Vincenzio Galilei, carried out a number of experiments to refute the belief common among musical theorists that the small number fractions, 2:1, 3:2 and 4:3, were always associated with agreeable tones. Vincenzio Galilei agreed that these numbers will give octaves, fifths and fourths for equally tense strings of the same material when their lengths are in these ratios, but he found by experiment that if the lengths are equal and the tensions are varied, then the weights required to produce the tensions giving the same intervals are as the square of the numbers. In addition, he experimented with strings of different materials and different weights and discovered that unison cannot be consistently obtained between two strings if they differ in any respect whatever. It is not unlikely that his son Galileo, who was also an accomplished musician, was fully informed of his research. The evidence is circumstantial but it is heightened by the fact that music was still considered at the time a special branch of mathematics, and that Galileo was interested by the problem of ratios. We have no indication, however, that he conducted any of the experiments mentioned by his father. . . .

His early orientation was mathematical; all that he wrote between 1584, the date of his first acquaintance with mathematics, and 1592, when he went to Padua to embark upon a new venture, confirms this.

GALILEO IS FREER AS A MATHEMATICIAN

The originality of Galileo's position is best understood against the background of the structure of the university in the latter part of the sixteenth century. His appointment as professor of mathematics may have been less lucrative than that of his colleagues who taught philosophy but it suffered from less intellectual constraints. A lecturer in philosophy was expected to explicate the thought of Aristotle, and the chief end of his scholarly endeavours was to master his writings. The assumption present in this, of course, was that if Aristotle were correctly understood and properly taught, the students would be equipped with the conceptual tools and the basic categories with which to interpret the physical world. Galileo's own situation was different. As a teacher of mathematics he had a much less clearly defined assignment than a philosopher who had to contend with the totality of earlier Aristotelian commentaries. His task was to understand and explain the works of [Greek mathematician] Euclid and [Alexandrian astronomer and mathematician] Ptolemy, the two authors whom he discussed in his formal lectures, but he was not fettered by several centuries of institutional philosophical tradition.

The distinctive mental perspectives of the philosophers and the mathematicians implied a different way of looking at the world. On the one hand, philosophers, following Aristotle, saw the universe on the model of a living, biological entity, teleologically oriented and best understood through experience and syllogistic reasoning.[4] Their system was close-knit, and to live in this world, where every aspect of every question was dealt with in meticulous order and detail, was in itself a fascination. On the other hand, mathematicians, under the guidance of Euclid and Archimedes, viewed the world in terms of geometrical shapes which obeyed mathematically expressible laws. Although many Aristotelians saw the importance of experiments, they failed to appreciate the significance of mathematics, and, to their lasting misfortune, the proper method in physics turned out to be quantitative and not qualitative.

In his *De Motu*, which is not a textbook for students but a scholarly essay on motion, Galileo enjoyed the relative freedom of an independent thinker from whom no rigid doctrinal commitment was expected. 'As a teacher of mathematics he leaned heavily toward the methodology of Euclid and Archimedes, it is true, but, as an investigator of questions concerning the motion of heavy and light bodies, he was essentially searching for a new approach to a problem—i.e., motion—which had for centuries fallen within the province of the Aristotelian-Scholastic philosophers. He thus shows a more "open" attitude toward introducing non-traditional elements into his investigation.'

He could also be completely fearless in his attack on Aristotle, and the *De Motu* is a work of protest as well as an attempt to introduce a new solution. Six chapters begin with

---

4. Teleology is the use of ultimate purpose or design as a means of explaining natural phenomena. A syllogism is a form of deductive reasoning, from a general premise to a particular instance.

the somewhat pugnacious phrase '*in quo contra Aristotelem concluditur*' [in which Aristotle argues the opposite], and Galileo declares that 'Aristotle, in practically everything that he wrote about local motion, wrote the opposite of the truth'. In another passage, he states that he is 'weary and ashamed of having to use so many words to refute such childish arguments and such inept attempts at subtleties as those which Aristotle crams in the whole book of *De Coelo*.' He takes Aristotle to task for failing to grasp the significance of mathematics and relying on mere experience. 'Aristotle was ignorant not only of the profound and more abstruse discoveries of geometry, but even of the most elementary principles of this science'. Those who try to defend him are 'even more inept in geometry'. The real master to turn to is the 'divine', the superhuman Archimedes, whose name I never mention without a feeling of awe'. In fact, explanation in the *De Motu* is conceived almost exclusively along the lines of an Archimedean solution to a geometrical problem. For instance, Galileo assumes that a volume can be considered as a summation of an infinite number of plane segments, and he uses the lever as an interpretative model to explain the behaviour of rising and falling bodies.

> Since it is most useful to compare bodies in natural motion with weights on a balance, this correspondence will be shown throughout the entire discussion on natural motion.

In providing Galileo with the lever (of which the balance is merely a special case) as a means of reducing motion to quantitative treatment, Archimedes became the father of the modern science of dynamics. By means of the principle of virtual velocities, Galileo extended the principle of the lever to problems of hydrostatics and later to all the simple machines. . . .

It seems clear, therefore, that the role of experience and experiment as a regulative factor was practically absent from Galileo's early writings. He considered a mathematically orientated approach to be more fruitful, and it is only gradually during the Paduan period that he began to realise the importance of devising systematic experiments.

VENETIANS ASK GALILEO TO SOLVE PRACTICAL PROBLEMS

In 1592, with the aid of his friend the Marquis Guidobaldo del Monte, Galileo exchanged his Pisan chair for the corresponding one in Padua, vacant since the death of [mathematics professor] Giuseppe Moletti in 1588.

nete, they discussed and repeated his experiments with a loadstone [a piece of magnetite that has magnetic properties]. Sagredo himself had a bent for instrument-making. He devised a machine to make screws, and he relied on Galileo's help to secure tools and skilled craftsmen. Paolo Sarpi was more concerned with theoretical problems, and it is in reply to one of his queries that Galileo first formulated the correct law of free fall, which he deduced, however, from the wrong assumption that the speed is directly proportional to the distance.

A large number of students to whom Galileo gave private tuition were young noblemen who were mainly interested in the relevance of geometry and mathematics to practical problems of military warfare. Galileo supplied them with an elementary handbook on castrametation [camp measurements], fortifications and sieges. For their use, he also improved and incorporated several features of earlier sectors in a military and geometrical compass which he began selling, for a handsome sum, as early as 1597. Two years later Marcantonio Mazzoleni, a skilled craftsman, entered his service, and from that time seems to have been mainly responsible for the compasses, surveying instruments and later the lenses that came out of Galileo's workshop.

In addition to lecturing on Euclid and Ptolemy as he had done at Pisa, Galileo also taught [John Holywood] Sacrobosco's *Sphere* and Aristotle's *Mechanics.* This latter series of lectures gave rise to a small but important work *On Mechanics* in which Galileo extended the principle of the lever by means of the principle of virtual velocities to simple machines: the windlass, the capstan, the pulley, the screw and the Archimedean screw. Galileo mentioned the useful applications that can be derived from the science of mechanics and from its instruments, but he mainly intended to dispel the illusion of some engineers who believed that they could cheat nature by overcoming a greater force with a smaller one. . . .

GALILEO REMAINS AT HEART A MATHEMATICIAN

The seventeenth century was above all an age in which the idea of experimenting came into its own, and the young Galileo is often credited with having seen that experiment is the main route to the advancement of learning. We can conclude that this view is an over-simplification. Galileo became interested, but by no means absorbed, in some as-

One could not be a professor of mathematics in the University of Italy's greatest seafaring nation without coming in contact with the docks and the shipyard. The rulers of the Republic believed in using their scientific manpower—something about which Galileo was later to complain—and he had not been in Padua long when his professional advice was sought by Venetian noblemen. Giacomo Contarini, who later became one of the overseers of the shipyard, asked him whether it was preferable to place the rowlock on the side of a ship or on a projecting strut. Galileo explained that the oar functioned as a lever with the fulcrum at the blade, and that the position of the rowlock was immaterial as long as the ratios of the distances between the fulcrum, the force and the weight remained the same. He also made it clear that it was important to avoid expending force in moving the water which should be kept at rest as much as possible. A few months later another leading Venetian patrician, Alvise Mocenigo, asked him to explain the construction of an oil lantern mentioned by Hero. Galileo replied by forwarding a paraphrase of Hero's text, and admitting that he was not too clear about its meaning.

Although these are the only semi-official requests we know for certain Galileo received from members of the Venetian ruling class, it is probable that he was also consulted on irrigation, which had become a pressing problem with the development at the end of the sixteenth century of rice and corn growing in the Venetian territories of the Po valley. In any case, Galileo soon became interested in the problem and by the end of 1593 he applied for a patent for a horse-driven pump to hoist water and irrigate land. On 18 February 1594, the patent officers reported that they had not seen Galileo's machine or a model of it, and recommended that he be given a patent for twenty years instead of the forty he had requested. This was granted by the Senate on 15 September of the same year. Galileo, however, does not seem to have built a working model of his machine until 1602. This would seem to indicate that he was not very keen on applying the fruits of his invention or that there was only slight incentive to do so. If Galileo was not pressed by demands for practical applications of his mathematical science, he had friends, especially Gianfrancesco Sagredo and Paolo Sarpi, who were interested in various aspects of technology. From 1602 when they first heard of [William] Gilbert's *De mag-*

pects of the craft tradition during his twenty years in Padua. He answered questions on the most suitable position of rowlocks and on the construction of lanterns, he built compasses, he discussed problems of military engineering, he experimented with loadstones, he designed a model for a waterpump and he invented a primitive thermometer. He remained, however, a mathematician in his method and in his outlook. His instinctive reaction was to work out the properties of the behaviour of bodies in good Archimedean fashion from geometric considerations of motion or of equilibrium on the model of a lever. When he did perform an experiment it was usually to illustrate a conclusion arrived at through mathematical reasoning. What was novel in Galileo's approach, when contrasted with that of his Aristotelian opponents, was not so much his attitude to experimentation as his faith in the relevance of mathematics.

CHAPTER 2

Galileo's Contribution to Physics

Formulating a New Scientific Method

Allen G. Debus

Allen G. Debus explains the method Galileo developed to show how, not why, an event happens in nature. To illustrate, Debus follows Galileo's steps designed to investigate the motion of falling bodies. Though Galileo's conclusions proved correct, there is speculation that he conducted only thought experiments and omitted real experimentation, a weakness in his method. According to Debus, other scientists conducted the actual experiments and found that Galileo's conclusions proved true. Allen G. Debus taught history of science and medicine at the University of Chicago. He is the author of *Science and Education in the Seventeenth Century: The Webster-Ward Debate* and *The Chemical Dream of the Renaissance.*

[French philosopher and mathematician René] Descartes was to have an influence on Continental science that was not to decline until the mid-eighteenth century. But if the defect of [English philosopher Francis] Bacon's new science was an overemphasis on experiment, that of Descartes failed as a result of its overemphasis on deduction. Truly effective only when applied to subjects that did in fact lend themselves to a mathematical treatment, few of his cosmological or biological speculations proved to have lasting value for the future development of science.

The influence of Bacon and Descartes [on modern science] notwithstanding, both were wedded to methodologies that were badly flawed from the standpoint of the modern scientist. What was needed was more of a real interplay between the inductive and deductive processes.[1] This ap-

1. Induction: The process of deriving general principles from particular facts or instances. Deduction: The process of reasoning in which a conclusion necessarily follows from the stated premises; inference by reasoning from general to the specific.

proach is seen best in the work of Galileo—not in the form of a discussion of scientific method, but rather in the actual development of his subject. For our purpose the most useful volume to examine is the *Mathematical Discourses and Demonstrations Concerning Two New Sciences* (1638). There is no need to summarize its contents because it is not our intent to follow the physics of motion of the seventeenth century in detail. Nevertheless, Galileo's development of the problem of free fall presents an excellent example of his methodological procedure.

GALILEO DEVELOPS A SCIENTIFIC METHOD

Beginning with the observation that in most studies of natural phenomena it is customary to seek their causes, Galileo rejects this and suggests rather that

> "The present does not seem to be the proper time to investigate the cause of the acceleration of natural motion, concerning which various opinions have been expressed by various philosophers, some explaining it by attraction to the center, others to repulsion between the very small parts of the body, while still others attribute it to a certain stress in the surrounding medium which closes in behind the falling body and drives it from one of its positions to another. Now all these fantasies, and others too, ought to be examined; but it is not really worth while. At present it is the purpose of our Author merely to investigate and to demonstrate some of the properties of accelerated motion (whatever the cause of this acceleration may be) . . ."

The primary question has changed from "why" to "how," and to implement this Galileo turned to a mathematical description of natural phenomena.

In the course of his investigation Galileo wrote the equivalent of a modern scientific monograph. First he stated his intention—to set forth a new science dealing with an ancient subject: change in motion. In the discussion of free fall proper, Galileo noted that it was well known that bodies accelerate as they fall. What was to be determined was just how this acceleration occurs. At this point he introduced definitions he planned to use (including those of "uniform motion," "velocity," and "uniformly accelerated motion"). The reader is next informed that Galileo will limit his discussion to falling bodies alone: "We have decided to consider the phenomena of bodies falling with an acceleration such as actually occurs in nature." Note how different this is from the Baconian method, in which all examples of motion would have been gathered prior to the determination of scientific laws.

At this point Galileo introduced a rule of simplicity before proceeding further: "Why should I not believe that such increases [in velocity] take place in a manner which is exceedingly simple and rather obvious to everybody?" That is, if bodies accelerate in free fall, we might make the assumption that they accelerate in the simplest possible way, uniformly. A test now seemed imperative and in the dialogue Galileo's friend, Sagredo,[2] admitted that

> "I can offer no rational objection to this or indeed to any other definition . . . [but] . . . I may nevertheless without offense be allowed to doubt whether such a definition as the above corresponds to and describes that kind of accelerated motion which we meet in nature in the case of freely falling bodies."

Galileo's answer was to deduce a series of theorems required if free fall is actually a case of uniform acceleration. Included are the familiar equations $s = \frac{1}{2} vt$ and $s \propto t^2$,[3] where s is distance, v is velocity, and t is time. An experimental proof is offered through the inclined plane, which permits the retardation of the descent motion so that both distance and time may be measured. Using a water clock as a timing device, Galileo obtained results that upheld his derived formula, $s \propto t^2$. Here then was a case of uniformly accelerated motion, even though he readily admitted that it was not free fall.

To proceed further, Galileo next made the assumption that a body that falls through a height of an inclined plane attains the same velocity as one that falls through its length. After presenting the logic for this, he again turned to experimental proof. In this case he turned to a pendulum, noting that it swung from a given height on one side to the same height on the other (after making some allowance for the resistance of air). But the motion of a pendulum describes the arc of a circle and therefore may be viewed as a descent along a series of inclined planes of different inclinations. These hypothetical planes were approximated by pegging nails in the board behind the pendulum. In all cases the pendulum bob came close to reaching the original height (therefore attaining nearly the original velocity on the descent). In this way it seemed possible to deduce that the times of descent along the lengths of inclined planes are in

2. Galileo presented his ideas in the form of dialogues, using the character Sagredo to state the common sense view and Simplicio to state the view he refutes, usually the Aristotelian view.   3. The mathematical symbol $\propto$ means proportional to, or varies as.

simple proportion to their heights, and that the accelerations are inversely proportional to the times of descent. That is, $\dfrac{t_1}{t_2} = \dfrac{h_1}{h_2}$

but $v = a$ (acceleration) t

or $a \propto \dfrac{1}{t}$

therefore $\dfrac{t_1}{t_2} = \dfrac{a_2}{a_1}$

All of this leads to the conclusion that free fall is uniformly accelerated. The result of course is basic for the physics of motion, but here it is of special interest to us for an example of procedural method. Galileo first stated his problem and then carefully enunciated the definitions he intended to use. Then he made a fundamental assumption regarding free fall and uniform acceleration that must be tested. This was done by checking theorems that must hold true if free fall is indeed uniformly accelerated. The experiment was then carried out and a further assumption made and tested before the original one was accepted.

GALILEO CONDUCTS THOUGHT EXPERIMENTS

All of this is carried on in the form of a dialogue, with lengthy digressions on the part of the participants. A weakness from our point of view is that the demonstrations are given in the form of thought experiments: that is, suggested experiments with no evidence of their actual completion. But the importance of it all is that here we see how a working scientist investigates a specific problem through the constant interplay of hypothesis and experiment. The suggested procedure is one that could be followed today. Indeed, many college students will recall that Galileo's inclined plane and pendulum are still used in laboratories as an introduction to the physics of motion.

Bacon and Descartes had both called for the destruction of the ancient philosophies. No one could deny their impact on the scientific world of the late seventeenth century, but in the end the influence of Galileo may well have been greater in the development of modern scientific method. The men of the Royal Society of London did not hesitate to designate themselves as "Baconian," but their Galilean heritage is no less evident.

Galileo's study of free fall involved two fundamental experiments: the inclined plane and the pendulum. Yet, as presented to the reader, Galileo's work emphasized the logic of the conclusions rather than their experimental foundation. Accordingly, Galilean scholars have debated at length whether or not Galileo actually performed the experiments. Although this question need not detain us, Galileo clearly left himself open to criticism, a criticism that is evident in his discussion of the earth's motion. Here a question frequently asked was: Where would a stone fall when dropped from the mast of a swiftly moving ship? When at anchor it is obvious that it falls parallel to the mast, but when in motion one might conceivably expect it to fall far to the rear since

GALILEO SAW THE NEED TO GO BEYOND LOGIC

In a lecture entitled "On the Method of Theoretical Physics," published in Ideas and Opinions, *physicist Albert Einstein credits Greek mathematician Euclid with providing science a logical system, but he attributes to Galileo the insight of seeing that the direct experience of experimentation is necessary to arrive at truth in nature.*

We reverence ancient Greece as the cradle of western science. Here for the first time the world witnessed the miracle of a logical system which proceeded from step to step with such precision that every single one of its propositions was absolutely indubitable—I refer to Euclid's geometry. This admirable triumph of reasoning gave the human intellect the necessary confidence in itself for its subsequent achievements. If Euclid failed to kindle your youthful enthusiasm, then you were not born to be a scientific thinker.

But before mankind could be ripe for a science which takes in the whole of reality, a second fundamental truth was needed, which only became common property among philosophers with the advent of Kepler and Galileo. Pure logical thinking cannot yield us any knowledge of the empirical world; all knowledge of reality starts from experience and ends in it. Propositions arrived at by purely logical means are completely empty as regards reality. Because Galileo saw this, and particularly because he drummed it into the scientific world, he is the father of modern physics—indeed, of modern science altogether.

Albert Einstein, *Ideas and Opinions.* Ed. Carl Seelig. New York: Wings Books, 1954.

the ship has moved ahead during the time of fall. The problem was of real interest to both Aristotelians and Copernicans,[4] for both saw in the example a possible analogy with the moving earth. Galileo, employing the medieval term of "impetus," stated firmly that in the moving ship the stone continued to fall parallel to the mast, explaining that the stone partook of the forward impetus of the ship. In the dialogue Simplicio, the Aristotelian spokesman, replied that, "Not only haven't you made a hundred tests of this, you have not even made one." Quite so, replied Galileo's spokesman, "I am certain without experiment that the event will be as I have told you; for it must be so." The conclusion may have been correct, but the argument was not completely convincing in 1638. . . .

OTHER SCIENTISTS CONFIRM GALILEO'S CONCLUSIONS

Aristotle had also suggested that bodies of different weights move in the same medium with velocities that stand to one another in the same ratio as their weights. For one who had observed objects falling in liquids and oils—or a stone and a feather dropped simultaneously in the air—this would indeed seem to be the commonsense answer. But what would happen in a vacuum, assuming that one could be produced? Galileo pointed out that the less dense a medium, the closer the velocities of the falling bodies become, regardless of their weight. Therefore, he argued, in a vacuum all bodies would fall at the same rate. Consequently the discussion of the relative velocities of falling objects of different weights was associated with the question of the existence of a vacuum. . . .

Galileo's discussion of a vacuum obviously had led to experimental work confirming his conclusions. But the same realization of the need for experimental proof will be seen if we return to the ship experiment. The argument of the moving ship had been one of the more powerful ones advanced by the opponents of Copernicus, and although Galileo had rejected their Aristotelian argument, he admittedly had not carried out the experiment to prove his case. Galileo's discussion had appeared in his *Dialogue on the Two Principal World Systems* in 1632. Prior to publication he had circulated his manuscript and it is clear from the ensuing correspondence that among those most interested were [French scientist Father Marin] Mersenne and [French scientist Pierre] Gassendi. Mersenne immediately tried, in 1633, to determine the velocities of stones dropped from a cathedral tower. But, also seriously concerned about the ship experiment, he wrote to a friend who often crossed the English Channel. During a crossing made in 1634 this correspondent arranged to have a sailor climb the mast and drop weights. The results confirmed the work of Galileo, as the stones fell at the foot of the mast. But this work was not published, and it was Gassendi who next turned to the ship experiment. Convinced of its importance, he determined to have it carried out with an audience so that there could be no doubt as to the outcome. He found a patron in the new governor of Provence, who had an interest in the sciences.

An elaborate series of tests discussed by Galileo was planned by Gassendi and carried out in October, 1640. Men on horseback and in chariots threw stones in the air and across to each other, and it was seen that these missiles followed the forward motion of the horses as well as the transverse motion of the throw. Objects dropped from a horse in full gallop were found to fall in a straight line from the point of view of the rider. These and a series of other tests all confirmed the work of Galileo, but surely the most spectacular demonstrations were made aboard a naval trireme [warship]. After the ship had reached its highest speed it was found that, whether the stone was dropped from the mast or projected straight up, in both cases it fell to the foot of the mast rather than far behind in the stern. In his description of the results, Gassendi gave the speed of the boat and described all of the experiments in detail. He then suggested that the reader might carry out similar tests by throwing a ball in the air on his balcony while pacing—or by taking a small sailboat out on the river and testing the facts as he had on the trireme. . . .

Galileo's works were eagerly sought and read by a large contemporary audience. And when he admitted that he had not tried the ship experiment, there were those who realized that it had to be done—and that it had to be done with witnesses.

One senses a far different climate in the 1640s than that existing in the opening years of the century. With Bacon, Descartes, and Galileo criticism of Aristotle and the scholastic tradition had become far more sophisticated. And while we may point to flaws in their results as well as their methods, it is evident that their discussions regarding the need for a new science, the role of experiment, the proper use of mathematics, and the interplay of the inductive and the deductive processes in the role of discovery directly and dramatically affected the development of science.

Galileo's study of local motion rightly makes him a key figure in the rise of modern science not only for his methodology, but also for the consequences of his work. He had attacked a fundamental aspect of Aristotelian natural philosophy and had developed in its stead a new science of motion carefully built upon experiment and the consequences to be deduced from his evidence.

A Broad Investigation into Physics

Lynn Thorndike

Lynn Thorndike provides a thumbnail review of Galileo's *Dialogues Concerning Two New Sciences,* in which Galileo explains his scientific research in the form of dialogues among three fictitious scientists named Salviati, Simplicio, and Sagredo. Although Galileo is not directly present in these dialogues, it is his discoveries and scientific conclusions that the trio discusses and ultimately puts forth. In giving his account of *Dialogues,* Thorndike is struck by the great number and variety of Galileo's experiments and by the sense of wonder that Galileo conveys even in the most rigidly academic sections of his treatise. Lynn Thorndike was professor of history at Columbia University. He is the author of *The History of Medieval Europe,* and *A Short History of Civilization.*

[In his *Dialogues Concerning Two New Sciences*] Galileo repeatedly asserts that bodies are composed of an infinite number of very minute corpuscles or atoms. The extremely fine particles of fire are able to penetrate the slender pores of metals, although these are too small to admit even the finest particles of air or of many liquids, while a vast number of tiny vacant spaces bind together the least particles of a metal. Bodies are composed of an infinite rather than a finite number of atoms. Similarly a continuous quantity contains an infinite number of indivisibles. Gold and silver may be reduced "into their ultimate, indivisible, and infinitely small components." Or again, many examples show that *materie fisiche* [physical matter, or objects] are made up "of infinitely small indivisible particles." Thus Galileo favored atomism before or contemporaneously with [French scientist Pierre] Gassendi and [French philosopher and mathe-

Excerpted from *A History of Magic and Experimental Science,* vol. 7, by Lynn Thorndike (New York: Columbia University Press, 1958). Reprinted by permission of the Copyright Clearance Center on behalf of the publisher.

matician René] Descartes, and foreran the "corpuscular philosophy" of [British physicist and chemist] Robert Boyle [which dealt with particles in atoms].

THE *DIALOGUES* INITIATES EXPERIMENTATION

Although abounding also in mathematical demonstrations, the *Two New Sciences* of Galileo perhaps more than any other single book, marks the advent of modern experimental method. There are experiments with a wooden rod fitted into a wall at right angles, with weights supported by two nails of different size driven into a wall, with a weight attached to a cylinder hanging vertically. The binding effect of spirals is illustrated by a device used in sliding down a rope. The experiment with two smooth flat surfaces which will slide over each other readily but are difficult to lift apart, is still attributed to avoidance of a vacuum and not to air pressure, and apparatus is devised to measure the *forza del vacuo* [strength of a vacuum]. There are experiments to find to what length cylinders of metal, stone, wood, glass etc. of any diameter can be elongated without breaking of their own weight, and experiments with molten gold, silver and glass. A rather crude experiment is described to determine whether the propagation of light is instantaneous, but it was a first step towards the Morley-Michelson experiment.[1]

There are experiments with falling bodies, including one from a tower two hundred cubits high, but those to show that a vacuum might be produced by violence "would here occupy too much time" and so are omitted. Two bodies which differed very little in speed falling through the air, in water sank with a speed ten times as great for one as for the other. Sagredo "often tried with the utmost patience to add grains of sand to a ball of wax until it should acquire the same specific gravity as water" and maintain equilibrium therein, but with all his care was never able to accomplish this. When physicians perform a similar experiment in testing waters, the addition of two grains of salt to six pounds of water is enough to bring the ball from the bottom to the surface. Evidently others than Galileo were performing exact and meticulous experiments. If a globe full of water with a very narrow mouth—"about the same diameter as a straw"—is

1. an experiment using light beams to test Aristotle's view that a substance called aether filled all the space between planets and stars

inverted, the water will not run out nor the air enter, but if a vessel of red wine is applied to the opening, the water and wine will very slowly interchange places.

There follow experiments with compressed air and an air-pump, weighing water against air, experiments with pendulums, showing that the time of descent is the same along all arcs, and "some easy and tangible experiments" concerning marvelous accidents in the matter of sound,—all these before even the first of the four days of the dialogues is over. Those with sound included the scraping of a brass plate with an iron chisel which produced rows of fine parallel marks when it made a noise. When the tones were higher, the marks were closer together and when deeper, farther apart. An experiment noted in the dialogue of the second day was producing a parabola by rolling a perfectly spherical brass ball on a metallic mirror held somewhat inclined.

EXPERIMENTS CONCERNING MOTION

The experiments of the remaining two days are concerned with motion, and Galileo claims to have discovered notable properties of motion not hitherto observed or demonstrated, such as that "the distances traversed during equal intervals of time by a body falling from rest stand to one another in the same ratio as the odd numbers beginning with unity," and that the path of projectiles is a parabola. Experiments are made with a ball rolling in a channel down inclined planes and the time measured by a water clock. We are told on the one hand that principles which have once been established by intelligent experiments become the foundation of the entire superstructure, but on the other hand that understanding why a thing happens far outweighs the mere information received from others or even gained by repeated experiment, and that the knowledge of a single fact by discovering its causes enables one to understand and ascertain other facts without need of recourse to experimentation, and further that "the same experiment which at first glance seemed to show one thing, when more carefully examined, assures us of the contrary." Thus Galileo recognized the existence of certain perils in experimentation and set limitations to the use of the experimental method, preferring rigid geometrical demonstration where that was possible.

Professor Lane Cooper in *Aristotle, Galileo and the Tower of Pisa* (1935), noted that the story of Galileo's employing the campanile or leaning tower of Pisa in experiments with falling bodies, first appeared in Vincenzio Viviani, *Racconto istorico de la Vita del Signor Galileo Galilei,* which was com-

THE SIGNIFICANCE OF GALILEO'S RESEARCH

In The Age of Reason Begins *Will and Ariel Durant enumerate the principles of physics Galileo established through his researches and experiments and explain their meaning for the development of science.*

Now he made the researches and experiments that he gathered together only toward the end of his life in his *Dialogues Concerning Two New Sciences*—i.e., concerning statics and dynamics. He affirmed the indestructibility of matter. He formulated the principles of the lever and the pulley, and showed that the speed of freely falling bodies increases at a uniform rate. He made many experiments with inclined planes; he argued that an object rolling down one plane would rise on a similar plane to a height equal to its fall if it were not for frictional or other resistance; and he concluded to the law of inertia (Newton's first law of motion)—that a moving body will continue indefinitely in the same line and rate of motion unless interfered with by some external force. He proved that a projectile propelled in a horizontal direction would fall to the earth in a parabolic curve compounding the forces of impetus and gravity. He reduced musical tones to wave lengths of air, and showed that the pitch of a note depends upon the number of vibrations made by the struck string in a given time. Notes, he taught, are felt as consonant and harmonious when their vibrations strike the ear with rhythmic regularity. Only those properties of matter belong to matter that can be dealt with mathematically—extension, position, motion, density; all other properties—sounds, tastes, odors, colors, and so on—"reside only in consciousness; if the living creature were removed, all these qualities would be wiped away and annihilated." He hoped that in time these "secondary qualities" could be analyzed into primary physical qualities of matter and motion, mathematically measurable.

These were basic and fruitful contributions. They were hampered by inadequacy of instruments; so, for example, Galileo underestimated the factor of air resistance in the fall of objects and projectiles. But no man since Archimedes had ever done so much for physics.

Will and Ariel Durant, *The Age of Reason Begins: A History of European Civilization in the Period of Shakespeare, Bacon, Montaigne, Rembrandt, Galileo, and Descartes: 1558-1648.* Part VII of *The Story of Civilization.* New York: Simon & Schuster, 1961.

posed in 1654 but not published until 1717, and that this original statement had been greatly enlarged upon and embroidered by subsequent imaginative writers. In a passage cited above concerning experiments with falling bodies, Galileo spoke of a tower 200 cubits or 300 feet high whereas the leaning tower is only 181 feet. The figure of 200 may have been selected for purposes of easy computation, but it seems clear that Galileo had often experimented with dropping bodies from heights and that towers would provide the most convenient and sheer drops. In his *De motu* [*On Motion*], discussing why less heavy bodies at first fall faster than heavier bodies, he asserts that wood at first drops faster than lead, but after a little the motion of the lead is so accelerated that it leaves the wood behind, "and, if they are released from a tall tower, precedes it by a great space; and of this I have often made trial."

Despite the rigid mathematical demonstration and experimental proof which are said to characterize the two new sciences, an element of the marvelous, not to say magical, is not entirely lacking in them, or at least in their exposition. We are told that "sometimes a wonder is diminished by a miracle." When Sagredo, speaking of burning glasses, remarks, "Such effects as these render credible to me the marvels accomplished by the mirrors of [Greek mathematician and physicist] Archimedes," Salviati retorts that it was Archimedes' "own books (which I had already read and studied with infinite astonishment) that rendered credible to me all the miracles described" by other writers. Or we have explained "a phenomenon upon which the common people always look with wonder," while even Salviati's "surprise is increased," when he sees every day enormous expansions occurring almost instantaneously, as in the explosion of gunpowder. Later he alludes to the supernatural violence with which projectiles are launched from fire-arms. Even secret mysteries are still the order of the day.

> The fact that one can take the origin of motion either at the inmost center or at the very top of the sphere

leads Simplicio to think

> that there may be some great mystery hidden in these true and wonderful results, a mystery related to the creation of the universe (which is said to be spherical in shape), and related also to the seat of the First Cause.

And Salviati agrees with him.

EXPERIMENTS WITH MAGNETS

Writing in 1606 of his own experiments with the magnet, Galileo said that he had made it sustain twice its own weight and that he had in mind (*nella fantasia*) "some other artifices to render this yet more marvelous." Twenty years later he wrote that for three months he had been busy with an admirable device of multiplying artificially and extremely the virtue of the magnet in sustaining iron. A piece weighing six ounces which by its natural force would not sustain more than an ounce of iron, by art sustains 150 ounces. At first he had been thrilled to support forty times more than its innate strength would, but now he is not content with 150 times it. Thus experimental science has not yet freed itself from the appeal of the surprising, the unexpected, the marvelous, the secret and the mysterious, which had always been characteristic of magic.

Galileo's "Clocks"

J. Bronowski and Bruce Mazlish

J. Bronowski and Bruce Mazlish provide historical and scientific background for Galileo's inventions to measure time. Establishing laws of mechanics and navigating at sea were hampered by the lack of any instruments to keep time more accurately than looking at the sun's position. Galileo used the pendulum to measure small intervals of time in mechanical experiments, and he charted the moons of Jupiter to give sailors a better measure of time at sea. J. Bronowski taught biology and statistical research at Oxford University in England and Yale University. He is the author of *The Identity of Man* and *The Common Sense of Science.* Bruce Mazlish taught history at the University of Maine and Columbia University. He is the author of *The Revolutionary Ascetic.*

If the planets run as a machine runs, then they must be moved and controlled by mechanical forces. The laws which these forces obey must be laws of mechanics. These celestial laws might, of course, be different from the laws of mechanics which are obeyed by forces on earth. The Middle Ages would have taken it for granted that they are different. By the year 1600, however, minds which had been shaken by the new stars and the new speculations found it natural to ask whether the laws of mechanics in the sky might not be the same as the laws of mechanics on earth. At the least, they found it natural to ask, with more persistence than had been used before, what precisely are the laws of mechanics on earth.

SPECULATION ABOUT FALLING OBJECTS

A central question in mechanics, because it was a question of fact and not of theory, asked at what rate an object falls to the ground. [Greek philosopher] Aristotle had said that a

Excerpted from *The Western Intellectual Tradition: From Leonardo to Hegel,* by Jacob Bronowski and Bruce Mazlish. Copyright © 1960 Jacob Bronowski and Bruce Mazlish. Reprinted by permission of HarperCollins Publishers, Inc.

heavy object falls faster than a light one, and [Italian philosopher and Dominican friar] St. Thomas Aquinas had followed him in this as in other opinions. The opinion had not gone quite unchallenged after Aquinas. As [historian] Pierre Duhem has shown in his work on the school of [William] Ockham, first [French physicist] Jean Buridan and then Nicholas of Oresme in the fourteenth century put forward the view that unequal objects fall equally fast; and their view was held in the University of Paris for the next century and longer. More recently, other scholars have found this view expressed even earlier, about 1335, by the Mertonians in Oxford.

In spite of these historical debates, however, the established view until the seventeenth century remained that of Aristotle, that heavier objects fall faster than light ones. Then, about 1600, the accepted view was challenged and defeated rather quickly. The story goes that it was defeated by Galileo, who is said to have dropped two cannon balls of unequal masses from the Leaning Tower of Pisa, and to have shown that they reached the ground together. Alas, there is little evidence for this story: if cannon balls were dropped from the Tower of Pisa, they were not dropped by Galileo, and it is unlikely that they reached the ground triumphantly together.

It is, in fact, foolish to suppose that the doctrine of unequal rates of fall proposed by Aristotle was as brazenly out of step with the facts as this, and might have been overthrown at any time in 2000 years simply by dropping two unequal masses. Objects which are dropped from any height, if they are unequal, also meet unequal resistance from the air, and they do not, therefore, fall equally fast. On the contrary, if the new mechanics claimed that they should, then the old mechanics could point to the fact that they did not. Deeper thinking was needed to challenge Aristotle, and more subtle experiments. One reason why such experiments had been difficult hitherto, and why all experiments in mechanics were difficult, was that there did not exist until this time any reliable clockwork to measure the passing of time in small intervals.

THE NEED FOR ACCURATE TIME MEASUREMENT

The work of Galileo, therefore, begins rightly with a more searching discovery: how to measure small intervals of time. This is the robust approach which marks off Galileo from his contemporaries, and makes him a first leader of practical science and pioneer of the empirical method. [Nicolaus] Copernicus and [Johannes] Kepler were theoretical minds: Copernicus appealed to mathematicians, Kepler to the courtly interest in astrology which then drew educated men. By contrast, Galileo was grounded in the practical outlook of

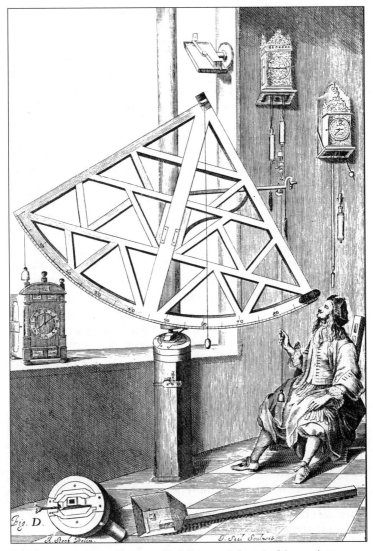

Galileo used the uniform swing of a pendulum in his motion experiments to formulate a law which governs the fall of an object.

the trading republics of northern Italy; he appealed particularly to the interest of Venice in navigation and in gunnery. He spent his most active years, from 1592 to 1610, at the University of Padua, which was under the protection of the Republic of Venice.

This was the age of Mediterranean commerce and, fanning out from the Mediterranean and the Atlantic coast, of the voyages of discovery by Italians, by Spaniards, and by Englishmen. Until the sixteenth century, the records of earlier travelers had been treated as curiosities. For example, Marco Polo had written a book about his travels in the East in 1298; yet, it was not till almost the sixteenth century that an Italian cosmographer Paolo Toscanelli, a friend of Christopher Columbus, used Marco Polo's book seriously as a source for geographical and navigational information.

Astronomy was now an important aid to navigation; but astronomy is not complete without accurate means of keeping time. For example, the latitude of a ship at sea can be found simply by observing the astronomical heavens; but the longitude can be found only if we know what time it is on some fixed longitude—say, on the longitude of Greenwich. For lack of a clock which could keep time at sea, navigators had to guess their longitude by what they called "dead reckoning" until well into the eighteenth century.

When Galileo Galilei was born, in 1564, there was not even a clock which could keep time accurately on land. The medieval clocks were not designed to be precise instruments which would run uniformly day in and day out. Medieval clocks were, in the first place, monastery clocks, whose purpose was to divide the day of prayer into equal parts or canonical hours, from the first matins to the evening vespers and the last complin. The day that was so divided ran essentially from dawn to dusk, and it was, therefore, a different day in summer and in winter. The clocks of the Middle Ages were a convenient means for dividing a day, but not for measuring time in any absolute sense. And these clocks were not capable of measuring time absolutely; they were clockworks, but they had no means of control to make them run uniformly—they had no escapement.

GALILEO USES THE PENDULUM TO MEASURE TIME

Galileo was not yet 20 when, as he reports, he noticed the regular swing of a lamp during a service in the cathedral at

Pisa in 1583. How could he test its regularity? Galileo put his finger on his pulse, and he observed that the swinging pendulum and the beating pulse kept equal time. He had established an underlying uniformity in nature, on which many clocks run to this day: the uniform motion of a pendulum, which keeps virtually the same time whether it swings in a large or a small arc.

Galileo was not the first to guess that a pendulum keeps almost perfect time: it had been guessed by Leonardo [da Vinci], a hundred years earlier. And Galileo did not strictly prove his guess: that was done mathematically by [Dutch physicist and astronomer] Christian Huygens a hundred years later. What Galileo did was to use the pendulum. He probably made it a basic means for measuring time in experiments in mechanics, and thereby he brought time and the clock into the practical business of carrying out experiments on earth. This was many times more useful than any demonstration on the Leaning Tower of Pisa.

Galileo was, therefore, able to measure the fall of objects through quite small distances: more precisely, he measured the time which they take to roll down a slope. He was able to show that, whatever the slope, a ball rolls in such a way that the total distance it has gone from rest is proportional to the square of the time it has been traveling. For counting time in this way, of course, the beats of a pendulum are ideal. And Galileo proved his law to be true whatever the mass of the ball: Aristotle was defeated, as it were by the way. As a result of this work, Galileo was able to show, between 1604 and 1609, that a thrown or falling object travels to earth along a parabola.

The Paris school of philosophers had produced arguments long before to cast doubt on Aristotle's mechanics. For example, they had asked the following question. Suppose that three equal balls are dropped together; then it is clear that they will fall steadily side by side. Suppose now that two of these balls are joined: surely all three will continue to fall side by side. Is it then, they asked, not clear that a single ball, and an object made of two balls joined together, will fall side by side? And does it, therefore, not follow that Aristotle is wrong in believing that heavier objects fall faster than light ones?

Now these elegant but abstract speculations, and the arguments on the Leaning Tower, were at an end. Galileo had done more than compare the fall of one object with another: he had formulated a precise law which governs the fall, in a form which was mathematically beautiful and convincing. His practical ingenuity with the pendulum and his mathematical skill in writing the law combined to give his work a finality which nothing before had reached. Galileo had perfectly joined logic to experiment.

GALILEO INVENTS A PULSILOGIUM

In an essay entitled "The Instruments of Galileo Galilei," Silvio Bedini describes how Galileo got the idea for an instrument to measure a patient's pulse, how he made the instrument, and why it was important.

The first scientific instrument with which Galileo's name was associated is the *pulsilogium,* which he produced shortly after his alleged observation of the isochronism of the pendulum in 1582 in the cathedral at Pisa. At this time Galileo was a medical student, and it is entirely logical that in his mind he would associate the phenomenon of the pendulum with his studies in medicine. There is an obvious similarity between the beat of a pendulum and a patient's pulse, and it is easy enough to understand how Galileo would have seen the relationship and visualized how the pendulum could serve as a measurer for the pulse rate. He constructed a small pendulum suspended from a string, the upper end of which was attached to a scale marked with diagnostic terms. By swinging the pendulum at the same time that he was counting the patient's pulse rate, he was able to obtain a direct reading for the patient's pulse-beats per minute by stopping the string with his thumb at the point of the scale which coincided with the patient's pulse rate. The device was later greatly elaborated, perhaps by Galileo and certainly by others, into several more complex forms. The basic source for Galileo's work with the *pulsilogium* is Viviani's letter of August 20, 1659, to Prince Leopold de'Medici, in which he described the history of the pendulum-regulated clockwork. . . .

Galileo's invention of the *pulsilogium* is of significance for two reasons. The instrument was the first actual application made of the discovery of the pendulum, and as such became a milestone in the history of measurement. At the same time, it was a pioneering effort in the new tendency toward the achievement of accuracy in the field of medicine.

Silvio Bedini, "The Instruments of Galileo Galilei." In *Galileo: Man of Science.* Ed. Ernan McMullin. New York: BasicBooks, 1967.

MORE OF GALILEO'S DISCOVERIES

At the same time, Galileo's work also implied a breach with Aristotle's belief that an arrow is kept in flight only so long as the air pushes it. This belief also had been doubted long ago by Jean Buridan and Nicholas of Oresme in Paris. Now Galileo proved it false by experiment. He proved that a mass which is moving will go on moving until some force acts to stop it. This demonstration was equally important in the development of the new mechanics.

About the year 1609, Galileo had news from Holland that people there had put two lenses together and had been able to see distant objects as if they were close at hand. Galileo had worked in optics, and this and the information he obtained enabled him to make a telescope for himself. He went on improving the telescope, and he also made what we should now call a compound microscope.

Galileo showed his telescope in Venice and at once created a sensation. Its usefulness to the merchant seamen there, for example, to identify distant ships, was patent.

But Galileo used the telescope more spectacularly to look into the sky with fresh, sharp eyes. He saw the craters of the moon, the spots on the sun, the phases of Venus, and what later turned out to be the rings of Saturn. The heavens were suddenly opened and transformed.

Characteristically, Galileo later proposed a still more subtle use of the telescope. Early in 1610, he had observed that Jupiter has four moons, and that they change their positions from one side of the planet to the other in a rapid and complex sequence. Therefore, Galileo proposed that a table of the positions of the moons of Jupiter should be made, to show where they will be at any time on any future night. In this way, it would be possible to read the time simply by looking at the moons of Jupiter through the telescope. Jupiter was to be turned into a divine clockwork, and the mariner at sea would be able to fix his longitude simply by looking at its face.

This suggestion did not turn out to be very practical, but it is revealing. It shows again how important a part the clock played in Galileo's thought, and in the ambitions of the merchant seamen of his time. Galileo's thought, here as elsewhere, was practical: no one else could have turned the casual observations of a lens grinder in Holland into a reasoned scheme for telling the time at sea.

CHAPTER 3

Galileo, the Telescope, and Astronomy

Practical and Scientific Uses of the Telescope

Timothy Ferris

In Timothy Ferris's exploration of Galileo's uses of the telescope, he discovers both Galileo's expediency and his genius. Able to devise an improved instrument, Galileo persuaded traders to use telescopes for spotting incoming ships while he used his own to study the night sky, studies which led him to revise concepts of gravitation and inertia. Ferris suggests that Galileo's discoveries may have been even greater had he collaborated with German astronomer Johannes Kepler, whose offers Galileo rejected. Timothy Ferris teaches science writing and astronomy at the University of California, Berkeley. He is the recipient of many science awards and the author of *The Red Limit, Galaxies,* and *The Mind's Sky.*

By the age of forty-five, Galileo was a respected scientist and teacher with a couple of books to his credit, but his contract [at the University of Padua] was coming up for renewal, his debts were mounting, and he needed something to elevate his career from the creditable to the extraordinary. It came to him in 1609. It was the telescope.

During one of his frequent visits to nearby Venice, Galileo learned that telescopes were being constructed in Holland. Quick to grasp the principles involved, he returned home to Padua and built a telescope for himself. "Placing my eye near the concave lens," he recalled, "I perceived objects satisfactorily large and near, for they appeared three times closer and nine times larger than when seen with the naked eye alone. Next I constructed another one, more accurate, which represented objects as enlarged more than sixty times."

Galileo did not need to be told that the telescope would have great practical value. Venice was an unwalled city, and its citizens depended for their defense upon their ability to spot approaching enemy ships in time to dispatch a fleet to engage them while they were still at sea; the telescope would greatly improve this early-warning system. The Venetians, furthermore, made their living from sea trade, and frequently kept an anxious watch, from the lookout towers (*campanili*) that dotted the city, for galleys returning with their holds full of cornmeal from the Levant, spices from Constantinople, and silver from Spain; an investor might be ruined if his ship were lost, or double his money once "his ship came in." A lookout using a telescope could spot the flag flying from an incoming trading ship much sooner than with the unaided eye.

Galileo accordingly arranged a demonstration for the authorities. On August 25, 1609, he led a procession of Venetian senators across the Piazza San Marco and up the Campanile for their first look through his first telescope. As he recalled the scene:

> Very many were the patricians and senators who, although aged, have more than once climbed the stairs of the highest campanili of Venice, to detect sails and vessels on the sea, so far away that coming under full sail toward the harbor, two hours or more passed before they could be seen without my eyeglass; because in fact the effect of this instrument is to represent an object that is, for example, fifty miles off, as large and near as if it were only five miles away.

The senators, suitably impressed, doubled Galileo's salary and granted him a lifelong appointment at Padua; as we would say today, Galileo got tenure. But his triumph was darkened by a cloud of deception. He permitted the senators to assume that he had *invented* the telescope. This was not strictly true, and his silence as to the stimulus of his greatest invention became embarrassing once telescopes produced by Dutch and Italian spectacle-makers began turning up in the marketplaces of Venice. . . .

But while the senators trained their telescopes on the horizon, Galileo trained his on the night skies. He was the first scientist to do so (or one of the first; Thomas Harriot in England observed the moon through a telescope that same summer) and what he saw spelled the beginning of the end of the closed, geocentric [earth-centered] cosmos, and the opening up of the depths of space.

GALILEO USES TELESCOPE FOR ASTRONOMY

As beginning observers have done ever since, Galileo looked first at the moon, and the sight of its mountains and craters immediately impressed him with the fact that it was not a wafer composed of heavenly aether, but a rocky, dusty, sovereign world. Aristotle to the contrary, the moon is "not robed in a smooth and polished surface," wrote Galileo, but is "... rough and uneven, covered everywhere, just like the earth's surface, with huge prominences, deep valleys, and chasms."

Turning his telescope to Jupiter, Galileo discovered four moons orbiting that giant planet, their positions changing perceptibly in the course of just a few hours' observation. Jupiter, he

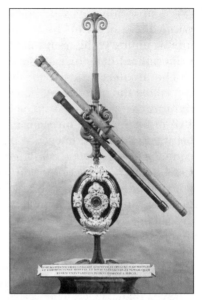

Galileo constructed a telescope similar to the one pictured.

was to conclude, constituted a Copernican solar system in miniature, and proof as well that the earth is not unique in having a moon. Galileo called it

> a fine and elegant argument for quieting the doubts of those who, while accepting with tranquil mind the revolutions of the planets about the sun in the Copernican system, are mightily disturbed to have the moon alone revolve about the earth and accompany it in an annual rotation about the sun. Some have believed that this structure of the universe should be rejected as impossible. But now we have not just one planet rotating about another while both run through a great orbit around the sun; our own eyes show us the four stars [i.e., *satellites*, a term coined by Kepler] which wander around Jupiter as does the moon around the earth, while all together trace out a grand revolution about the sun in the space of twelve years.

When Galileo observed the bright white planet Venus, he found that it exhibits phases like those of the moon, and that it appears much larger when in the crescent phase than when almost full. The obvious explanation was that Venus orbits the sun and not the earth, exhibiting a crescent face when it stands nearer to the earth than does the sun and a gibbous [more than half but not entirely illuminated] face when it is on the far side of the sun. "These things leave no room for doubt about the orbit of Venus," Galileo wrote.

"With absolute necessity we shall conclude, in agreement with the theories of the Pythagoreans [followers of Greek philosopher Pythagoras] and of Copernicus, that Venus revolves about the sun just as do all the other planets."

The greatest surprise was the stars. The telescope suggested, as the unaided eye could not, that the sky has *depth*, that the stars are not studded along the inner surface of an Aristotelian sphere, but range out deep into space. "You will behold through the telescope a host of other stars, which escape the unassisted sight, so numerous as to be almost beyond belief," Galileo reported. Moreover, the stars were organized into definite structures, of which the most imposing was the Milky Way:

> I have observed the nature and the material of the Milky Way.
> . . . The galaxy is, in fact, nothing but a congeries of innumerable stars grouped together in clusters. Upon whatever part of it the telescope is directed, a vast crowd of stars is immediately presented to view. Many of them are rather large and quite bright, while the number of smaller ones is quite beyond calculation.

Galileo's account of his visions through the telescope were first published in March 1610, in his *Sidereus Nuncius,* or *Starry Messenger.* The book was an instant success, and soon readers as far away as China were reading its reports of the rocky reality of the moon, the satellites of Jupiter, and the multitude of previously unseen stars in the sky. Here was observational evidence that we live in a Copernican solar system in a gigantic universe.

Galileo, who was principally a physicist and had been a Copernican before he ever looked through a telescope, understood that the task now facing science was to bring physics into accord with the reality of a moving Earth. The old anti-Copernican arguments had been turned inside out: Given that the earth really *does* rotate on its axis, why *don't* arrows shot into the air fly off to the west, or east winds constantly blow across the land? Why, in short, does a moving Earth act *as if* it were at rest? Finding the answers to these questions would require a greatly improved understanding of the concepts of gravitation and inertia. Galileo struggled with both.

GALILEO STUDIES NEW CONCEPTS OF GRAVITATION

In Aristotelian physics, heavy objects were said to fall faster than light ones. Early on, probably while still at Pisa, Galileo had realized that this commonsensical view was wrong—

that in a vacuum, where air resistance would have no effect, a feather would fall as fast as a cannonball. Having no means of creating a vacuum, Galileo tested his hypothesis by rolling spheres of various weights down inclined planes. This slowed their rate of descent as compared to free fall, making it easier to observe that all were accelerating at approximately the same rate.

But these experiments, which form the basis for the myth of the Leaning Tower, served to verify rather than to instigate Galileo's thesis. More important were his "thought experiments," the careful thinking through of procedures that he could not actually carry out. To be sure, Galileo recognized, as he put it, that "reason must step in" only "where the senses fail us." But since he lived in a time when the senses were aided by none but the most rudimentary experimental apparatus—he had, for instance, no timepiece more accurate than his pulse—Galileo found that reason had to step in rather often. In the words of [physicist] Albert Einstein, the greatest all-time master of the thought experiment, "The experimental methods of Galileo's disposal were so imperfect that only the boldest speculation could possibly bridge the gaps between empirical data." Consequently it was more by thinking than by experimentation that Galileo arrived at new insights into the law of falling bodies.

His reasoning went something like this: Suppose that a cannonball takes a given time—say, two pulse beats—to fall from the top of a tower to the ground. Now saw the cannonball in half, and let the two resulting demiballs fall. If Aristotle is right, each demiball, since it weighs only half as much as the full cannonball, should fall more slowly than did the original, full-size cannonball. If, therefore, we drop the two demiballs side by side, they should descend at an identical, relatively slow velocity. Now tie the demiballs together, with a bit of string or a strand of hair. Will this object, or "system," in Galileo's words, fall fast, as if it knew it were a reconstituted cannonball, or slowly, as if it still thought of itself as consisting of two half cannonballs?

Galileo phrased his *reductio ad absurdum* [carrying something to an absurd extreme] this way, in his *Dialogues Concerning Two New Sciences:*

> [Were Aristotle right that] a large stone moves with a speed of, say, eight while a smaller moves with a speed of four, then when they are united, the system will move with a speed of

less than eight; but the two stones when tied together make a stone larger than that which before moved with a speed of eight. Hence the heavier body moves with less speed than the lighter; an effect which is contrary to [Aristotle's] supposition. Thus you see how, from your assumption that the heavier body moves more rapidly than the lighter one, I infer that the heavier body moves more slowly.

GALILEO STUDIES NEW CONCEPTS OF INERTIA

This line of reasoning pointed directly to the second major question facing post-Copernican physics, that of inertia. If a cannonball and a feather fall at the same rate in a vacuum, then what is the difference between them? There must be *some* difference: The cannonball, after all, weighs more than the feather, will make more of an impression if dropped on one's head from atop the Leaning Tower, and is harder to kick along the ground. We would say today that the feather and the cannonball have differing *mass*, and that the amount of their mass determines their *inertia*—their tendency to resist changes in their state of motion. It is precisely because the heavier object possesses greater inertia that it takes longer for gravity to get it going, which is why it falls no faster than the lighter object. But these are Newtonian conceptions [based on discoveries by Issac Newton], unknown to Galileo, who had to make his way on his own.

Aristotle had defined half of the concept of inertia, that bodies at rest tend to remain at rest. This was sufficient for dealing with an immobile Earth, but was of no use in explicating the physics of an earth in motion in a Copernican universe. Galileo groped his way toward the other half of the concept—that bodies in motion tend to remain in motion, i.e., that the cannonball's inertial mass makes it just as difficult to stop as to start. Sometimes he came close, as in his charming comparison of the residents of planet Earth with voyagers aboard a ship:

> Shut yourself up with some friend in the main cabin below decks on some large ship, and have with you there some flies, butterflies, and other small flying animals. Have a large bowl of water with some fish in it; hang up a bottle that empties drop by drop into a wide vessel beneath it. With the ship standing still, observe carefully how the little animals fly with equal speed to all sides of the cabin. The fish swim indifferently in all directions; the drops fall into the vessel beneath; and, in throwing something to your friend, you need throw it no more strongly in one direction than another, the

distances being equal; jumping with your feet together, you pass equal spaces in every direction. When you have observed all these things carefully . . . have the ship proceed with any speed you like, so long as the motion is uniform and not fluctuating this way and that. You will discover not the least change in all the effects named, nor could you tell from any of them whether the ship was moving or standing still.

GALILEO ERRS BY CLINGING TO OLD IDEAS

But here Galileo bogged down. He was still a captive of Aristotle's erroneous supposition that the behavior of objects results from an internal tendency, or "desire," rather than simply from their inertial mass and the application of force:

> I seem to have observed that physical bodies have physical inclination to some motion (as heavy bodies downward), which motion is exercised by them through an intrinsic property and without need of a particular external mover, whenever they are not impeded by some obstacle. And to some other motion they have a repugnance (as the same heavy bodies to motion upward), and therefore they never move in that manner unless thrown violently by an external mover. Finally, to some movements they are indifferent, as are these same heavy bodies to horizontal motion, to which they have neither inclination . . . or repugnance. . . . And therefore, all external impediments removed, a heavy body on a spherical surface concentric with the earth will be indifferent to rest and to movements toward any part of the horizon. And it will maintain itself in that state in which it has once been placed; that is, if placed in a state of rest, it will conserve that; and if placed in movement toward the west (for example) it will maintain itself in that movement.

Some of these words anticipate Newton's explanation of inertia; bodies "placed in movement" tend to remain in motion, those "at rest" to remain at rest. Others remain ensnared in Aristotle's dusty web, as when Galileo asserts that objects have an inherent "inclination" or "repugnance" for certain sorts of motion. Galileo never really freed himself of confusion on this point, and his "law" of falling bodies, stated in 1604 and often called the first law of classical physics, was fraught with error.

Galileo might have made more progress in understanding inertia and gravitation had he collaborated with [German astronomer Johannes] Kepler. Kepler, too, had only part of the answer; he, like Galileo, thought of inertia chiefly as a tendency of objects to remain at rest, and, consequently, he conceived of gravity as having not only to hold planets in thrall to the sun but also to tug them along in their orbits. But he was ahead of Galileo in some ways, as when he proposed that the gravitational attraction of the moon is responsible for the tides. Galileo dismissed Kepler's theories of gravity as mere mysticism. "I am . . . astonished at Kepler," he wrote. ". . . Despite his open and acute mind, and though he has at his fingertips the motions attributed to the earth, he has nevertheless lent his ear and his assent to the moon's dominion over the waters, to occult properties, and to such puerilities [childish ideas]."

GALILEO REJECTS KEPLER

The differences between the two men were pronounced. Galileo was an urbane gentleman who loved wine (which he described as "light held together by moisture"), women (he had three children by his mistress, Marina Gamba), and song (he was an accomplished musician). Kepler sneezed when he drank wine, had little luck with women, and heard his music in the stars. The deep organ-tones of religiosity and mysticism that resounded through Kepler's works struck Galileo as anachronistic and more than a bit embarrassing. Kepler suspected as much, and pled with Galileo to please "not hold against me my rambling and my free way of speaking about nature." Galileo never answered his letter. Einstein remarked near the end of his life that "it has always hurt me to think that Galilei did not acknowledge the work of Kepler. . . . That, alas, is vanity," Einstein added. "You find it in so many scientists."

Nowhere is Galileo's disdain for Kepler more painful to recount than in the matter of the telescope. Kepler was by this time recognized as the most accomplished astronomer in the world, and his enthusiastic endorsement of Galileo's *Starry Messenger* had helped stave off criticism by those who dismissed the telescope as a kaleidoscopelike toy that produced not magnification but illusion. (This was not an entirely unreasonable suspicion; Galileo's early telescopes produced spurious colors, and they presented such a dim image, in so narrow a field of view, that it was not immediately obvious that they magnified at all.) But astronomy hereafter would require telescopes, and Kepler, though he understood the optical principles involved much better than Galileo did, could not obtain lenses of quality in Prague. With his customary earnestness and lack of restraint, Kepler wrote to Galileo in 1610, asking him for a telescope or at least a decent lens, "so that at last I too can enjoy, like yourself, the spectacle of the skies."

> O telescope, instrument of much knowledge, more precious than any scepter! . . . How the subtle mind of Galileo, in my opinion the first philosopher of the day, uses this telescope of ours like a sort of ladder, scales the furthest and loftiest walls of the visible world, surveys all things with his own eyes, and, from the position he has gained, darts the glances of his most acute intellect upon these petty abodes of ours—the planetary spheres I mean—and compares with keenest reasoning the distant with the near, the lofty with the deep.

Galileo ignored Kepler's entreaties. Possibly he feared that his observations might be eclipsed by what an astronomer of Kepler's abilities could accomplish if he, too, had a telescope at hand. In any event, he had other fish to fry. He was busy parlaying his rapidly growing celebrity into a position at Cosimo de' Medici's court in Tuscany. He passed the request along to Cosimo's ambassador, who advised him to, by all means, send the estimable Kepler a spyglass. Galileo instead told Kepler that he had no telescopes to spare, and that to make a new one would require too much time. Meanwhile, he was making presents of telescopes to royal patrons whose favor might advance his career. One of the beneficiaries of Galileo's gifts, the elector of Cologne, summered in Prague that year and loaned Kepler his telescope. For one month, Kepler could gaze with delight at the craters of the moon and the stars of the Milky Way. Then the elector left town, taking the telescope with him.

Just when Galileo might have done the most to help bring physics to a Copernican maturity, he instead diverted his efforts to a quixotic campaign aimed at converting the Roman Catholic Church to the Copernican cosmology.

Galileo's Telescope and the Copernican Revolution

Thomas S. Kuhn

Thomas S. Kuhn explains that with Galileo's telescope astronomers discovered new information
about the stars, the moon, Jupiter's moons, the orbit
of Venus, and most importantly, the position of the
sun and the earth in the solar system. Kuhn argues
that the major impact of Galileo's telescope was not
proof of Copernicus' theory of a sun-centered solar
system, but rather its effectiveness as a propaganda
tool to promote the Copernican view and discount
the Ptolemaic view of an earth-centered solar system. This change in attitude, however, took more
than a century to complete primarily because of
church doctrine which favored placing the earth—
and thus humans—at the center of the universe.
Thomas S. Kuhn taught philosophy and the history
of science at Harvard, Berkeley, and Princeton Universities. He is the author of *Black-Body Theory and
the Quantum Discontinuity* and *The Structure of Scientific Revolutions 1894–1912*.

In 1609 the Italian scientist Galileo Galilei (1564–1642)
viewed the heavens through a telescope for the first time,
and as a result contributed to astronomy the first qualitatively new sort of data that it had acquired since antiquity.
Galileo's telescope changed the terms of the riddle that the
heavens presented to astronomers, and it made the riddle
vastly easier to solve, for in Galileo's hands the telescope disclosed countless evidences for Copernicanism. But Galileo's
new statement of the riddle was not formulated until after
the riddle had been solved by other means. If it had been announced earlier, the story of the Copernican Revolution
would be quite different. Coming when it did, Galileo's as-

Reprinted by permission of the publisher from pp. 219–227 in *The Copernican Revolu-
tion: Planetary Astronomy in the Development of Western Thought*, by Thomas S. Kuhn
(Cambridge, MA: Harvard University Press). Copyright © 1957 by the President and
Fellows of Harvard College; Copyright © 1985 by Thomas S. Kuhn.

tronomical work contributed primarily to a mopping-up operation, conducted after the victory was clearly in sight.

In 1609 the telescope was a new instrument, though it is not clear just how new it was. Galileo heard that some Dutch lens grinder had combined two lenses in a way that magnified distant objects; he tried various combinations himself and quickly produced a low-power telescope of his own. Then he did something which, apparently, no one had done before: he directed his glass to the heavens, and the result was astounding. Every observation disclosed new and unsuspected objects in the sky. Even when the telescope was directed to familiar celestial objects, the sun, moon, and planets, remarkable new aspects of these old friends were discovered. Galileo, who had been a Copernican for some years before he knew of the telescope, managed to turn each new discovery into an argument for Copernicanism.

THE TELESCOPE DISCLOSES THE STARS

The telescope's first disclosure was the new worlds in the firmament about which [poet John] Donne, only two years later, complained. Wherever he turned his glass, Galileo found new stars. The population of the most crowded constellations increased. The Milky Way, which to the naked eye is just a pale glow in the sky (it had frequently been explained as a sublunary phenomenon, like comets, or as a reflection of diffused light from the sun and moon) was now discovered to be a gigantic collection of stars, too dim and too little separated to be resolved by the naked eye. Overnight the heavens were crowded by countless new residents. The vast expansion of the universe, perhaps its infinitude, postulated by some of the Copernicans, seemed suddenly less unreasonable. [Italian scientist Giordano] Bruno's mystical vision of a universe whose infinite extent and population proclaimed the infinite procreativeness of the Deity was very nearly transformed into a sense datum [a conclusion based on the facts of the sense of sight].

Observation of the stars also resolved a more technical difficulty that had confronted the Copernicans. Naked-eye observers had estimated the angular diameter of stars and, with the aid of the accepted figure for the distance between the earth and the sphere of the stars, had transformed the angular diameter into an estimate of linear dimensions. In a Ptolemaic universe these estimates had given not unreasonable results: the stars might be as large as the sun, or there-abouts. But, as Brahe[1] repeatedly emphasized in his attacks upon Copernicanism, if the Copernican universe were as large as the absence of stellar parallax[2] demanded, then the stars must be incredibly large. The brighter stars of the heavens must, Brahe computed, be so large that they would more than fill the entire orbit of the earth, and this he not unnaturally refused to believe. But when the telescope was directed to the heavens, Brahe's problem turned out to be an apparent problem only. The stars did not need to be so large as he had estimated. Though the telescope immensely in-creased the number of stars visible in the skies, it did not in-crease their apparent size. Unlike the sun, moon, and plan-ets, all of which were magnified by Galileo's glass, the stars retained the size they had had before. It became apparent that the angular diameter of stars had been immensely over-estimated by naked-eye observation, an error now explained as a consequence of atmospheric turbulence which blurs the images of stars and spreads them over a wider area in the eye than would be covered by their undistorted image alone. The same effect makes the stars seem to twinkle; it is largely suppressed by the telescope, which gathers a larger number of rays to the eye.

THE TELESCOPE SHOWS THE SURFACE OF THE MOON

The stars did not, however, provide the only, or even the best, evidence for Copernicanism. When Galileo turned his telescope to the moon, be found that its surface was covered by pits and craters, valleys and mountains. Measuring the length of the shadows cast into craters and by mountains at a time when the relative positions of the sun, moon, and earth were known, he was able to estimate the depths of the moon's declivities and the height of its protuberances and to begin a three-dimensional description of the moon's topog-raphy. It was not, Galileo decided, very different from the earth's topography. Therefore, like the measurements of the parallax of comets, telescopic observations of the moon raised doubts about the traditional distinction between the terrestrial and the celestial regions, and those doubts were

---

1. Tycho Brahe proposed a compromise between the Ptolemaic and Copernican sys-tems, in which the earth remained fixed while the sun and moon traveled around it, and the planets in turn revolved around the sun.   2. an apparent change in the direc-tion of stars caused by a change in the observational position that provides a new line of sight

reinforced almost immediately by telescopic observations of the sun. It too showed imperfections, dark spots which appeared and disappeared on its surface. The very existence of the spots conflicted with the perfection of the celestial region; their appearance and disappearance conflicted with the immutability of the heavens; and, worst of all, the motion of the spots across the sun's disk indicated that the sun rotated continually on its axis and thus provided a visible paradigm for the axial rotation of the earth.

JUPITER'S MOONS AND VENUS'S ORBIT

But this was not the worst. Galileo looked at Jupiter with his telescope and discovered four small points of light quite close to it in the sky. Observations made on successive nights showed that they continually rearranged their relative positions in a manner that could most simply be explained by supposing that they revolved continually and quite rapidly about Jupiter. These bodies were the four principal moons of Jupiter, and their discovery had an immense impact upon the seventeenth-century imagination. There were, it appeared, new worlds "in the Planets" as well as in "the Firmament." More important, these new worlds could not be conceived, on either the Ptolemaic or the Copernican hypothesis, to move in roughly circular orbits about the center of the universe. Apparently they moved around a planet, and their behavior was therefore the same as that of the earth's moon in Copernican astronomy. The discovery of Jupiter's moons therefore reduced the force of one more objection to the Copernican system. The old astronomy, as well as the new, would have to admit the existence of satellites, governed by planets. In addition, and perhaps most consequential of all, the observations of Jupiter provided a visible model of the Copernican solar system itself. Here in planetary space was a heavenly body surrounded by its own "planets," just as the planets previously known encircled the sun. The arguments for Copernicanism were multiplied by the telescope almost as rapidly as the heavenly bodies themselves.

Many other arguments were derived from telescopic observation, but only the observations of Venus provide sufficiently direct evidence for Copernicus' proposal to concern us here. Copernicus himself had noted in Chapter 10 of the First Book of the *De Revolutionibus* that the appearance of Venus could, if observable in detail, provide direct information about the shape of Venus's orbit. If Venus is attached to an epicycle [a circle describing the orbit of the planets around the earth] moving on an earth-centered deferent, and if the center of the epicycle is always aligned with the sun, then . . . an observer on the earth should never be able to see more than a crescent edge of the planet. But if Venus's orbit encircles the sun . . . then an earthbound observer should be able to see an almost complete cycle of phases, like the moon's; only phases near "new" and "full" would be imperceptible, because Venus would then be too close to the sun. Venus's phases can not be distinguished with the naked eye, which sees the planets as mere shapeless points. But the telescope enlarges planets sufficiently to give them shape, and . . . its shape provides strong evidence that Venus moves in a sun-centered orbit.

THE TELESCOPE BECOMES A TOOL OF PROPAGANDA

The evidence for Copernicanism provided by Galileo's telescope is forceful, but it is also strange. None of the observations discussed above, except perhaps the last, provides direct evidence for the main tenets of Copernicus' theory—the central position of the sun or the motion of the planets about it. Either the Ptolemaic or the Tychonic universe contains enough space for the newly discovered stars; either can be modified to allow for imperfections in the heavens and for satellites attached to celestial bodies; the Tychonic system, at least, provides as good an explanation as the Copernican for the observed phases of and distance to Venus. Therefore, the telescope did not prove the validity of Copernicus' conceptual scheme. But it did provide an immensely effective weapon for the battle. It was not proof, but it was propaganda.

After 1609 the main psychological force of the Ptolemaic system was its conservatism. Those who held to it would not be forced to learn new ways. But if the Ptolemaic system required extensive revisions to adjust it to the results of telescopic observation, it would lose even its conservative appeal. It was very nearly as easy to make the full transition to Copernicanism as to adjust to the requisite new version of Ptolemy, and many of those who took the observations seriously did make the full transition. These new converts may also have been impelled by another consideration: the Copernicans, or at least the cosmologically more radical ones, had anticipated the sort of universe that the telescope was disclosing. They had predicted a detail, the phases of Venus, with precision. More important, they had anticipated, at least vaguely, the imperfections and the vastly increased population of the heavens. Their vision of the universe showed marked parallels to the universe that the telescope made manifest. There are few phrases more annoying or more effective than "I told you so."

For the astronomically initiate the evidence of the telescope was, perhaps, superfluous. [German astronomer Johannes] Kepler's Laws and his *Rudolphine Tables*[3] would have been equally, though far more slowly, effective. But it is not on the astronomically initiate that the telescope had the greatest immediate impact. The first unique role of the telescope was providing generally accessible and nonmathematical documentation for the Copernican point of view. After 1609 men who knew only a smattering of astronomy could look through a telescope and see for themselves that the universe did not conform to the naïve precepts of common sense, and during the seventeenth century they did look. The telescope became a popular toy. Men who had never before shown interest in astronomy or in any science bought or borrowed the new instrument and eagerly scanned the heavens on clear nights. The amateur observer became a well-known figure, a subject for both emulation and parody. With him came a new literature. The beginnings of both popular science and science fiction are to be discovered in the seventeenth century, and at the start the telescope and its discoveries were the most prominent subjects. That is the greatest importance of Galileo's astronomical work: it popularized astronomy, and the astronomy that it popularized was Copernican.

THE DECLINE OF PTOLEMAIC ASTRONOMY

Kepler's ellipses and Galileo's telescope did not immediately crush the opposition to Copernicanism. On the contrary, as we noted at the start of this chapter, the bitterest and most vociferous opposition was not organized until after both Kepler and Galileo had made their principal astronomical discoveries. Kepler's work, like Copernicus' sixty-five years earlier, was accessible only to trained astronomers, and, in

3. new improved astronomical tables that supported the notion that planets revolve in ellipses, not circles

spite of the great accuracy that Kepler was known to have achieved, many astronomers found his noncircular orbits and his new techniques for determining planetary velocities too strange and uncongenial for immediate acceptance. Until after the middle of the century a number of eminent European astronomers can be found trying to show that Kepler's accuracy can be duplicated with mathematically less radical systems. One tried to revert to epicycles; another consented to ellipses but insisted that the speed of a planet was uniform with respect to the unoccupied focus of the ellipse; still others tried orbits of another shape. None of these attempts was successful, and as the century continued fewer and fewer of them were made. But not until the last decades of the seventeenth century did Kepler's Laws become the universally accepted basis for planetary computations even among the best practicing European astronomers.

Galileo's observations met initially even greater opposition, though from a different group. With the advent of the telescope Copernicanism ceased to be esoteric. It was no longer primarily the concern of highly trained mathematical astronomers. Therefore it became more disquieting and, to some, more dangerous. The new worlds discovered by the telescope were a primary source of Donne's malaise. A few years later telescopic observations provided part of the impetus necessary to set in motion the ecclesiastical machinery of official Catholic opposition to Copernicanism. After Galileo had announced his observations in 1610, Copernicanism could not be dismissed as a mere mathematical device, useful but without physical import. Nor could even the most optimistic still regard the concept of the earth's motion as a temporary lunacy likely to vanish naturally if left to itself. The telescopic discoveries therefore provided a natural and appropriate focus for much of the continuing opposition to Copernicus' proposal. They showed the real cosmological issues at stake more quickly and more clearly than pages of mathematics.

The opposition took varied forms. A few of Galileo's more fanatical opponents refused even to look through the new instrument, asserting that if God had meant man to use such a contrivance in acquiring knowledge, He would have endowed men with telescopic eyes. Others looked willingly or even eagerly, acknowledged the new phenomena, but claimed that the new objects were not in the sky at all; they were apparitions caused by the telescope itself. Most of Galileo's opponents behaved more rationally. Like [Cardinal] Bellarmine, they agreed that the phenomena were in the sky but denied that they proved Galileo's contentions. In this, of course, they were quite right. Though the telescope argued much, it proved nothing.

RELUCTANCE TO GIVE UP A CHERISHED BELIEF

The continuing opposition to the results of telescopic observation is symptomatic of the deeper-seated and longer-lasting opposition to Copernicanism during the seventeenth century. Both derived from the same source, a subconscious reluctance to assent in the destruction of a cosmology that for centuries had been the basis of everyday practical and spiritual life. The conceptual reorientation that, after Kepler and Galileo, meant economy to scientists frequently meant a loss of conceptual coherence to men like Donne and [poet John] Milton whose primary concerns were in other fields, and some men whose first interests were religious, moral, or aesthetic continued to oppose Copernicanism bitterly for a very long time. The attacks were scarcely abated by the middle of the seventeenth century. Many important tracts insisting on a literal interpretation of Scripture and upon the absurdity of the earth's motion continued to appear during the first decades of the eighteenth century. As late as 1873 the ex-president of an American Lutheran teachers' seminary published a work condemning Copernicus, [English physicist Isaac] Newton, and a distinguished series of subsequent astronomers for their divergence from scriptural cosmology. Even today the newspapers occasionally report the dicta of a dotard who insists upon the uniqueness and stability of the earth. Old conceptual schemes never die!

But old conceptual schemes do fade away, and the gradual extinction of the concept of the earth's uniqueness and stability clearly, if almost imperceptibly, dates from the work of Kepler and Galileo. During the century and a half following Galileo's death in 1642, a belief in the earth-centered universe was gradually transformed from an essential sign of sanity to an index, first, of inflexible conservatism, then of excessive parochialism, and finally of complete fanaticism. By the middle of the seventeenth century it is difficult to find an important astronomer who is not Copernican; by the end of the century it is impossible. Elementary astronomy responded more slowly, but during the closing decades of the century Copernican, Ptolemaic, and Tychonic astronomy were taught side by side in many prominent Protestant universities, and during the eighteenth century lectures on the last two systems were gradually dropped. Popular cosmology felt the impact of Copernicanism most slowly of all; most of the eighteenth century was required to endow the populace and its teachers with a new common sense and to make the Copernican universe the common property of Western man. The triumph of Copernicanism was a gradual process, and its rate varied greatly with social status, professional affiliation, and religious belief. But for all its difficulties and vagaries it was an inevitable process. At least it was as inevitable as any process known to the historian of ideas.

Galileo and Kepler

Arthur Koestler

Arthur Koestler narrates the events surrounding the publication of Galileo's *Starry Messenger*, the report on his first observations with the telescope. Written in a readable, factual style, Galileo's little book set scientists, laymen, and poets buzzing as far away as England, but his academic colleagues in Italy rejected his work. According to Koestler, astronomer Johannes Kepler came to Galileo's aid and defended the work, but Galileo never acknowledged the help or thanked Kepler for it. Arthur Koestler, a Hungarian novelist and journalist, is best known for writing the controversial anticommunist novel *Darkness at Noon*.

It was the invention of the telescope that brought [German astronomer Johannes] Kepler and Galileo, each traveling along his own orbit, to their closest conjunction. To pursue the metaphor, Kepler's orbit reminds one of the parabola of comets which appear from infinity and recede into it; Galileo's as an eccentric ellipse, closed upon itself.

The telescope was, as already mentioned, not invented by Galileo. In September 1608 a man at the annual Frankfurt fair offered a telescope for sale which had a convex and a concave lens, and magnified seven times. On October 2, 1608, the spectacles maker Johann Lippershey of Middleburg claimed a license for thirty years from the Estates General of the Netherlands for manufacturing telescopes with single and double lenses. In the following month, he sold several of these, for three hundred and six hundred gilders respectively, but was not granted an exclusive license because in the meantime two other men had claimed the same invention. Two of Lippershey's instruments were sent as a gift by the Dutch government to the king of France; and in April 1609 telescopes could be bought in spectacles makers' shops in Paris. In the summer of 1609 [mathematician] Thomas Harriot in England made telescopic observations of the moon, and drew maps of the lunar surface. In the same year several of the Dutch telescopes found their way to Italy and were copied there.

GALILEO PROMOTES HIS TELESCOPE IN VENICE

Galileo himself claimed in the *Messenger from the Stars* that he had merely read reports of the Dutch invention, and that these had stimulated him to construct an instrument on the same principle, which he succeeded in doing, "through deep study of the theory of refraction." Whether he actually saw and handled one of the Dutch instruments brought to Italy is a question without importance, for once the principle was known, lesser minds than Galileo's could and did construct similar gadgets. On August 8, 1609, he invited the Venetian Senate to examine his spyglass from the tower of St. Marco, with spectacular success; three days later, he made a present of it to the Senate, accompanied by a letter in which be explained that the instrument, which magnified objects nine times, would prove of utmost importance in war. It made it possible to see "sails and shipping that were so far off that it was two hours before they were seen with the naked eye, steering full sail into the harbor," thus being invaluable against invasion by sea. It was not the first and not the last time that pure research, that starved cur, snapped up a bone from the warlords' banquet.

The grateful Senate of Venice promptly doubled Galileo's salary to a thousand scudi per year, and made his professorship at Padua (which belonged to the Republic of Venice) a lifelong one. It did not take the local spectacles makers long to produce telescopes of the same magnifying power, and to sell in the streets for a few scudi an article which Galileo had sold the Senate for a thousand a year—to the great amusement of all good Venetians. Galileo must have felt his reputation threatened, as in the affair of the military compass; but, fortunately, this time his passion was diverted into more creative channels. He began feverishly to improve his telescope, and to aim it at the moon and stars, which previously had attracted him but little. Within the next eight months he succeeded, in his own words: "by sparing neither labor nor expense, in constructing for myself an instrument so superior that objects seen through it appear magnified nearly a thousand times, and more than thirty times nearer than if viewed by the natural powers of sight alone."

GALILEO PUBLISHES HIS FINDINGS IN *STAR MESSENGER*

The quotation is from *Sidereus Nuncius,* the *Messenger from the Stars,* published in Venice in March 1610. It was Galileo's first scientific publication, and it threw his telescopic discoveries like a bomb into the arena of the learned world. It not only contained news of heavenly bodies "which no mortal had seen before"; it was also written in a new, tersely factual style which no scholar had employed before. So new was this language that the sophisticated imperial ambassador [George Fugger] in Venice described the *Star Messenger* as "a dry discourse or an inflated boast, devoid of all philosophy." In contrast to Kepler's exuberant baroque style, some passages of the *Sidereus Nuncius* would almost qualify for the austere pages of a contemporary "Journal of Physics."

The whole booklet has only twenty-four leaves in octavo [92 pages]. After the introductory passages, Galileo described his observations of the moon, which led him to conclude:

"that the surface of the moon is not perfectly smooth, free from inequalities, and exactly spherical, as a large school of philosophers considers with regard to the moon and the other heavenly bodies, but that, on the contrary, it is full of irregularities, uneven, full of hollows and protuberances, just like the surface of the earth itself, which is varied everywhere by lofty mountains and deep valleys."

He then turned to the fixed stars, and described how the telescope added, to the moderate numbers that can be seen by the naked eye, "other stars, in myriads, which have never been seen before, and which surpass the old, previously known stars in number more than ten times." Thus, for instance, to the nine stars in the belt and sword of Orion he was able to add eighty others which he discovered in their vicinity; and, to the seven in the Pleiades, another thirty-six. The Milky Way dissolved before the telescope into "a mass of innumerable stars planted together in clusters"; and the same happened when one looked at the luminous nebulae [mass of interstellar dust or gas or both].

But the principal sensation he left to the end.

"There remains the matter which seems to me to deserve to be considered the most important in this work, namely, that I should disclose and publish to the world the occasion of discovering and observing four planets, never seen from the very beginning of the world up to our own times."

The four new planets were the four moons of Jupiter, and

the reason why Galileo attributed to their discovery such capital importance he explained in a somewhat veiled aside.

"Moreover, we have an excellent and exceedingly clear argument to put at rest the scruples of those who can tolerate the revolution of the planets about the sun in the Copernican system, but are so disturbed by the revolution of the single moon around the earth while both of them describe an annual orbit round the sun that they consider this theory of the universe to be impossible."

In other words, Galileo thought the main argument of the anti-Copernicans to be the impossibility of the moon's composite motion around the earth, and with the earth around the sun; and further believed that this argument would be invalidated by the composite motion of the four Jupiter moons. It was the only reference to Copernicus in the whole booklet, and it contained no explicit commitment. Moreover, it ignored the fact that in the Tychonic system [cosmic theory of Danish astronomer Tycho Brahe] *all* the planets describe a composite motion around the sun, and with the sun around the earth; and that even in the more limited "Egyptian" system at least the two inner planets do this.

Thus Galileo's observations with the telescope produced no important argument in favor of Copernicus, nor any clear committal on his part. Besides, the discoveries announced in the *Star Messenger* were not quite as original as they pretended to be. He was neither the first nor the only scientist who had turned a telescope at the sky and discovered new wonders with it. Thomas Harriot made systematic telescopic observations and maps of the moon in the summer of 1609, before Galileo, but he did not publish them. Even the Emperor Rudolph [of Prague] had watched the moon through a telescope before he had heard of Galileo. Galileo's star maps were so inaccurate that the Pleiades group can only be identified on them with difficulty, the Orion group not at all; and the huge dark spot under the moon's equator, surrounded by mountains, which Galileo compared to Bohemia, simply does not exist.

THE *STAR MESSENGER* HAD A DRAMATIC EFFECT

Yet when all this is said, and all the holes are picked in Galileo's first published text, its impact and significance still remain tremendous. Others had seen what Galileo saw, and even his priority in the discovery of the Jupiter moons is not established beyond doubt; yet he was the first to publish what he saw, and to describe it in a language which made everybody sit up. It was the cumulative effect that made the impact; the vast philosophical implications of this further prising open of the universe were instinctively felt by the reader, even if they were not explicitly stated. The mountains and valleys of the moon confirmed the similarity between heavenly and earthly matter, the homogeneous nature of the stuff from which the universe is built. The unsuspected number of invisible stars made an absurdity of the notion that they were created for man's pleasure, since he could see them only armed with a machine. The Jupiter moons did not prove that Copernicus was right, but they did further shake the antique belief that the earth was the center of the world around which everything turned. It was not this or that particular detail but the total contents of the *Messenger from the Stars* that created the dramatic effect.

The booklet aroused immediate and passionate controversy. It is curious to note that Copernicus' *Book of Revolutions* had created little stir for half a century, and Kepler's Laws [based on Tycho Brahe's observations] even less at their time, while the *Star Messenger*, which had only an indirect bearing on the issue, caused such an outburst of emotions. The main reason was, no doubt, its immense readability. To digest Kepler's magnum opus required, as one of his colleagues remarked, "nearly a lifetime"; but the *Star Messenger* could be read in an hour, and its effect was like a punch in the solar plexus on those grown up in the traditional view of the bounded universe. And that vision, though a bit shaky, still retained an immense, reassuring coherence.

Even Kepler was frightened by the wild perspective opened up by Galileo's spyglass. "The infinite is unthinkable!" he repeatedly exclaimed in anguish.

The shock waves of Galileo's message spread immediately, as far as England. It was published in March 1610; [British poet John] Donne's *Ignatius* was published barely ten months later, but Galileo (and Kepler) are repeatedly mentioned in it.

I will write [quoth Lucifer] to the Bishop of Rome:
He shall call Galileo the Florentine to him . . .

But soon, the satirical approach yielded to the metaphysical, to a full realization of the new cosmic perspective.

Man has weav'd out a net, and this net throwne
Upon the Heavens, and now they are his owne . . .

[British poet John] Milton was still an infant in 1610; he grew up with the new wonders. His awareness of the "vast unbounded Deep" that the telescope disclosed reflects the end of the medieval walled universe.

Before [his] eyes in sudden view appear
The secrets of the hoary Deep—a dark
Illimitable ocean, without bound,
Without dimension . . . [from Paradise Lost]

ITALIAN ACADEMICS REJECT GALILEO'S WORK

Such was the objective impact on the world at large of Galileo's discoveries with his "optick tube." But to understand the reactions of the small academic world in his own country, we must also take into account the subjective effect of Galileo's personality. Copernicus had been a kind of invisible man throughout his life; nobody who met the disarming Kepler, in the flesh or by correspondence, could seriously dislike him. But Galileo had a rare gift of provoking enmity—not the affection alternating with rage which Tycho aroused, but the cold, unrelenting hostility which genius plus arrogance minus humility creates among mediocrities.

Without this personal background, the controversy that followed the publication of the *Sidereus Nuncius* would remain incomprehensible. For the subject of the quarrel was not the *significance* of the Jupiter satellites, but their *existence,* which some of Italy's most illustrious scholars flatly denied. Galileo's main academic rival was [astronomer Giovanni] Magini in Bologna. In the month following the publication of the *Star Messenger,* on the evenings of April 24 and 25, 1610, a memorable party was held in a house in Bologna, where Galileo was invited to demonstrate the Jupiter moons in his spyglass. Not one among the numerous and illustrious guests declared himself convinced of their existence. Father Clavius, the leading mathematician in Rome, equally failed to see them; [Cesare] Cremonini, teacher of philosophy at Padua, refused even to look into the telescope; so did his colleague [Guglielmo] Libri. The latter, incidentally, died soon afterward, providing Galileo with an opportunity to make more enemies with the much-quoted sarcasm: "Libri did not choose to see my celestial trifles while he was on earth; perhaps he will do so now he has gone to heaven."

These men may have been partially blinded by passion and prejudice, but they were not quite as stupid as it may seem. Galileo's telescope was the best available, but it was still a clumsy instrument without fixed mountings, and with a visual field so small that, as somebody has said, "the marvel is not so much that he found Jupiter's moons, but that he was able to find Jupiter itself." The tube needed skill and experience in handling, which none of the others possessed. Sometimes a fixed star appeared in duplicate. Moreover, Galileo himself was unable to explain why and how the thing worked; and the *Sidereus Nuncius* was conspicuously silent on this essential point. Thus it was not entirely unreasonable to suspect that the blurred dots which appeared to the strained and watering eye pressed to the spectacles-sized lens might be optical illusions in the atmosphere, or somehow produced by the mysterious gadget itself. This, in fact, was asserted in a sensational pamphlet, *Refutation of the Star Messenger*, published by Magini's assistant, a young fool called Martin Horky.

Thus, while the poets were celebrating Galileo's discoveries, which had become the talk of the world, the scholars in his own country were, with very few exceptions, hostile or skeptical. The first, and for some time the only, scholarly voice raised in public in defense of Galileo was Johannes Kepler's.

KEPLER DEFENDS GALILEO

It was also the weightiest voice, for Kepler's authority as the first astronomer of Europe was uncontested—not because of his two Laws, but by virtue of his position as imperial mathematicus and successor to Tycho. John Donne, who had a grudging admiration for him, has summed up Kepler's reputation "who (as himselfe testifies of himselfe) ever since Tycho Brahe's death hath received it into his care, that no new thing should be done in heaven without his knowledge."

The first news of Galileo's discovery had reached Kepler when [amateur poet and philosopher Johannes Matthaeus] Wackher von Wackenfeld called on him on or around March 15, 1610. The weeks that followed he spent in feverish expectation of more definite news. In the first days of April, the Emperor received a copy of the *Star Messenger*, which had just been published in Venice, and Kepler was graciously permitted "to have a look and rapidly glance through it." On April 8, at last, he received a copy of his own from Galileo, accompanied by a request for his opinion.

Galileo had never answered Kepler's fervent request for an opinion on the *Mysterium,* and had remained equally silent on the *New Astronomy.* Nor did he bother to put his own request for Kepler's opinion on the *Star Messenger* into a personal letter. It was transmitted to Kepler verbally by the Tuscan ambassador in Prague, Julian de Medici. Although Kepler was not in a position to verify Galileo's disputed discoveries, for he had no telescope, he took Galileo's claims on trust. He did it enthusiastically and without hesitation, publicly offering to serve in the battle as Galileo's "squire" or "shield bearer"—he, the imperial mathematicus, to the recently still unknown Italian scholar. It was one of the most generous gestures in the annals of science.

The courier for Italy was to leave on April 19; in the eleven days at his disposal Kepler wrote his pamphlet, *Conversation with the Star Messenger,* in the form of an open letter to Galileo. It was printed the next month in Prague, and a pirated Italian translation appeared shortly afterward in Florence.

It was precisely the support that Galileo needed at that moment. The weight of Kepler's authority played an important part in turning the tide of the battle in his favor, as shown by Galileo's correspondence. He was anxious to leave Padua and to be appointed court mathematician to Cosimo de Medici, Grand Duke of Tuscany, in whose honor he had called Jupiter's planets "the Medicean stars." In his application to Vinta, the duke's secretary of state, Kepler's support figures prominently.

> "Your Excellency, and their Highnesses through you, should know that I have received a letter—or rather an eight-page treatise—from the Imperial Mathematician, written in approbation of every detail contained in my book without the slightest doubt or contradiction of anything. And you may believe that this is the way leading men of letters in Italy would have spoken from the beginning if I had been in Germany or somewhere far away."

He wrote in almost identical terms to other correspondents, among them to [scientist] Matteo Carosio in Paris.

> "We were prepared for it that twenty-five people would wish to refute me; but up to this moment I have seen only one statement by Kepler, the Imperial Mathematician, which confirms everything that I have written, without rejecting even an iota of it; which statement is now being reprinted in Venice, and you shall soon see it."

Yet, while Galileo boasted about Kepler's letter to the

grand duke and his correspondents, he neither thanked Kepler nor even acknowledged it. . . .

Galileo's reaction to the service Kepler had rendered him was, as we saw, complete silence. The Tuscan ambassador at the imperial court urgently advised him to send Kepler a telescope to enable him to verify, at least *post factum*, Galileo's discoveries, which he had accepted on trust. Galileo did nothing of the sort. The telescopes his workshop turned out he donated to various aristocratic patrons. . . .

Kepler's dearest wish, to see for himself the new marvels, was at last fulfilled. One of Kepler's patrons, the Elector Ernest of Cologne, Duke of Bavaria, was among the select few whom Galileo had honored with the gift of a telescope. In the summer of 1610 Ernest was in Prague on affairs of state, and for a short period lent his telescope to the imperial mathematicus. Thus from August 3 to September 9 Kepler was able to watch the Jupiter moons with his own eyes. The result was another short pamphlet, *Observation Report on Jupiter's Four Wandering Satellites,* in which Kepler confirmed, this time from firsthand experience, Galileo's discoveries. The treatise was immediately reprinted in Florence, and was the first public testimony by independent, direct observation, of the existence of the Jupiter moons. It was also the first appearance in history of the term "satellite," which Kepler had coined in a previous letter to Galileo.

At this point the personal contact between Galileo and Kepler ends. For a second time Galileo broke off their correspondence.

CHAPTER 4

Galileo's Confrontation with the Church

PEOPLE
WHO MADE
HISTORY

GALILEO

Galileo Tests the Pope for Approval

Giorgio de Santillana

Giorgio de Santillana analyzes Galileo's 1624 audiences with his former friend Maffeo Barberini, now Pope Urban VIII. During these meetings Galileo tested whether or not the Pope would agree that Galileo may write about Copernicanism. According to Santillana, Galileo first assessed the Pope's attitude in his new position; second, he elicited the Pope's approval to write about Nature; third, he realized the Pope did not understand his ideas; and fourth, Galileo measured his gains and losses in the argument and decided to go ahead and write the *Dialogue*. Giorgio de Santillana, who taught at the Massachusetts Institute of Technology, is the author of *The Origins of Scientific Thought* and co-author with Hertha von Dechend of *Hamlet's Mill: An Essay on Myth and the Frame of Time*.

At the end of April, 1624, after a leisurely voyage and a stay of two weeks with Cesi[1] at his castle in Acquasparta, Galileo arrived in Rome. He was bringing with him a delightful novelty, the first microscope (he called it simply "occhialino"), with which one could see all sorts of "horrendous things" moving about in a drop of water. He was received by the Pope with "infinite demonstrations of love" and in the course of six weeks had as many long conversations with him. Very soon, however, he realized that he was not going to get very far. He was talking no longer to Maffeo Barberini, but to Urban VIII.

Urban felt himself, with some reason, to be of the stuff of which the great Popes of the Renaissance had been made. In

---

1. Federico Cesi was founder of the Lynceans, scholars fighting those who believed the earth was the center of the universe. Cesi was later to supervise the printing of Galileo's *Dialogue*, but he died before the book was published.

Excerpted from *The Crime of Galileo*, by Giorgio de Santillana. Copyright 1955 The University of Chicago. Reprinted by permission of the University of Chicago Press.

that critical period early in the Thirty Years' War, when the fate of the Reformation hung in the balance, he was planning a great political campaign which would change the balance of Europe. Splendor and power were going to be his insignia. . . .

In those days Urban was still dreaming of spectacular successes. It was the morning of his reign, a morning full of magnificence and confidence. Amid the turmoil of the affairs of state he found time for long audiences with Galileo.

What took place in those audiences will forever remain a matter for speculation. But from scattered data we may infer that the conversation went something like this. On being copiously complimented on the *Saggiatore* and being told by the Pope that he had had it read aloud at table, Galileo deprecated the poor merit of these feeble excursions on a perforce limited subject, whereupon the Pontiff exclaimed his wish that more such incomparable creations should flow from his magical pen. Thereupon Galileo tactfully alluded to the malice of his many enemies and to the many disadvantages under which he labored, and the Pope reassured him that, if he remained such a dutiful son of the Holy Church as he had shown himself hitherto, his enemies would bark in vain. The System of the Schools, in intelligent hands, ought to fear nothing from the new science, for it was established on natural evidence itself; and he, the Pope, could show it quite easily. He expanded on that subject. The campaign against Galileo was really alarm born of the incompetence of certain people who usurped the privileges of the scholar, and it would be kept in check.

Frustrated, thus, in his first approach, the scientist bethought himself of indirect pressure. Some time later Cardinal Hohenzollern, on his leave-taking audience, was moved to represent to the Pope what difficulties he had in converting German noblemen who had been shocked by the prohibition of 1616.[2] The Holy Father was sympathetic. But he remarked that the Church neither had condemned nor would condemn the doctrine of Copernicus as heretical, but only as rash (*temeraria*), and that there was no chance that it would ever be proved wrong, for a convincing proof was impossible. The statement of fact, we may observe, was less than accurate, for, in the first place, the Congregation of the

---

2. In February 1616 the General Congregation of the Inquisition ruled that Galileo must abandon the notion that the sun is at the center of the universe and that the earth moves. Galileo was not to teach or defend this idea or he would be imprisoned.

Index is not "the Church," and, in the second place, it had declared the opinion *false*, not *rash*; in the third place, its Qualifiers had specified reservedly that it was "foolish and absurd philosophically and formally heretical."

Be that as it may, the Pope could, even without pronouncing himself *ex cathedra* [with the authority derived from his office] for the first time on the subject, have had the findings corrected or reversed. He did neither. He somewhat attenuated the content and at the same time confirmed it as a juridical precedent. The main objective was lost. But those remarks left a slight opening.

GALILEO TRIES TO WIN THE POPE'S APPROVAL

Galileo in his contacts had "begun to discover new land," as he wrote. This appears to mean, from other allusions, that the prelates he consulted (Cobelluzzi, Barberini, Borghese) agreed that there had been entirely too much fuss about this affair, that it was a purely juridical matter, and that the decree could not be revised for reasons of prestige but that anyone could go and be as Copernican as he pleased, provided he gave no scandal and played the game. The Roman hierarchy knew itself too well not to countenance a skeptical worldly conformism in others.

Fortified by these opinions, Galileo in the next audiences again approached the subject. He steered through many mutual deplorations on the decline of good writing toward the remark that a number of very wonderful conceits and effects of Nature were still waiting to be written about, were it only for the delight of the mind—if he understood the decree rightly to read that a free discussion of natural hypotheses was still allowed. He was assured that this was the very spirit of the decree, as everyone should know: not to restrain the mind in its ingenious conjectures but to prevent the wrong philosophical conclusions from being drawn. We Ourselves, said the Pope, have validly defended Copernicus in 1616, and he pointed out that it would expose the Church to the ridicule of the heretics if the very man who gave such a valid contribution to the reform of the calendar carried through by Pope Gregory were declared heretical in his thoughts. So long as he reigned, insisted the Pontiff, the memory of Copernicus had nothing to fear. The Church knew very well how much prudence is required in this delicate matter of the interpretation of Scripture. Surely, it was not her intention to clip the wings of Signor Galileo's subtle speculations and admirable discoveries, which were an adornment of the true faith and might also lead to remarkable improvements in engineering, as long as he was quite sure he intended to leave theology alone.

But, then, suggested Galileo hastily before the Pope could revert to discoursing of absent friends, the decree must have been misunderstood by many, for there was ill-informed muttering at home and sneering abroad that it had been the work of uninformed consultors. —Nonsense, said the Pope, We Ourselves were part in it. There were then high reasons. But it was certainly a regrettable necessity, most regrettable. And, then, urged Galileo, would it not be to the benefit of the true faith if the many natural reasons for and against could be probed carefully and dispassionately so as to show that the issue, maturely examined, needed a higher decision? That, agreed the Pope, would be a good idea. To prove that all the ingenuity of man could devise in the matter of the heavens could lead to no conclusive statement was all to the benefit of obedience. Let the Signor Galileo assay theories with that exquisite balance of scruples wherewith he was wont to test the truth, and show again that "we are not to find out the work of His hands."

Better still, suggested Galileo, supposing that one took the following line, which had occurred to him while writing a poetic conceit which perhaps His Beatitude remembered from years back, a curious fantasy on the ebb and flow of the sea to which he was attached and which had been possibly too much appreciated by certain foreigners who had taken it for their own: supposing that one could produce proofs of the Pythagorean theory that imposed themselves as physically necessary, if not metaphysically. . . .

Urban VIII cut him short with a little lecture: "Let Us remind you of something that We had occasion to tell you many years ago, speaking as one philosopher to another; and, if We remember, you were not willing then to offer Us any definite refutation.

"Let Us grant you that all of your demonstrations are sound and that it is entirely possible for things to stand as you say. But now tell Us, do you really maintain that God could not have wished or known how to move the heavens and the stars in some other way? We suppose you will say 'Yes,' because We do not see how you could answer otherwise. Very well then, if you still want to save your contention, you would have to prove to Us that, if the heavenly movements took place in another manner than the one you suggest, it would imply a logical contradiction at some point, since God in His infinite power can do anything that does not imply a contradiction. Are you prepared to prove as much? No? Then you will have to concede to Us that God can, conceivably, have arranged things in an entirely different manner, while yet bringing about the effects that we see. And if this possibility exists, which might still preserve in their literal truth the sayings of Scripture, it is not for us mortals to try to force those holy words to mean what to us, from here, may appear to be the situation.

"Have you got anything to object? We are glad to see that you are of Our opinion. Indeed, as a good Catholic, how could you hold any other? To speak otherwise than hypothetically on the subject would be tantamount to constraining the infinite power and wisdom of God within the limits of your personal ideas [*fantasie particolari*]. You cannot say that this is the only way God could have brought it about, because there may be many, and perchance infinite, ways that He could have thought of and which are inaccessible to our limited minds. We trust you see now what We meant by telling you to leave theology alone."

GALILEO KNOWS HE HAS LOST

It was only then, probably, that Galileo was able to measure the chasm which separated his thought from that of the Pontiff; for the latter's words, taken seriously, would have implied that all investigation of Nature was bound to lead to nothing. He might have objected as he does in the *Dialogue*: "Surely, God could have caused birds to fly with their bones made of solid gold, with their veins full of quicksilver, with their flesh heavier than lead, and with wings exceeding small. He did not, and that ought to show something. It is only in order to shield your ignorance that you put the Lord at every turn to the refuge of a miracle."

But this was no time to argue. He kept his peace. He must have been familiar already with that type of argument and known how difficult it was to cope with. From the point of view of Church philosophy, it was sound and orthodox doctrine. [Philosopher] Robert Grosseteste had provided the epistemological part of it back in the thirteenth century. Taken on the pragmatic level, it did not make much sense, for it permitted, while not permitting, science to proceed, with the proviso that it would not be getting anywhere. For all his literary sympathies, the Pope was utterly unable to grasp the implications of the new thought. A humanist of the sixteenth century, schooled by the Jesuits in Peripatetic principles, Urban lived in a world of significant forms and sensuous substances, varied and multiple, with many wonderful names and qualities apt for the learned discourse; the paradox of mathematical physics, the bridge thrown directly from the extreme abstraction of geometry to basic monotone matter defined only by mass and measure, remained beyond his conceiving. The new "natural conclusions," he felt, had their proper place in enriching the world, not in reducing it to geometric space.

This is where his thinking was backed by the great schemes of the Renaissance and its hope in unknown harmonies. "There is nothing that is incredible," [philosopher] Marsilio Ficino had said. "For to God all things are possible, and nothing is impossible. There are numberless possibilities that we deny because we do not happen to know them." This was also what [philosopher] Pico della Mirandola had maintained, hinting at reaches of "natural magic" beyond our dreams; and [philosopher Tommaso] Campanella, too, was supporting Galileo in the hope of results such as no scientist could ever produce. It was "Platonic theology" itself, urging man to extend his imagination beyond what he could see and test; it was Leonardo's belief in the creative power of artistic "fantasy." And this is clearly, even more than subtle Scholastic theories, the idea behind Urban's words: We cannot suppose that Nature has to be contained within the limits of our "particular fantasy," for she is all the possible as well. Moreover, in good Christian religion, no creature can "necessitate" its maker, were it even by true knowledge; and the transcendence of God makes it impossible that from this world we should ever know His ways. It was known that we are not allowed, for example, to think of space as infinite by nature, for then it would become a necessary part of the nature of God and thus lose its creatureliness.

Surely, it is written: *Dominus scientiarum Deus,* "God is the Lord of sciences." But this does not allow us to try to impose the seeming "necessities" of one science upon all the other ones, and it does not go without a certain arbitral role assigned to His vicar on earth.

All these things Sanctissimus had learned in his time. Therefore, he concluded, the Church is not doing any damage to science if she precludes a serious treatment of such ideas which would give scandal to the faithful. They cannot be really true and should be labeled "fantasy." As such, they may have their charm; and the Pope could show that he was able to appreciate it, for it was he who had restored Campanella, the incorrigible maverick Dominican, to freedom and literary activity.

Urban's thought was a late version, even as he himself was a late copy of the Renaissance Popes. No one could explain to him that, under his very reign, the Church was going to face things that his philosophy had never dreamed of. As a humanist, he felt he had given an adequately ample answer. As a lawyer, he decided the case was settled and turned to more urgent business. . . .

As he departed, loaded with favors, holy medals, "Agnus Dei," [a prayer to Jesus] and pensions for his family, escorted by an orotund papal parchment of commendation for His Most Serene Highness the Grand Duke (". . . We embrace with paternal love this great man whose fame shines in the heavens and goes on earth far and wide . . ."), Galileo felt that he had not been wholly unsuccessful. He was sixty years old by now, and he had learned what one could expect from the world. Eight years of prudence had taught him the way of devious implication. If he had pulled through with the *Saggiatore*, he could hope, this time with papal favor, to mention his subject in a more explicit manner and let it quietly sink in. He had confidence in the force of the truth, once it is intrusted to the pen, which, as he used to say, "is the touchstone of the mind." Copernicanism was not heretical. It was not even so wild as all that. So far so good. He now had permission to present his brief to the public. From what he understood of the authorities, they were interested only in formal clauses of submission that would safeguard their prestige and punctilio. "If we cannot get past *that* outfit, call me Grassi,[3] he must have said to [Giovanni] Ciàmpoli, or the Florentine equivalent of it, for that certainly was the way he felt. The *Dialogue on the Great World Systems* had been decided upon.

---

3. In his book *Saggiatore*, Galileo attacked Horatio Grassi's views regarding comets, complaining that Grassi's idea was wrong and his method of argument faulty.

On Trial for Heresy

Hermann Kesten

Hermann Kesten describes the publishing problems
Galileo encountered and the measures he took to
avoid trial and punishment for his controversial
writings. According to Kesten, Galileo successfully
manipulated church authorities to receive permission to publish *Dialogue Concerning the Two Chief
World Systems*. This work endorsed the Copernican
view of a sun-centered solar system and scientifically dismissed the prevailing, church-sponsored,
Ptolemaic belief in an earth-centered universe. Once
the Pope and the Inquisition had examined the dialogues, however, they discovered Galileo's real views
and the insults he leveled against church authorities.
As Kesten notes, from then on Galileo's trial became
a certainty. Hermann Kesten, a German scholar, has
published *Die Fremden Gallere* and *Roman, Die
Zwillinge von Nurnberg: Roman.*

In April, 1630, he [Galileo] finally completed his main work,
his *Dialogo dei due massimi sistemi del mondo,* Dialogue of
the two greatest world systems.

He was sixty-six years old and he thought his time had
come. Until then he had published only pamphlets and occasional writings. His pupils were already university professors and were giving public lectures about him. He was the
chief of the modern school in Europe. He was the great enemy of the Aristotelians, the scholastics and the reactionaries.[1] He had become the representative man of his century,
and his greatest work was still in manuscript form.

1. Scholastics were adherents of the dominant Christian theological and philosophical
school of the Middle Ages, based on the authority of the Latin Fathers and of Aristotle.
Reactionaries were extreme conservatives, opposed to progress or liberalism.

Reprinted from *Copernicus and His World*, by Hermann Kesten, translated by E.B. Ash-
ton and Norbert Guterman. Copyright © 1945 by Roy Publishers, A.N., New York.

THE FORM AND STYLE OF THE *DIALOGUE*

In his Dialogue three characters converse about the systems of the world: Salviati, Sagredo and Simplicio. They are in the palace of a Venetian nobleman, they sail in a gondola, they read and they argue. Salviati and Sagredo are portraits of two of Galileo's deceased friends. Salviati is the spokesman for the Copernican theory; Sagredo, with his common sense, his *buon naturale* [good nature], is the mediator between Salviati and Simplicio, the Copernican and the Aristotelian; Simplicio is so named after the famous Sicilian commentator on Aristotle, Simplicius; he is a scholastic and defends the systems of Aristotle and Ptolemy.

Galileo wrote this book in a popular manner. He wanted to prove the truth of the Copernican system and defend it against all the arguments of the old school. . . .

The great merit of these dialogues is that they founded the new physics. Aristotle, in his physics, determined the nature and mechanics of the heavens assuming that the earth was motionless. Galileo created the new mechanics and dynamics of the heavens assuming that the earth moved. Here he presents the new science coherently, as applied to the Copernican theory. And he taught that scientific knowledge permits human reason to partake of divine reason. The Inquisition[2] termed this idea heretical. Indeed, this idea implied the concept of unlimited progress, although it was also responsible for the fragmentary nature of Galileo's work.

Galileo grasped the philosophical, moral and scientific revolutions initiated by Copernicus.

[Pope] Urban VIII once said casually to Thomas Campanella [a philosopher who admired Galileo's work] who, finally released from thirty years' imprisonment, had come to Rome in 1629 and been graciously received by the Pope: "If it had depended upon us, that decree [of 1616] would not have been issued." And to Cardinal Zollern he said: "Out of sheer respect for the memory of Copernicus I would not have permitted his condemnation, if I had been Pope at that time!"

GALILEO EXPLAINS HIS BOOK TO THE POPE

Galileo heard of this and went to Rome with his manuscript. He arrived on May 3, 1630, and during an audience with the Pope explained the intention of his book: he wanted to pro-

---

2. formerly a Roman Catholic tribunal directed at suppression of heresy

duce all the existing proofs of the Copernican theory in order to show the world that Rome had not acted from ignorance when it condemned the Copernican theory.

Urban demanded that the book contain no theological considerations; that the Copernican system be represented only as a mathematical hypothesis; that Galileo clearly stress the purpose of the dialogues, that is, to make it clear that Rome had not acted from ignorance of the Copernican proofs and that he replace the title "Dialogues About the Ebb and Flow of the Tides" by another.

Galileo found it hardest of all to renounce his title; as is often the case in such matters, he clung to his false hypotheses about the tides more passionately than to many of his correct discoveries. He submitted his manuscript to the censorship of Riccardi, Master of the Sacred Palace, who received the Pope's instructions.

Galileo was also willing to write a preface and conclusion recognizing the omniscience of the Church without reservations. Riccardi demanded only minor changes; Galileo gave his consent, and Riccardi his *imprimatur* [official approval]. Since the title and certain passages still had to be modified, the permission could only be conditional.

PUBLICATION PROBLEMS AND DELAYS

Galileo entrusted his friend [Federico] Cesi with the printing, returned home contented and soon afterward received the news of Cesi's death and a warning from his friend [Benedetto] Castelli advising him to publish his book in Florence, "and as soon as possible . . . and for many cogent reasons that I do not wish at present to trust to paper."

On September 11, the Florentine Inquisition put its *imprimatur* under the Roman one, but to Galileo's request to Riccardi for permission from the Roman Inquisition to print the book in Florence, the Master of the Sacred Palace replied that he had to undertake a new revision and asked for the manuscript or a copy of it.

The horrified Galileo wrote that the plague and the quarantine made it almost impossible to send such a bulky manuscript to Rome and asked permission to send only the introduction and conclusion, adding that these could be changed at will.

Thanks to the tender solicitude of the wife of the Tuscan ambassador, [Francesco] Niccolini, Riccardi agreed to Galileo's proposal, provided that an expert theologian of the Dominican order revised the manuscript in Florence. Months went by. The introduction and conclusion did not return from Rome nor did Father Stefani, the consultant of the Florentine Inquisition, receive the order to revise the manuscript from Rome.

Meanwhile the winter passed. "And so my work is in a trap," wrote Galileo, "my life is passing away, and I spend it in constant pain.". . .

Finally, by the end of May, the Florentine Inquisitor received the conditions for printing the manuscript; he was allowed to proceed independently of the Roman revision and to give or refuse his *imprimatur.*

He gave it. The title and a few expressions were changed. A few weeks later the printing began. But months still had to pass before Riccardi sent in the revised introduction and conclusion. . . .

In February, 1632, the book was published with the double *imprimatur* of Rome and Florence. The preface inserted upon the insistence of the Church authorities contradicted the book both in its tone and in its contents, just as [Andreas] Osiander's preface had contradicted the Revolutions. . . .

The book at once aroused intense passions of love and hate. It made many readers feel, as Sagredo puts it in the dialogues, like liberated prisoners. Others took pleasure in the many physical experiments described, still others enjoyed the animated dialogue, the changing scenes, the comic situations, anecdotes and fairy-tales. The work gained immediate popularity and renown. [Dutch politician and theologian] Hugo Grotius declared that it could not be compared to any book of modern times while Thomas Campanella saw "the true system of the world assured."

In the dialogues Galileo again ridiculed his old enemy, the Jesuit Father, Christoph Scheiner of Ingolstadt, as a plagiarist. It was said of this man that because he was secretly convinced of the truth of the Copernican world system, he publicly persecuted the Copernicans with particular fury. Later everyone held this Scheiner responsible for Galileo's second trial by the Inquisition.

THE *DIALOGUE* ANGERS CHURCH AUTHORITIES

By the end of July Galileo learned that the Pope and the Inquisition were examining his dialogues. As early as August,

1632, only a few months after their publication, the Roman Inquisition forbade Galileo and Landini, the printer, to sell copies of the book. The remaining copies were to be handed over to the Inquisition.

The Tuscan government, through its representative in Rome, immediately expressed its surprise that a book so thoroughly scrutinized before publication and approved by the Roman and Florentine Inquisitor should be suspended. Rome replied that out of regard for the Grand Duke the book had been submitted for investigation not to the Inquisition but to a special Congregation.

The Jesuits in Rome were already circulating reports that the teachings expounded in the dialogues were most reprehensible, worse than all the heresies of [protestant reformers Martin] Luther or [John] Calvin; that despite all the submissive pious additions the book was still Copernican; that the censors had been bluffed by the preface and conclusion; and that Galileo had only made fun of them. Worst of all, they convinced the Pope that Galileo had held him up to ridicule in the character of Simplicio. Urban was an Aristotelian; he had often argued with Galileo about the Copernican theory, and could not fail to recognize his own arguments in many of Simplicio's arguments; in fact, Simplicio refutes the proof of the earth's motion by the existence of the tides with the Pope's own words, and makes it unmistakably clear that he had adopted this counter-argument from an *eminentissima persona* [distinguished person].

Urban VIII now made it his own business to persecute Galileo.

On October 1 the Florentine Inquisitor summoned Galileo, and in the presence of a notary and witnesses informed him that he must appear before the Commissioner of the Inquisition in Rome before the end of the month. Galileo was horrified. He appealed to the Minister and to the Grand Duke. He was advised to obey.

To Cardinal Barberini, a relative of the Pope, Galileo wrote: "When I think that the fruit of all my work and efforts now result in a subpoena by the Holy Office, such as is issued only to those found guilty of severe crimes, I am so affected that I curse the time I have spent on these studies, by which I hoped to rise somewhat above the beaten path of science. I regret that I have communicated part of my results to the world and I feel inclined to suppress and consign to the flames what I still have on hand, thus completely satis-fying the wishes of my enemies to whom my ideas are so burdensome."

Galileo asked that he be spared the trip to Rome on ac-count of his advanced age—he had attained seventy years—and his many ailments, to which insomnia had now been added. The plague and the long quarantine, he said, would make this trip mortally dangerous for him. Could he not be granted an examination of his case by correspondence, or could he not be heard in Florence? Naturally he would travel if the authorities insisted on it, for he valued obedience to them higher than his own life.

He won only a few weeks' delay by these entreaties. He was still tarrying in Florence when a second order was fol-lowed by a third one, even more peremptory. Now Galileo sent in the report of three highly reputed physicians, ac-cording to whom the slightest accident might cause the death of the sick and aging man.

GALILEO URGED TO COMPLY WITH THE POPE'S ORDERS

Urban VIII who was directing the proceedings against Galileo gave orders to inform the Florentine Inquisitor that His Holiness and the Holy Office could not tolerate any ex-cuses, and that, if necessary, they would send a commis-sioner and a physician to examine Galileo. If they found him transportable they would bring him to Rome in chains as a prisoner. Should the trip really be dangerous for him because of his condition, "his intermittent pulse, weakened senses and humors, frequent spells of fainting, melan-cholies, weak stomach, insomnia, stitches in the side and severe rupture," that is, should a delay be found to be im-perative, he would be brought to Rome in chains as a pris-oner immediately upon his recovery or the elimination of immediate danger to his life. And Galileo himself was to pay the travelling expenses of the commissioner and the physician!

The Grand Duke is said to have been indignant at the tone of this order, but he severely admonished Galileo to submit to the Pope. In the middle of the winter (January 26, 1633) he set out on his journey.

He was surprised by the indictment. He had discussed his manuscript with the Pope and the Roman and Florentine In-quisitors, he had submitted to their revisions on every point, he had obtained a double imprimatur, his book was formally justified and protected. If it nevertheless proved dangerous later, it could after all be prohibited. But the author was guilty of no crime—except the one that had been manufactured to do him injury. . . .

When a tangible proof of Galileo's guilt was lacking, it was—found. Now the later permission granted by the Inquisition, the double *imprimatur* lost all value. The censors had given it without knowledge of the order of 1616 [a suspicious document ordering Galileo to give up his ideas about the universe and his support of Copernicus]. According to the indictment Galileo had fraudulently concealed this order.

On February 3, 1633, after a long quarantine Galileo reached Rome in the Grand Duke's sedan chair—a mark of his favor. For the time being he was allowed to stop in the Tuscan ambassador's palace; but he was already under house arrest and forbidden to receive visitors.

GALILEO QUESTIONED IN THE PALACE OF THE INQUISITION

Only two months later, on April 12, was he summoned for the first questioning in the palace of the Inquisition. As in all Inquisition trials, what was in question was not the defense of the accused or the clarification of the facts, but a confession of guilt. If the accused confessed his guilt the Inquisition might order him to be burned and confiscate his possessions; but if he failed to confess, he was burned and his possessions confiscated for that failure.

Galileo was supposed to confess his guilt, that is to say, the violation of the forged order dated February 26, 1616.

The technique of the Inquisition is well known. Galileo never saw the bill of indictment against him, he never saw the dubious record of the proceedings of February 26, 1616. His persecutors only alluded darkly to his dark guilt. Confess, they demanded, confess! Confess everything! What words had been used sixteen years before; which witnesses had been present at the time; what this one or that one had said according to the minutes, all these matters were discussed. At no point was Galileo's book or his theory discussed.

Urban directed the examination of the defendant, he never presided at the trial.

During the first examination Galileo declared spontaneously that his dialogues did not defend the Copernican theory, but rather refuted it; that desirous of doing every-

Galileo is accused of heresy in the palace of the Inquisition for publishing a book on Copernican ideas.

thing in the proper fashion he had submitted his manuscript to the Roman and Florentine Inquisitions and humbly accepted every change they suggested. True, he had not mentioned Bellarmin's admonition, because, after all, it did not occur to him that it was applicable to this book in which he demonstrated the untenability of the Copernican arguments. And he submitted a copy of Bellarmin's testimonial of May, 1616, to the effect that no penalty had been imposed on Galileo and that only the text of the decree against Copernicus had been transmitted to him.

Now the Inquisition kept Galileo in its palace as a prisoner, from April 12 to April 30. He fell sick in jail, and appeared for the second examination completely broken. He declared that he had just reread his book for the first time in three years; that he had noticed that in certain passages he had been led astray by his pleasure in his own skill in debate, so that some arguments against Simplicio had turned out to be fairly cogent, even quite credible. But he intended, he said, to expand the book in order to make it quite clear that he did not then and did not now in any way share the condemned opinion that the earth moves. "Since on this occasion I will have to add one or two dialogues, I promise to take up again the arguments in favor of the opinion considered false and condemned and to refute them in the most conclusive manner that our merciful Lord will inspire in me. Accordingly I beg this high court to assist me in this good resolve and to enable me to carry it out."

On April 30 he was allowed to return from the jail of the Inquisition to Ambassador Niccolini's palace where he remained under house arrest. He brought a document containing his defense to his third examination on May 10. He stated that the text of the order of 1616 was entirely new to him; that he had obeyed Bellarmin's order and that he would do every penance imposed upon him by the Holy Office. He asked the cardinals "to consider his wretched health and his constant anguish of heart during the last ten months, and the discomfort of his long hard trip during the worst season, at the age of seventy, and the fact that he had already lost the greater part of the year, and that all these sufferings were already a sufficient punishment for his errors which they should ascribe to his senility. He also recommended to them his honor and reputation against the slanders of his enemies intent upon besmirching his good name."

GALILEO RETURNS FOR THE VERDICT

Six weeks later he received his last summons, on June 21. Galileo expected to be acquitted. The examining magistrate made him give the usual oath that he would speak the truth. He asked Galileo whether he had anything to say. Galileo answered: "I have nothing to say."

Once again he was asked whether he held for true, had held for true and since when he had held for true that the sun was the center of the world and that the earth daily moved around it.

Once again Galileo declared that before the decree of the Index in 1616 he had held that both opinions, those of Ptolemy and of Copernicus, were worthy of consideration; after the decree "every doubt vanished from my mind, and I held and still hold Ptolemy's opinion that the earth is motionless and that the sun moves as absolutely true and incontestable."

Once again he was told that it was clear from his dialogues that even after that time he had believed in the motion of the earth; and he was asked freely to tell the truth: whether he now considered this opinion true or had considered it to be true.

Galileo reiterated that after the decision of the authorities he had not considered the condemned opinion true.

The judge reiterated that, nevertheless, the dialogues suggested that he did consider Copernicus' opinion true; and that if he did not make up his mind finally to confess the truth, the proper legal proceedings would be taken against him.

Galileo declared: "I do not consider Copernicus' opinion true and have not considered it true, since I was ordered to renounce it; for the rest, I am here in your hands, do with me what you please."

GALILEO THREATENED WITH TORTURE

Once again the magistrate asked him to speak the truth, and said that if he did not, he would be tortured.

Galileo replied: "I am here to submit, but I have not held this opinion for true since the decision, as I have said."

According to the text of the minutes as it stands today he was thereupon sent back to his dungeon in the palace of the Inquisition. But the minutes seem to have been tampered with at this point. From the verdict against Galileo it can be inferred that at least the "first degree of torture," the *territio realis*, that is to say, a cross-examination in the torture chamber in view of the instruments of torture, was applied to him.

Thus, by order of Pope Urban, the employees of the famous international institute for torture displayed before the creator of modern mechanics their latest machines for dispensation of "justice" and explained to him in the minutest detail what parts of his flesh they would twinge and which of his bones they would break unless he finally confessed his belief in the motion of the earth. Galileo must have cast a long glance at the Church's mechanical arguments before finally admitting in the torture chamber under duress what the very next day he was compelled to recant in the monastery under the same duress, to wit, the Copernican theory of the earth's motion.

According to another record the verdict had already been prescribed on June 16, five days before its final examination, by order of the Pope. Here we read: "Sanctissimus gave orders that Galileo be questioned *de intentione* [of his intentions], under threat of torture, as though he were to be submitted to it, and then that he be made to recant before the full Congregation of the Holy Office, and be sentenced to imprisonment, at the discretion of the Holy Office."

On the day following his last examination the seventy-year-old Galileo who was suffering from several ailments, was compelled to kneel down in a penitential robe in the presence of seven cardinals at a solemn session of the Inquisition in the great hall of the Dominican monastery of Santa Maria Sopra Minerva in Rome; he was compelled to take a Bible in his hands to abjure the error of thinking that the earth moves by reciting a long and ignominious formula: "I recant, curse and execrate with sincere heart and non-hypocritical faith all these errors and heresies, as well as all other errors and opinions, which are contrary to the teachings of the Holy Catholic and Roman Apostolic Church; I also swear that in the future I will neither orally nor in writing say or maintain anything that might justify a similar suspicion of heresy against me; and should I know a heretic or anyone suspect of heresy, I will report him to the Holy Office or the Inquisitor or the bishop of my diocese."

The Inquisitors then read the verdict. Galileo was condemned to formal imprisonment in the dungeons of the Holy Office for an undetermined period at the discretion of the Inquisition. For three years he was to recite the seven penitential psalms once a week; he was "extremely suspect to heresy." The Dialogues were prohibited.

The Significance of the Order of 1616

Richard J. Blackwell

Richard J. Blackwell analyzes how Galileo was found guilty. In 1616 the pope ordered Galileo to be silent on Copernicanism because it violated sacred scripture. Blackwell argues that communication of this order misled Galileo: The account of the trial given to him stated only that he was told that Copernicanism violated the Bible, but a secret account filed in the Holy Office stated explicit orders for silence on Copernicanism. In 1633 Galileo was tried on the basis of the secret document. By that time he had already arqued for Copernicanism in *Dialogue;* consequently, he was found guilty of disobedience. Richard J. Blackwell, who teaches humanities at St. Louis University, has published numerous articles and books, including *Discovery in the Physical Sciences.*

Galileo's trial was an immensely complex affair. To fully understand it one would need to examine the trial and its antecedents at many levels: the scientific, theological, and philosophical issues involved, the legal basis and procedural rules which governed it, the ecclesiastical politics and intrigues behind the scenes, and the personalities of the main actors. It is beyond the scope of this [article] to take on an examination of all these factors. Rather we will limit ourselves to a discussion of only one of the theological issues involved; namely, the role of the Bible in the proceedings against Galileo.

The situation is further complicated by the fact that there were really two trials, separated by seventeen years, or perhaps better, two quite distinct phases of what was really one and the same trial. The first took place in 1616, and focused on the indictment and judgment of Copernicanism as false and clearly contrary to the Scriptures, with Galileo being involved only indirectly. The second took place in 1633, and focused on Galileo personally over the question of whether he had disobeyed an injunction placed on him individually as part of the proceedings of 1616. This two-phase character of the trial had the effect of neatly separating the conceptual issues regarding the relation of science and the Bible from the question of Galileo's personal responsibility and culpability, a separation which does not appear to have happened accidentally.

THE ORIGIN OF THE CHARGES AGAINST COPERNICANISM

The Catholic Church decided to brand Copernicanism as erroneous in February 1616. The roots of this calamitous decision went back exactly one year, to 7 February 1615, when [Dominican priest Niccolò] Lorini initiated the first involvement of the Holy Office with his complaint against the orthodoxy of Galileo's *Letter to Castelli*.[1] Lorini's specific complaint was dismissed, but unfortunately that episode did not end the affair. Tommaso Caccini then went to Rome and met with Cardinal Aracoeli to arrange an appearance before the Holy Office to testify about events which had occurred in Florence.[2] On 19 March Pope Paul V ordered the Holy Office to conduct an interrogation of Caccini because he was "informed about the errors of Galileo, and insists on testifying about them to exonerate his conscience." The interrogation took place the next day in Rome in the great hall of the Holy Office before Fr. Michelangelo Sighizzi, O.P. (1585–1625), the Commissary General of the Roman Inquisition.

As was customary, a scribe, who remains unnamed in this case, prepared a deposition of the substance of the interview, which was then signed by the witness to verify its authenticity. The resulting document is thus not a strictly *verbatim* account of the witness's testimony, but its accuracy on content is quite dependable. A close examination of Caccini's deposition explains a great deal about the condemnation of Copernicanism one year later.

---

1. After hearing about a conversation regarding Copernicanism between the Grand Duchess Christina and his friend Benedictine priest Benedetto Castelli, Galileo explained his thoughts on the subject in a letter to Castelli. He later expanded his thoughts in a letter to the Grand Duchess Christina.   2. On the Sunday before Christmas, 1614, Dominican priest Tommaso Caccini delivered a sermon in Florence railing against Copernicanism, Galileo, and all mathematicians. Because he was so rude, his superior sent Galileo an apology.

The first topic on which Caccini testified was his sermon against Copernicanism in the Church of Santa Maria Novella in Florence on 20 December 1614. He began by relating that the passage of Scripture under discussion on that Fourth Sunday of Advent was the miracle of God's stopping the motion of the sun at Joshua's request, as related in Joshua 10:12. . . .

The import of this testimony is unmistakable. The Fathers of the Church have all interpreted Joshua 10:12, and similar passages, in their proper literal sense, that is, the sun is in motion. Furthermore the Church teaches, specifically at the Council of Trent,[3] Session IV, that one may not interpret Scripture contrary to the common agreement of the Fathers. Therefore Copernicanism is formally heretical, i.e., directly contrary to the explicit word of God. And Galileo is mentioned by name as an advocate of this heresy. Caccini's logic was impeccable. . . .

THE POPE ORDERS GALILEO TO OBEY

Galileo, of course, would not have known anything firsthand about the interrogations and documents discussed earlier in this [article]. They were all secret proceedings of the Holy Office. But he may well have been suspicious that things were going against his interests because, contrary to the advice of the Tuscan ambassador at Rome and of several friends, Galileo went to Rome in December 1615 specifically to argue his case. Had he somehow heard that his *Letters on Sunspots* had been denounced just a few weeks earlier by [Florentine parish priest Giannozzo] Attavanti?

Galileo's main maneuver at the time was to try to formulate a definitive proof of heliocentricism. To that end he wrote out in January 1616 a first version of his hopefully conclusive (but defective) argument to explain the tides by the double motion of the earth, which was later to become the foundation of the Fourth Day of the *Dialogue*. He managed to persuade the young Cardinal Alessandro Orsini (1593–1626) to present this document to Pope Paul V in the hope of winning the pope's support. This maneuver had exactly the opposite effect; yet as late as early February Galileo was still optimistic.

On 25 February, the day after the consultors submitted

---

3. Councils were convened by the Catholic Church to settle disputes. The Council of Trent focused on Catholic dogma and reforming the discipline, training, and life-style of the clergy.

their censures of the two suspect propositions, the results were reported to the pope, who immediately ordered Cardinal Bellarmine to arrange a private meeting with Galileo on the issue of Copernicanism. His instructions to Bellarmine were quite specific.

> The Most Holy has ordered the illustrious Cardinal Bellarmine to call before him the said Galileo and to advise him to abandon the said opinion; and if he should refuse to obey, the Commissary, before a notary and witnesses, should impose upon him an injunction to abstain completely from teaching or defending that doctrine and opinion or from discussing it; and if he should not agree, he is to be imprisoned.

The pope's instructions to Bellarmine were very explicit. He envisioned three successive steps. First Bellarmine was to inform Galileo of the condemnation of heliocentricism by the Holy Office and to ask Galileo to drop his commitment to that position. If Galileo agreed to obey, the meeting was to be concluded. Second, if he refused to obey, then the Commissary General was to place Galileo under an injunction to obey. If Galileo accepted the injunction agreeably, then the meeting would be over, with Galileo restrained by the injunction. Third, if Galileo opposed the injunction, he was to be imprisoned.

The meeting between Bellarmine and Galileo took place the next day at the cardinal's residence. The Commissary General mentioned in the pope's instructions and also present at the meeting was Michaelangelo Seghizzi, O.P., the same official who had presided at Caccini's deposition one year earlier.

What happened at that meeting? Did Galileo agree to abandon Copernicanism in light of the Church's condemnation when initially asked to do so? If so, the meeting should have ended at that point. Or did Galileo object and refuse to obey? If so, Galileo should have been placed under an injunction. Did that happen? If so, who issued the injunction, Seghizzi or Bellarmine? Was the injunction served legally? What were the specific orders contained in the injunction placed on Galileo?

We do not know the answers to these questions. The meeting certainly took place; and we also know that the order of imprisonment in step three of Pope Paul's instructions was not given. However it is significant to note that even at this early stage the pope had envisioned the possibility of imprisoning Galileo, and he must have been prepared to carry out such a drastic action. Galileo's obedience was a serious matter.

TWO VERSIONS OF THE MEETING WITH GALILEO

The reason for our lack of knowledge of precisely what happened is that the two surviving documents summarizing the meeting are flatly inconsistent with each other. Furthermore one of the documents is ambiguous at the critical point of delineating what happened just after Bellarmine's initial request of Galileo.

These documents originated as follows. In the next two months after the meeting the rumor mills of Rome carried the report that Galileo had abjured [renounced under oath] his opinion and that he had been censured and punished. To clear his reputation Galileo very prudently asked Bellarmine for his help in the form of a letter to certify what had happened at the meeting. Bellarmine had no hesitations in supplying Galileo with the following letter:

> We, Robert Cardinal Bellarmine, hearing that it has been calumniously rumored that Galileo Galilei has abjured in our hands and also has been given a salutary penance, and being requested to state the truth with regard to this, declare that this man Galileo has not abjured, either in our hands or in the hands of any other person here in Rome, or anywhere else as far as we know, any opinion or doctrine which he has held; nor has any salutary or any other kind of penance been given to him. Only the declaration made by the Holy Father and published by the Sacred Congregation of the Index has been revealed to him, which states that the doctrine of Copernicus, that the earth moves around the sun and that the sun is stationary in the center of the universe and does not move east to west, is contrary to Holy Scripture and therefore cannot be defended or held. In witness whereof we have written and signed this letter with our hand on this twenty-sixth day of May, 1616.

Meanwhile another account of the meeting, a memorandum written apparently by an unnamed scribe in attendance at the session, was placed in the file of the Holy Office. This document, which is irregular in some significant ways, reads as follows:

> At the Palace, the usual residence of the aforenamed Cardinal Bellarmine, the said Galileo, having been summoned and standing before His Lordship, was, in the presence of the Very Reverend Father Michael Angelo Seghiti de Lauda, of the Order of Preachers, Commissary-General of the Holy Office, admonished by the Cardinal of the error of the aforesaid opin-

ion and that he should abandon it; and later on—*successive ac incontinenti*—in the presence of myself, other witnesses, and the Lord Cardinal, who was still present, the said Commissary did enjoin upon the said Galileo, there present, and did order him (in his own name), the name of His Holiness the Pope, and that of the Congregation of the Holy Office, to relinquish altogether the said opinion, namely, that the sun is in the center of the universe and immobile, and that the earth moves; nor henceforth to hold, teach, or defend it in any way, either verbally or in writing. Otherwise proceedings would be taken against him by the Holy Office. The said Galileo acquiesced in this ruling and promised to obey it.

The ambiguity in the documents referred to above resides in the words "successive ac incontinenti," which [historian Jerome I.] Langford translates as "and later on." This phrase, which has been interpreted in many ways, introduces the critical discussion of what happened after Bellarmine had carried out stage one of the pope's instructions.

But of much greater importance is the inconsistency between the two documents. Bellarmine's certificate states that Copernicanism "cannot be defended or held." Galileo reasonably took this to mean "defended as true" and "held to be true," which would still allow discussion of the arguments pro and con. However the memorandum at the Holy Office contained the much stronger wording, "nor henceforth to hold, *teach,* or defend it *in any way, either verbally or in writing.*" The added, emphasized words ruled out any and all discussion of the topic rather unequivocally.

Assuming that the injunction placed on Galileo was issued legally, which of the above did it order? No one knows. Unfortunately the crux of the trial in 1633 turned precisely on this point. And the one man whose mere word would have conclusively settled the issue at the trial, Cardinal Bellarmine, had died in 1621. The crucial development in many ways was the original decision made in 1616 which led to all this; namely, the decision to put Galileo to an explicit test of obedience to the Decree of 5 March,[4] rather than simply to include his *Letters on Sunspots* for correction in that Decree, or better yet, to let Galileo read it on his own and infer its unavoidable application to his own work. Unfortunately in conducting the private session with Galileo, an ambiguous and

---

4. The Decree of 5 March, 1616, declared Copernican theory "contrary to Sacred Scripture," ordered Copernicus's book suspended until corrected, and "also that all other books teaching the same thing are prohibited, as the present Decree prohibits, condemns, and suspends them all respectively."

dangerous situation was created which was to haunt all concerned for years to come.

GALILEO NAIVELY GOES AHEAD WITH *DIALOGUE*

Galileo, of course, had no way of knowing about the memorandum in the secret files of the Holy Office. For him Bellarmine's certificate defined the practical ground rules of what was and was not permitted under the Decree of 1616. Even at that, however, he did not broach the topic of Copernicanism for the next eight years.

Then the scene changed significantly for the better. In 1623 Galileo's acquaintance and admirer, Maffeo Cardinal Barberini of Florence, was elected pope and took the name of Urban VIII. The new pope was a well-educated man of letters and friend of artists and intellectuals. Encouraged by this development, Galileo journeyed to Rome, where he was warmly welcomed, and where he engaged in six long conversations with Urban VIII, who was comfortable with him taking up the topic of Copernicanism again, albeit hypothetically. The pope himself thought that such matters could never be demonstratively settled, since there are no restrictions on the power of God to create whatever kind of world that he might choose to create.

Galileo returned to Florence with the confidence and resolve to undertake his postponed book on the structure of the world. This project consumed the next eight years of his life, interspersed with many delays due to his chronic ill health and to protracted negotiations with the printers and with the censors for required permissions. Finally in February 1632 the book was published in Florence, with ecclesiastical permissions from the censors in both Rome and Florence. It was Galileo's masterpiece, his *Dialogue Concerning the Two Chief World Systems, Ptolemaic and Copernican.*

The book caused an immediate storm of protests over everything from personal effrontery to serious charges of religious heterodoxy. The latter were due mostly to the fact that the Copernican side clearly seems to win the argument among the interlocutors of the *Dialogue,* despite the author's claims to a balanced neutrality. Sales of the book were stopped, and copies confiscated, by the summer of 1632.

In September a Special Commission appointed by Urban VIII to look into the matter discovered the 1616 memorandum in the files of the Holy Office. Even the pope was surprised. A trial became unavoidable. For the publication of Galileo's book had rather clearly violated the injunction not "to hold, teach, or defend it in any way, either verbally or in writing." Various delays pushed the trial into the spring of 1633. The proceedings started on 12 April, and ended on 22 June.

THE 1633 TRIAL CONCERNING GALILEO'S OBEDIENCE

Since Galileo's trial was an immensely complex affair, we intend to look only at the role of the Bible in the proceedings. Regarding the events in the first phase of the trial in 1615–16, there is no doubt that the Bible is located at center stage. But when one studies the documents of the 1633 phase of the trial, one finds something unexpected. There is rather little mention of the Scriptures, and then almost always in the context of pointing out that the 1616 Decree had declared Copernicanism to be contrary to the Bible.

In these trial documents one finds little or no mention of the levels of meaning and truth value of the Scriptures, no use of the distinction between literal and figurative passages, no discussion of what is or is not a matter of faith and morals, no analysis of the criteria for determining the unanimous agreement of the Fathers, nor even quotations from Scripture in support of the Church's position. By 1633 all these topics had faded from the picture. The classic questions of biblical exegesis were no longer center stage.

Rather, almost all the references to the Bible are in the context of recalling the condemnation of heliocentricism in 1616; and then the concern is not to reexamine the substance of that decision but to reassert it, with both force and frequency. The proceedings in 1633 were not focused on science and the Scriptures; that issue had been settled beyond recall in 1616. The focus rather was on the person of Galileo. Was he loyal or was he disobedient?

In Galileo's depositions to the court attention is almost exclusively directed to the injunction, the Decree, and what had happened when he obtained the censors' permissions to publish. It was not the time or the place to reargue the views in the *Letter to Castelli*. The dramatic high point came when Galileo produced the testimony of Bellarmine's certificate, which he had prudently saved, to the effect that Copernicanism could "not be defended or held"—period. It then became a case of which documentary account of the Bellarmine Galileo meeting would predominate. The decision on this key issue was not surprising; but obviously it had nothing to do with the Scriptures.

The Trial Summary

The Bible did make its appearance in another way, which turned out to be quite damaging to Galileo. Toward the end of the proceedings a summary of the trial was drawn up, by an unknown author, to be sent to the pope and the cardinals who were to judge the case. This document was the main basis for their decisions. But it is an inaccurate account in certain subtle ways designed to reflect negatively on Galileo. The main device used by the author of this document was to recount Lorini's original complaint in 1615 against Galileo, including excerpts from his inaccurate copy of the *Letter to Castelli*, which made it appear that Galileo had said that some statements in the Bible are false and that others pervert important dogmas. Needless to say, those who argue that the 1633 trial was the product of a conspiracy have used this anti-Galileo trial summary as primary evidence.

There is no doubt that this slanted trial summary had its intended effect, for in the preamble to the sentence, Lorini's denunciation and the *Letter to Castelli* are mentioned as Galileo is charged with "interpreting Holy Scripture according to your own meaning in response to objections based on Scripture which were sometimes made to you." Although the Fourth Session of the Council of Trent is not mentioned here, not one of the judges would have failed to see that Galileo had thereby disobeyed the decree of the council. Further the *Letter to Castelli* is said to contain "various propositions against the authority and true meaning of the Holy Scripture."

The Bible is also mentioned in the formal sentence which comes a few pages later. Galileo is judged to be

> vehemently suspected of heresy, namely of having believed and held the doctrine which is false and contrary to the Sacred and Divine Scriptures, that the sun is the center of the world and does not move from east to west and that the earth moves and is not the center of the world; and that any opinion may be held and defended as probable after it has been declared and defined contrary to the Holy Scripture.

Both charges of heresy in this final judgment explicitly mention the Bible. The first is the familiar charge that Galileo has violated the 1616 condemnation of heliocentricism as contrary to the Scriptures, a prior decision which remained unquestionable at the 1633 trial. The second judgment goes one step further by asserting that one cannot even claim that heliocentricism is probable.

This is interesting for at least two reasons. First the point being made against Galileo is that he cannot take refuge in saying that the *Dialogue* treated Copernicanism merely as an open possibility. Note that this is quite different from treating it "hypothetically" in the sense of assuming it counterfactually for purposes of calculation. The latter concedes the non-reality of heliocentricism; the former allows that it might be the way things actually exist in the world. But if Copernicanism is contrary to the Bible, then it is not the existial state of affairs in the world, and thus cannot be said to be probable. This is an expansion on the 1616 rejection of Copernicanism.

Second the judges are invoking here what appears to be a methodological principle of biblical exegesis. What has been declared to be contrary to the Scripture is false. But the false cannot be said to be probable. To say otherwise is to conflate truth and falsity, for the probable is that which may well be true. This is not being said, however, primarily for methodological reasons, but for the theological concern to protect the truth status of the Bible from any shadow of falsity. For to say that the Bible contains falsity would surely be a heretical denial of the word of God.

GALILEO'S TWO-PHASED TRIAL

If we step back from the details of Galileo's two-phased trial, we can see that a pattern emerges. In the first stage the problems of the relations of science and religion and of biblical exegesis vs. scientific truth in general were central. This stage was characterized by foundational debates over the conceptual issues involved. This was followed by a decision (which became quickly unquestionable) which terminated debate at the conceptual level: Copernicanism is contrary to the Scriptures. This in turn was followed by a public announcement of the decision and of the general obligation to accept and obey it: the Decree of 1616. In the present case Galileo received in addition personal orders to agree to and observe the condemnation: the disputed injunction. From this point on, discussion of the merits of the original decision became taboo, and attention focused on issues of loyalty and obedience. When a violation of the decision occurred later, or was thought to have occurred, adjudication of the case was carried out in terms of how the individual responded to the obligations to agree and obey, and not in terms of the wisdom of the resolution of the original conceptual issues: the trial of 1633. This is how the Galileo affair developed. The cultural atmosphere at the end was quite different from that of the beginning. Cognitive disputes over truth and falsity gave way to authority disputes over loyalty and disobedience.

A Nontraditional Examination of the Galileo-Church Conflict

Rivka Feldhay

Rivka Feldhay analyzes the events of Galileo's "trial" by the Roman Catholic Church and historians' attempts to interpret them. Feldhay maintains that traditional interpretations have depended on opposing concepts: rationality/irrationality, disclosure/concealment, publicity/suppression. She advocates a new approach that rethinks these oppositions. Rivka Feldhay has done extensive scholarly work on the history and theology of the Middle Ages and the Renaissance.

The conflict between Galileo and the church took place in two stages. The first was in 1616, and ended with a warning to Galileo, although not with legal persecution. In popular literature and in certain historical works, this stage used to be called the "first trial". The second stage of the drama activated the elaborate judicial machine of the Inquisition, and has been known as the "second trial".

PART ONE: THE WARNING IN 1616

The first encounter begins some time after the publication of the *Sidereus nuncius* [*Starry Messenger*] (1610), when Galileo's great telescopic discoveries have gained him and the Copernican cosmology a certain amount of fame, together with some hostility. In 1614–1615, complaints are raised in Florentine circles about the incompatibility of the new discoveries with certain verses from the Scriptures. The rumours reach Galileo through a letter from his disciple, the monk Benedetto Castelli. In reply, Galileo writes a letter to Castelli, expressing his ideas about the relationship of knowledge aiming at an understanding of the universe to

Excerpted from *Galileo and the Church: Political Inquisition or Critical Dialogue?* by Rivka Feldhay. Copyright © 1995 by Cambridge University Press. Reprinted with the permission of Cambridge University Press.

knowledge connected with the attainment of salvation. The first kind of knowledge, he says, is based on evidence of the senses, and teaches us "how heaven goes", whereas the second, derived from the Scriptures, teaches us "how to go to heaven". Galileo questions Castelli about the validity and legitimacy of his explanations, and Castelli gives his assent with a recommendation to introduce some minor changes. Following this exchange, Galileo reformulates his ideas in the famous *Letter to the Grand Duchess Christina* (1615). The letter passes from hand to hand in circles sympathetic to the Galilean discoveries. Consequently, Galileo's name is twice denounced to the Inquisition. The Congregation of the Holy Office begins investigations, which culminate in official deliberations of the consultants of the Holy Office over the two main propositions of the Copernican theory: namely, that the sun is immobile in the centre of the universe, and that the earth is not the centre of the universe and moves around the sun at the same time performing daily revolutions. The deliberations end on 23 February 1616 with a decision to reject the Copernican theory and to deny it any philosophical or theological truth. The matter is now transferred to the Congregation of the Index, which issues a decree forbidding and suspending certain books whose subject-matter is connected with the Copernican theory. When the deliberations are at their height, Galileo goes to Rome to publicize his views and perhaps convince the church of the scientific truth of his opinions. However, on 26 February 1616, he is invited on the decision of the Congregation of the Holy Office to the residence of Robert Bellarmine, a prominent cardinal of the Inquisition, and is warned that he should abandon his position with regard to Copernicanism.

PART TWO: THE TRIAL IN 1633

The second act begins with Galileo's visit to Rome in 1630. He has recently finished the book which he had been working on for the prior twelve years, and in which he has presented all the arguments for and against the two great world systems—the Copernican and the Ptolemaic. Six years before (1624) he had a series of discussions touching on astronomical and cosmological matters with the new Pope Urban VIII (1568–1644), a liberal churchman well known for his love of the arts and sciences. In the course of these discussions Galileo was impressed by Urban's inclination to favour an astronomical dialogue. He has now come to Rome to ask for an imprimatur (permission of publication) for his book. The request is presented to Niccolo Riccardi, the Master of the Holy Apostolic Palace, who also functions as head censor of the Holy Office. Riccardi finds it necessary to consult with his friend and colleague Raffaello Visconti, who is better versed than himself in the mathematical sciences. Visconti recommends some corrections, all with the intention of emphasizing the hypothetical-mathematical character of the book, in the spirit of the wishes expressed by the pope. Galileo promises to follow Visconti's recommendations and to introduce the necessary changes. The imprimatur is given on condition that the new corrected version be submitted to Riccardi before printing.

Galileo is back in Tuscany, but finds it impossible to return with the new version to Rome owing to plague, quarantine, and poor health. From Tuscany he exerts enormous pressures in order to be allowed to have his book published in Florence. After a long period of hesitations and recurring procrastinations Riccardi gives in. The responsibility for a further reading of the manuscript is passed on to the Inquisitor of Florence, followed by precise instructions for the required introduction to the book. The manuscript is checked by the Florentine Inquisitor, is passed on to another censor named Giacinto Stefani for further examination, and after being approved by the two men finally goes to press and is out on the shelves by the spring of 1632.

Shortly afterwards, the first copies of the *Dialogue on the Two Chief World Systems* reach Rome. They are read by the pope, Riccardi, and some other church dignitaries, and are immediately confiscated. Further dissemination is forbidden. The pope appoints a special commission to decide upon the fate of both the book and its author, and Galileo is summoned to Rome. He arrives in the city in February 1633, after several delays. In March, he is incarcerated in the Inquisition building. It is there that the first two hearings of the "second trial" take place. Galileo is then transferred to the villa of Francesco Niccolini, the Tuscan ambassador to Rome. There he writes his self-defence, which is presented to the Commissary General of the Inquisition. This session is followed by one further hearing which finally leads to a sentence. Galileo is suspected of holding heretic opinions, which he is ordered to abjure; he is condemned to formal imprisonment at the pleasure of the Inquisition, his book is prohibited, and the sentence is sent to Inquisitors all over the Catholic world, to be read in full assembly and in the presence of the leading practitioners of the mathematical arts.

Two interpretive positions, two reading strategies have suggested themselves to Galilean scholars: one being that of the champions of scientific rationality, the other belonging to the apologetic voices of the church and to some opponents of Galileo. But at the heart of both readings there has always been one question: Was Galileo right? Was he right from a scientific point of view? Could he *really* prove what he claimed to discover? Was he right from a political point of view? In 1616, did he not, after all, give his word that he would abandon the Copernican doctrine? Was he right from an ecclesiastical point of view? How, after all, could the church be expected to give up the policies necessitated by the Protestant Reformation in order to stand up to his immense challenge?

ADVOCATES SAY GALILEO WAS RIGHT

Galileo was right, say the advocates, for he corroborated the Copernican theory and refuted Aristotelian cosmology and Ptolemaic astronomy. The church which opposed and censored him was blind to the effectiveness of his mathematical method and afraid of the truth of his physical hypotheses. But, whereas Galileo's correctness is usually described in terms drawn from his theories themselves, the church's position is explained in nondiscursive, political, and psychological terms. The church of the Counter Reformation, it is claimed, is known for its lack of tolerance towards unorthodox views, coupled with a persecution and oppression of intellectuals. Copernicanism was conceived as a direct threat to the traditional reading of the Scriptures and, as a consequence, to the whole authority of the church. The church could not afford to tolerate the sophisticated defence of a dangerous theory put forward by Galileo.

These institutional motives, however, were coupled with personal motivations. Galileo's bitter debates with some Jesuit astronomers made them into his enemies and pushed them into seeking vengeance by convincing the pope to bring Galileo to trial. Urban VIII, who had been criticized for his nepotistic policies and dubious involvement in the Thirty Years' War, vented his anger on poor Galileo, thereby trying to regain some lost political assets. So emotionally heated was the confrontation that some church officials deviated from common legal procedures, even going so far as to forge a document in order to justify their position.

Be the details as they may, the binary structure of the story is clear and simple: rationality is embodied in Galilean science, although not necessarily in the figure of the scientist; irrational modes of thought, institutions, and historical agents belong to the other side, the church, which is seen as an embodiment of political power.

OPPONENTS SAY GALILEO WAS WRONG

This strategy of reading the events, however, has its counterpart. Galileo was wrong, say the adversaries, for he ascribed absolute truth to the Copernican world system. No scientific theory can be really, absolutely true, let alone the Copernican theory which had been faulty from the very beginning. The most one can say is that heliocentrism was to be preferred to geocentrism, and that the church was late recognizing this. Copernicanism, however, contained no more truth than its rival world system, and Galileo, in fact, did rather poorly in his attempt to prove the superiority of the modern theory. It was R. Bellarmine, cardinal of the Holy Office, who really understood the hypothetical nature of scientific theories, and whose point of view has become a cornerstone of modern scientific thinking.

On the other side, we find a stubborn man, very arrogant, whose claims to knowledge have been grossly exaggerated. It is hardly surprising if he deliberately disregarded Bellarmine's instructions and then acted dishonestly towards the authorities, asking for permission to bring his book to the printer. It was his inability to compromise, his lack of modesty which pushed the church to take drastic steps, to humiliate him and censor his book.

The story is thus inverted, and yet the structure remains the same. The church, with its prudent attitude towards ephemeral scientific theories, becomes the vicar of rationality, whereas the stubborn Galileo embodies an all-too-human irrationality. It matters little that the advocates speak about rationality in terms drawn from Galilean science, while the opponents do so in terms drawn from a Catholic "image of knowledge". It matters little whether irrationality is ascribed to institutions or to individuals. What really matters is that both stories are but inverted interpretations of the same structure, the same clash between reason and unreason.

THE DOCUMENTS

We have a plot with diametrically opposed interpretations. And we have a body of documents with a story of their own. The documents of the trials were originally in the ownership of the Congregation of the Holy Office. The system of organization of the archives divided the documents into two groups, collected in two different kinds of files. . . .

The story of the unusual vicissitudes of the documents of Galileo's trials betrays the same kind of confusions and inconsistencies as characterize the attempts to interpret their meaning. There is an unresolved tension between the need to conceal and suppress, and the need to publish and disclose. What is disclosed is a formal, unitary facade of institutional authority and power, maintained by legal procedures. What is suppressed is a variety of voices representing contradictory interests, the sole evidence of which is the acts of manipulation revealed in the obvious incompleteness of the documents. The possible identities and interests of the representatives of these contradictory positions and the structured interrelationships between them have never been systematically investigated by historians. . . .

MOST INTERPRETATIONS OF DOCUMENTS INVOLVE INCONSISTENCIES

Three main difficulties are common to most interpretations of the documents. They involve three inconsistencies, one for each layer of the story: (1) the conceptual, (2) the institutional, and (3) the psychological.

(1) Among some of the documents there are conceptual contradictions. The Inquisition files contain *two* versions of the warning of 1616 and its meaning. There is a clear contradiction between the unsigned document containing the command of the Commissary of the Inquisition, in the presence of Bellarmine, prohibiting Galileo from *holding, teaching,* or *defending* the Copernican theory in any way whatsoever, and the admonition by Bellarmine himself which only forbade him to *hold* the Copernican theory as absolutely true. At least two conflicting notions of "the hypothetical" or "the probable" were implied by this inconsistency.

(2) The church was inconsistent in its attitude toward the

publication of the documents. This may appear to be an external fact, but it is directly related to the way both the documents and Galilean science itself were understood by the church establishment. The tension between the interest in revealing and the interest in concealing suggests a far more significant tension between a negative and preventive role and the positive and constructive role which the church in fact played, or at least could have played, in the production of scientific knowledge.

(3) Galileo was inconsistent in his reaction to the demands posed by the church authorities. The Inquisition would not have treated Galileo so harshly had it not conceived of him as a realist (i.e., believing in the absolute truth of Copernicanism). Galileo could not possibly have abided by the church's demands and obtained the imprimatur had he not presented his claims in a nonrealist way.

Traditionally, the inconsistencies in the story have been resolved by means of the supposed opposition between reason and unreason, common to all interpretations. Inconsistencies pose no problem for the irrational side of the story. Thus, it is only Galileo's advocates who need worry about inconsistency (3). The opponents simply tend to say that Galileo acted as a realist when it pleased him to do so, and that the church could not afford such a game. Similarly, the inconsistency implied in (2) need worry the opponents only. Galileo's advocates are quick to point to the arbitrariness of the power politics of the church. It is inconsistency (1), however, which poses a serious problem for both sides. If both documents are authentic, then both Galileo and the church were giving at least two different meanings to key concepts like "the hypothetical" or "the probable". The strategies of advocates and opponents alike in dealing with this problem are equally unconvincing. If the church had conducted the trials with goodwill, say the advocates, there would not have been such an embarrassing discrepancy between two of its documents; if Galileo had truly abided by the first warning, say the opponents, there would have been no need for a second trial. In order to exonerate Galileo of either disciplinary or conceptual transgressions, most of the advocates tend to withdraw to an ad hoc hypothesis, namely, that the church forged the 26 February document: it was found unsigned, many years after the event, and totally surprised the accused, who had not been aware of such a strong interdiction against discussing Copernicanism. The opponents, who insist upon Galileo's disciplinary error, resort to the hypothesis of duplicity on his side, which they try to corroborate by an analysis of his hidden intentions. This analysis is clearly at odds with everything Galileo explicitly and consistently expressed in writing and in his oral responses to the inquisitors.

Both the advocates and the opponents share three presuppositions, expressing the limitations of certain opposing concepts common to both parties: the concepts of reason versus unreason, unity versus diversity, and knowledge versus power. These presuppositions are:

1. The church with which Galileo was dealing was monolithic in its reaction to his intellectual and institutional challenge.
2. The church was dealing with the same Galileo in 1616 and in 1632–1633.
3. The church, which actually represented political power, suppressed knowledge; it never created knowledge.

A NEW APPROACH TO INTERPRETATION OF DOCUMENTS

But what if we put aside the common categories—reason, faith, church, science—and tried to concretize them, to embody them in personalities, institutional positions and roles, specific patterns of action, particular policies? What would happen if we suspended judgment of the rational and the irrational, and disregarded the binary structure of the myth? We should then free ourselves of the above three presuppositions and start anew, with the following assumptions:

(1) The church was not monolithic. Although the Reformation gave birth to a political and cultural counter-movement, the Counter Reformation was merely a common ideal allowing rival forces within the Catholic Church to strive for hegemony [domination]. Therefore, always ask who is speaking and from where; try to identify personalities, institutional positions, specific intellectual and political interests, not only in the case of the seemingly heretical rebel, but also within the church itself.

(2) Both Galileo and the church may have changed their views on key issues at stake; there is no a priori reason to exclude such a possibility. Therefore, allow all parties to change views and positions. Look for possible changes and try to account for them in intellectual and institutional terms.

(3) The effects of power on the production of knowledge

are not always negative; power is always constructive as well. Therefore, abandon the opposition between power and knowledge and look for interactions; look for the knowledge required in order to justify censorship and for the knowledge which censorship forces the censored to develop.

(4) Conflict and interaction are never restricted to a single domain: bodies of knowledge and images of knowledge, ideologies and positions within a structure of power relations are usually in question at the same time. Therefore, try to distinguish and then relate the different dimensions, without, however, allowing one dimension to be reduced to any of the others.

CHAPTER 5

Galileo Lives Under House Arrest

Remaining Intellectually Active

Ludovico Geymonat

Ludovico Geymonat portrays Galileo as a serene and intellectually alert man during his last years while under house arrest. Aided by two young scholars, he was able to carry on his researches and conduct experiments. According to Geymonat, Galileo's spirit was heightened and his personality was softened by correspondence with friends, especially by his friendship with his son's sister-in-law. Geymonat edited a volume of Galileo's *Discorsi* and authored the articles, "Il Dialogo di Galileo" and "Il Galileo della Storia e il Galileo di Brecht."

His prolonged confinement at Arcetri, his distressing loss of vision, and the many troublesome misfortunes of old age did not prevent Galileo from finishing his life in an atmosphere of serene and composed dignity. He knew how to teach his friends, his pupils, and even his adversaries a final lesson in humanity which was by no means the least of his many valuable services.

First of all, one may observe that the obvious deterioration of his physical condition had at least one good result for the aged scientist: it reduced the severity of the orders issued against him by the Church authorities. In 1639 he was allowed to have at his house in Arcetri a very young and extremely intelligent scholar, Vincenzio Viviani, who remained with him to the end, and who later wrote a biographical sketch of Galileo. This work was composed at the express request of Prince Leopold de' Medici, and its tiresome obsequiousness to the persecutors of Galileo is largely due to its official character. Still, its author's deep affection for his teacher cannot fail to move us.

Excerpted from *Galileo Galilei: A Biography and Inquiry into His Philosophy of Science*, by Ludovico Geymonat, translated by Stillman Drake (New York: McGraw-Hill, 1965). Copyright © 1957 by Giulio Einaudi Editore.

Young Scholars Help Galileo

Among the things that Viviani could offer which were especially welcome to Galileo were not only the devotion of an admiring pupil, but also his youthful and insatiable interest in scientific problems, his desire always to secure new explanations, and his ability to keep alive in Galileo the taste for research. There is no better evidence of this than Galileo's words in a letter to [his friend] Benedetto Castelli dated December 3, 1639: "It is obvious ... that in philosophy, doubt is the father of invention, opening the way to the discovery of truth. The objections raised for many months now by this youth, my present guest and pupil, against the principle[1] that I assumed in my treatise on accelerated motion, which he has been studying with great attention, forced me to think it over with a view to persuading him that he should accept it as an acceptable and true principle; and I have finally emerged, to his and my great delight, with the conclusive proof, which I have already discussed with several persons. This he next wrote out for me; for I am deprived of my eyes and would perhaps be confused about the diagrams and figures required." The stimulating company of this young student was doubtless one of the chief sources of the serenity achieved by the teacher. Gradually it enabled him to put aside bitter memories of the past and it gave him a keener sense of that invincible power by which human knowledge could progress from generation to generation without allowing itself ever to be checked by its adversaries, however strong, or by the death of any single contributor, however able.

In October 1641, another young scientist appeared at Arcetri to receive the last teachings of the master. This was Evangelista Torricelli, who was unquestionably the greatest genius among the direct heirs of the Galilean spirit. But by that time Galileo's voice was fading out, and he was no longer able to add anything new to what he had already written.

Galileo's Dispute with Fortunio Liceti

One of the most characteristic episodes of the final period in Galileo's life was his dispute with Fortunio Liceti, an Aristotelian scholar, professor of philosophy and medicine first

---

1. the principle that the relations of space and time demonstrated for the vertical fall of heavy bodies hold for the descent along any inclined plane

at Pisa, then at Padua, and finally at Bologna. Conspicuous in this debate was its change of feeling. Beginning with a sharpness not unlike that of his old polemics, Galileo after a short time adopted an unusually moderate tone; his deep serenity of mind is clearly evident together with a more mature awareness of his thought.

Fortunio Liceti had published a treatise with the title *Litheosphorus sive de lapide bononiensi (Litheosphorus, or Of the Bolognese Stone),* on the so-called light-bearing ore of Bologna, a species of barite discovered in 1604 on Mount Paderno near Bologna by an alchemist named Vincenzio Casciarolo. This stone had the singular property of becoming phosphorescent by exposure to sunlight—or, as was said then, of absorbing light and then giving it up again little by little. The fiftieth chapter of Liceti's book dealt with the ashen light discernable in the shadowed part of the moon, especially when it is near conjunction with the sun. After attempting to refute Galileo's theory (set forth in the *Starry Messenger)* that this phenomenon was no more than the effect of sunlight reflected from the earth to the moon, Liceti tried to explain it as a brilliance originating in an atmosphere surrounding the moon . . . which (like the Bolognese light-bearing stone) had the property of conserving for a certain time the light that had previously come to it from the sun. . . .

Liceti sent a copy of his book to Galileo with a request that he communicate his judgment of it. Meanwhile, Prince Leopold de' Medici had urgently asked Galileo to reply to the fiftieth chapter. In March 1640 Galileo decided to set forth his views on this interesting question. He dictated the reply to young Viviani in the form of a letter to Prince Leopold. This letter did not conceal his small respect for this adversary, whom he subjected to pungent criticisms. The attack was further sharpened by the fact that the letter was sent not only to Prince Leopold (as was proper) but also circulated among various friends before it came to Liceti's attention. Liceti accordingly wrote to the famous scientist, respectfully but without hiding his resentment, and asked permission to publish the letter with a reply.

GALILEO RECASTS HIS CRITICISM MORE COURTEOUSLY

At this point the debate might either have suffered a brusque interruption or assumed a progressively more acid character. Instead (on August 25, 1640) Galileo replied to his opponent with sincere cordiality (a cordiality that increased in the ensuing months) and promised to compose a new version of his letter as soon as possible. (This second version was couched in more courteous words than the original, though it still had a certain ironic tone.) In offering to write it, Galileo said:

"The modesty and delicacy in which you clothe your ideas are truly admirable. Though the ideas in themselves may contain some little bitterness, yet they are presented so sweetly that they have been kindly received, with delight and pleasure. . . . I had no thought of publishing that letter of mine [to Leopold] . . . but if you are resolved to print my replies, I will recast it without changing the content of what I wrote in any way, addressing my arguments, if you like, directly to you. . . . As to abstaining from goads: if (as I hope from your courtesy and generosity) this is to be done, I assure you that should it be neccesary for me to reply further, even if I am defeated by your doctrines, I shall not allow myself to overstep the bounds of the reverence that I owe your high merits."

Galileo was evidently not disposed, from mere courtesy to his opponent, to change his opinions in the least, nor would any such pretense make sense on the part of a serious thinker who was in full possession of his mental faculties despite his great age. What he did change was his approach. This was important, for the abandonment of his former asperity in favor of greater serenity placed him in a position to examine the significance of his own scientific position with increasing objectivity. Galileo's correspondence with Liceti not only continued after the first clash, but even broadened and became more serious. Eventually Galileo reconsidered in all its generality the problem of the spirit of the new science in relation to the true core of Aristotelian philosophy. Galileo's clarifications for Liceti—clarifications which represented not so much a summary as a deepening of his previous positions—offer us perhaps the best key to a rounded interpretation of his thought.

Yet his scientific position was unchanged. Even with respect to the touchy problem of Copernicanism, he remained faithful (despite the abjuration) to his old convictions, at least so far as prudence permitted. Proof is afforded by his letter to [scientist] Francesco Rinuccini on the twenty-ninth of March 1641, in which the sense of his words is so clear as to require no comment: "The falsity of the Copernican system should not be doubted on any account, especially by us Catholics. . . . And just as I consider the Copernican observations and conjectures insufficient, so I regard as even more fallacious and erroneous those of Ptolemy, Aristotle, and their followers, for (remaining always within the bounds of human reason) their inconclusiveness can be quite clearly shown."

GALILEO'S FRIENDSHIP WITH ALESSANDRA BOCCHINERI

The richness of Galileo's personality is further revealed by an entirely different kind of episode—his relations with Alessandra Bocchineri. This woman had the merit, in [modern Italian writer Antonio] Banfi's words, of touching with "ultimate grace the spirit of Galileo," drawing from him "with the fervor of her limpid, rich, vibrant vitality . . . an almost pure rage of this spirit at the forgotten exhaustion of his body [coupled with] a harmony of moving affection and tender courtesy, the sweetness of a serene enchantment like a dream (alas, only a dream) of spring in the last warmth of autumn."

Alessandra, sister of Geri Bocchineri and of Sestilia, the wife of [Galileo's son] Vincenzio Galilei, had experienced both pain and joy in her brief life. Widowed by the death of Lorenzo Nati of Bibiena, she had married Francesco Rasi of Aretino and accompanied him to the court of the Grand Duke of Mantova. But Rasi also died after a short time, and Alessandra was once again left alone in a strange city far from her own family. Rather than leave the Gonzagas, she entered into the service of Eleonora, the Duke's sister, whom she followed to Vienna as a lady of the court when Eleonora married the Emperor Ferdinand. At Vienna the Empress presented her to a brilliant Florentine diplomat, Gianfrancesco Buonamici, who became her third husband. In 1630 Alessandra returned suddenly to Italy, and (as her brother wrote to Galileo) "was able to escape by only eighteen days of travel from the evils of war and plague, to the delight of all who knew her."

Naturally, Vincenzio soon introduced his father to this beautiful and intelligent sister-in-law who had managed to arouse so much interest at the most elegant courts of Europe. In the correspondence of Galileo and Alessandra which soon began, there is a lively reciprocal spiritual sympathy which did not diminish with time. Rather, in the last year of Galileo's life it took on a particularly affectionate tone, and brought to him that restorative breath of disturbed tenderness mentioned above. Alessandra wrote from Prato on the twenty-seventh of March 1641: "I often wonder to myself how I shall be able before I die to find a way to be with you and spend a day in conversation without scandalizing or making those people jealous who have made fun of us for this wish. If I thought that you were in good health, and that you would not be fatigued by traveling in a carriage, I should like to send my horses and find a small carriage so that you might favor me by coming to stay a few days with us the next time we have good weather. Therefore I beg you to do me the favor of replying, that I may send for you at once; you may come slowly, and I do not believe you would suffer. . . . I do not wish to write further, in view of my hope that you will write and tell me when to send the carriage; then we shall say what the Arno [River] says when it is at flood and carries off great treasures."

It is hard not to feel the bitterness in Galileo's immediate reply, dated the sixth of April. After having spoken of his "inexpressible pleasure" on receiving the invitation, he has to admit that it cannot be accepted: "I can never tell you sufficiently the pleasure I should take in uninterrupted leisure to enjoy your conversation, elevated above usual feminine talk, so much so that little more significant and perceptive can be expected from the most experienced and practiced men in the world. I am sorry that your invitation cannot be accepted, not only because of the many indispositions that oppress me in my old age, but because I am held in prison for reasons well known to my lord your husband, the distinguished cavalier."

Although he could not see her again, it is certain that he felt her spiritual presence at the serene sunset of his life. It was to Alessandra that his last letter was written, on the twentieth of December 1641: "I have received your welcome letter at a time when it is a great consolation to me, as I have been confined to bed by serious illness for many weeks. My cordial thanks to you for the courteous affection that you show for my person, and for the condolence you send me in my miseries and misfortunes. . . . I beg you to excuse my involuntary brevity, and with most cordial affection I kiss your hands.". . .

From the beginning of November 1641, Galileo was confined to bed by a continual low fever, with pains in the kidneys and great palpitations of the heart. His two pupils Evangelista Torricelli and Vincenzio Viviani remained with him constantly; he enjoyed following their scientific discussions with an attentive mind, but he was less and less able to take a direct part in them.

On the night of the eighth of January 1642, as Viviani wrote, "with philosophic and Christian firmness he rendered up his soul to its Creator, sending it, as he liked to believe, to enjoy and to watch from a closer vantage point those eternal and immutable marvels which he, by means of a fragile device, had brought closer to our mortal eyes with such eagerness and impatience." It was only a month before his seventy-eighth birthday.

"His body," continued Viviani, "was taken from the villa at Arcetri to Florence, and by commission of our most Serene Grand Duke was separately interred in the temple of Santa Croce, where lies the ancient sepulcher of the noble family of Galilei, with the thought of erecting to him an august and sumptuous monument in the most conspicuous place in that church, that thus, after death no less than in life, might be generously honored the immortal fame of Florence's second Amerigo [Vespucci][2]—discoverer not of a little land, but of innumerable celestial globes and new lights, under the happy auspices of the most serene House [of Medici]."

The "august and sumptuous monument" could not yet be erected, however. On the twenty-fifth of January 1642, Francesco Cardinal Barberini, nephew of Pope Urban VIII, wrote to Father Giovanni Muzzarelli, the Inquisitor of Florence: "Monsignor the Assessor has read before His Holiness our Lord the letter of your Reverence in which you gave notice of the death of Galileo Galilei and mentioned what it is believed should be done concerning his tomb and obsequies; and His Blessedness, with the opinion of their Eminences [the Cardinals Inquisitors], has decided that you, with your usual skill, should get the ear of the Grand Duke and suggest that it is not good to raise a mausoleum over the corpse of one who has been punished in the Tribunal of the Holy Inquisition and has died while under that punishment,

2. Italian navigator and explorer of the South American coast. America was named in his honor.

because this might scandalize the good, with prejudice to the piety of His Highness. But if you cannot dissuade him from this idea, you should notify him that in the epitaph or inscription that is to be placed on the tomb, there must be no words which might injure the reputation of this Tribunal. You must give the same notification to him who will make the funeral oration; arrange to see it and consider it well before it is spoken or printed. His Holiness reposes the care of this affair in the wise prudence of your Reverence."

No doubt the "usual skill" of Father Muzzarelli was considerable, and so was the submissiveness of the Most Serene House of Medici. The monument to Galileo was not erected until about a century after his death. It was only in 1734 that the Holy Office, consulted on the matter, decided to authorize its construction: "It is to be written back to the Father Inquisitor that nothing prevents the construction of Galileo's tomb, but solicit his care that the inscription to be made on the said tomb be communicated to him, he to transmit it to the Holy Congregation, so that proper orders may be given concerning it before it is done."

Contending with His Confinement

Dava Sobel

Dava Sobel describes the conditions under which Galileo lived and worked while writing Dialogues Concerning Two New Sciences. *Sobel notes that the church was strict with Galileo; even simple requests for health care and for permission to attend Easter Mass were granted only with the church's severe restrictions. Because the church kept Galileo under such tight control, he made intricate plans to publish* Two New Sciences *in secret. By the time his work was finally published, Galileo had completely lost his sight and was unable to see his greatest scientific achievement. American writer Dava Sobel is the author of* Longitude, *and she is co-author of* The Illustrated Longitude.

The experience of resuming with Salviati, Sagredo, and Simplicio[1]—at age seventy—the topics that had engaged him since his first awakening as a philosopher doubly challenged Galileo. On the one hand, his ever-accumulating wisdom helped him regard certain ancient concepts in fresh ways, and this delayed his bringing the long unfinished work [*Two New Sciences*] to closure even now. "The treatise on motion, all new, is in order," he wrote to an old friend in Venice, "but my unquiet mind will not rest from mulling it over with great expenditure of time, because the latest thought to occur to me about some novelty makes me throw out much already found there."

On the other hand, his accumulated years hampered the alacrity of his thought. "I find how much old age lessens the vividness and speed of my thinking," Galileo wrote [his

1. the same three characters Galileo had used to discuss his ideas in *Dialogue on the Great World Systems* published in 1632.

friend] Elia Diodati while completing *Two New Sciences,* "as I struggle to understand quite a lot of things I discovered and proved when I was younger."

FINDING A PUBLISHER FOR *TWO NEW SCIENCES*

But where and how would he publish the product of all this effort? Certainly not in Rome or Florence. Shortly before Galileo returned to Arcetri, Pope Urban had issued a companion warning to the banning of the *Dialogue,* outlawing the reprinting of any of Galileo's earlier books. This action ensured that Galileo's works would gradually die out in Italy, where the Holy Office exerted its greatest influence.

"You have read my writings," Galileo complained of the prohibition against him to another correspondent in France,

> and from them you have certainly understood which was the true and real motive that caused, under the lying mask of religion, this war against me that continually restrains and undercuts me in all directions, so that neither can help come to me from outside nor can I go forth to defend myself, there having been issued an express order to all Inquisitors that they should not allow any of my works to be reprinted which had been printed many years ago or grant permission to any new work that I would print . . . a most rigorous and general order, I say, against all my works, *omnia edita et edenda* [everything published and everything I might have published in the future]; so that it is left to me only to succumb in silence under the flood of attacks, exposures, derision, and insult coming from all sides.

Galileo's friend Fra Fulgenzio Micanzio, theologian to the Venetian republic, thought he could get around the pontifical warnings to see *Two New Sciences* published in the more liberal atmosphere at Venice. Fra Micanzio soon discovered in preliminary conversations with the Venetian inquisitor, however, that Galileo faced the same obstacles there as in any other Italian duchy or papal state—that even the Credo or the Lord's Prayer might well be refused a printing license if Galileo were the one to seek it.

There ensued a multinational effort among Galileo's supporters to find a printer somewhere who could translate and safely publish *Two New Sciences.* Geneva-born Parisian Elia Diodati hoped at first to see this happen in France, in the city of Lyons, the home of Galileo's distant relative Roberto Galilei, a businessman who facilitated all French correspondence with the Italian scientist. However, Galileo soon had another offer of publication help in 1635 from an Italian engineer working for the Holy Roman Emperor and eager to have *Two New Sciences* printed in Germany. Grand Duke Ferdinando [of Italy] voluntarily lent his aid to this plan, commissioning his brother Prince Mattia, who was conveniently just leaving for Germany on a military mission, to hand-deliver sections of the contraband manuscript to Galileo's contact there. Alas, Father Christopher Scheiner, the Jesuit astronomer formerly known as "Apelles," had returned to Germany by this point, strengthening the anti-Galileo feelings in that country and making the licensing of the new book there highly unlikely.

SECRECY DURING PUBLICATION

At the end of various intrigues, Diodati found Galileo a Dutch publisher, Louis Elzevir, who visited him at Il Gioiello in May of 1636 to settle their agreement. (Although Galileo was now technically forbidden to receive visitors, Elzevir numbered among several distinguished foreign callers, including [British] philosopher Thomas Hobbes, who came after reading an unauthorized English translation of the *Dialogue,* and poet John Milton.) Fra Micanzio in Venice, who knew both parties to the publishing contract, volunteered to serve as conduit between Arcetri and Holland; this gave the old theologian the pleasure of reading *Two New Sciences* in installments as each finished part reached him.

"I see that you took the trouble to transcribe these in your own hand," Fra Micanzio once remarked with surprise upon receipt of certain pages, "and I don't see how you can stand it, for to me it would be absolutely impossible."

While Galileo refined the main themes, he also expanded the content of the book to include some seemingly unrelated sections. After all, who knew when he would ever secure another opportunity to publish anything?

"I shall send as soon as possible this treatise on projectiles," Galileo promised in December 1636 while finalizing Day Four of *Two New Sciences,* "along with an appendix [twenty-five pages long] on some demonstrations of certain conclusions about the centers of gravity of solids, found by me at the age of 22 after two years of study of geometry, for it is good that these not be lost."

In June of 1637, Galileo sent off the last pieces of dialogue for *Two New Sciences,* which ended with Sagredo's hopeful allusion to other discussion meetings the trio might enjoy "in the future." Printing began at Leiden, Holland, that fall, and the published volume came out the following spring.

Safe in a Protestant country, the Dutch publisher feared no reprisal from the Roman Inquisition. Galileo, however, remaining vulnerable in Arcetri, claimed ignorance of the book's publication until the ultimate moment. Even in his dedicatory note to French ambassador François de Noailles, he feigned surprise at how his manuscript had found its way to a foreign printing press. "I recognize as resulting from Your Excellency's magnanimity the disposition you have been pleased to make of this work of mine," Galileo wrote in a preface dated March 6, 1638,

> notwithstanding the fact that I myself, as you know, being confused and dismayed by the ill fortune of my other works, had resolved not to put before the public any more of my labors. Yet in order that they might not remain completely buried, I was persuaded to leave a manuscript copy in some place, that it might be known at least to those who understand the subjects of which I treat. And thus having chosen, as the best and loftiest such place, to put this into Your Excellency's hands, I felt certain that you, out of your special affection for me, would take to heart the preservation of my studies and labors. Hence, during your passage through this place on your return from your Roman embassy, when I was privileged to greet you in person (as I had so often greeted you before by letters), I had occasion to present to you the copy that I then had ready of these two works. You benignly showed yourself very much pleased to have them, to be willing to keep them securely, and by sharing them in France with any friend of yours who is apt in these sciences, to show that although I remain silent, I do not therefore pass my life in entire idleness.
>
> I was later preparing some other copies, to send to Germany, Flanders, England, Spain, and perhaps also to some place in Italy, when I was notified by the Elzevirs that they had these works of mine in press, and that I must therefore decide about the dedication and send them promptly my thoughts on that subject. From this unexpected and astonishing news, I concluded that it had been Your Excellency's wish to elevate and spread my name, by sharing various of my writings, that accounted for their having come into the hands of those printers who, being engaged in the publication of other works of mine *[Letter to Grand Duchess Cristina]*, wished to honor me by bringing these also to light at their handsome and elaborate press. . . . Now that matters have arrived at this stage, it is certainly reasonable that, in some conspicuous way, I should show myself grateful by recognizing Your Excellency's generous affection. For it is you who have thought to increase my fame by having these works spread their wings

freely under an open sky, when it appeared to me that my reputation must surely remain confined within narrower spaces.

GALILEO'S REQUESTS FOR MEDICAL TREATMENT AND MASS

Around the same time he wrote this fictitious scenario, Galileo appealed to the Holy Office for permission to seek medical treatment in Florence. Urban's brother Antonio Cardinal Sant' Onofrio, sternly denying this request via the Florentine inquisitor, ruled that Galileo had not described his illness in enough detail to be granted such an indulgence. Furthermore, the cardinal imagined, "Galileo's return to the city would give him the opportunity of having meetings, conversations, and discussions in which he might once again let his condemned opinions on the motion of the Earth come to light."

Galileo's failing health forced him to persist in this pursuit, however, and after he submitted to a surprise medical examination demanded by the Inquisition, he won the right to repair temporarily to Vincenzio's house on the Costa San Giorgio. On March 6 Cardinal Sant' Onofrio told the inquisitor at Florence that Galileo "may let himself be moved from the villa at Arcetri, where he now is, to his house in Florence in order to be cured of his maladies. But I give Your Eminence orders that he must not go out into the city and not have public or secret conversations at his house."

From the city, Galileo petitioned again, asking allowance to be carried in his chair by his family, over the few steps he could not walk in his present state, to hear mass at the neighborhood Church of San Giorgio. In the spirit of Easter, Cardinal Sant' Onofrio then instructed the Florentine inquisitor "according to his own judgment to give Galileo permission to attend Mass on feast days in the nearest possible church, provided that he does not have personal contacts."

Galileo returned to Arcetri later in the spring of 1638, before *Two New Sciences* came off the printing press at Leiden. Somehow his title for the book got changed, if not in translation, perhaps in translocation or by editorial fiat. Its title page names it:

Discourses
and
Mathematical
Demonstrations,
Concerning Two New Sciences
Pertaining to

Mechanics & Local Motions,
by Signor
Galileo Galilei, Lyncean
Philosopher and Chief Mathematician to His Serene Highness
The Grand Duke of Tuscany.
With an Appendix on the center of gravity in various Solids.

No record remains of Galileo's original title, but only his later lament over the substitution of "a low and common title for the noble and dignified one" he had selected. Nevertheless, the book sold briskly when it appeared in June of 1638. Weeks passed after its publication before Galileo himself received even a single copy. And by the time it reached his hands, he could not read or even see it. His eyes, vulnerable to infections and strains that had pained him much of his life, were now ruined by a combination of cataracts and glaucoma.

GALILEO'S PROGRESSIVE BLINDNESS

The blindness took first his right eye, in July 1637, forcing him to abandon the addition of a fifth day to *Two New Sciences,* and then the left the next winter. During the gloaming time when he had only one eye with which to observe the heavens or peruse his earlier notes and drawings, he wrote a final brief treatise on how best to gauge the diameters of stars and the distances between celestial bodies, and also made his last astronomical discovery, regarding the librations, or rocking, of the Moon.

"I have discovered a very marvelous observation in the face of the Moon," Galileo wrote to Venetian Fra Micanzio in November of 1637, "in which body, though it has been looked at infinitely many times, I do not find that any change was ever noticed, but that the same face was always seen the same to our eyes."

The Moon indeed keeps the same face—that of a smiling man's eyes, nose, and mouth—always turned toward the Earth. For although the Moon rotates about its axis as it revolves around the Earth, the time period of its rotation precisely matches the monthly period of its revolution, keeping the far side out of sight. Around the fringes of the Moon's face, however, a combination of curious effects affords occasional glimpses of parts otherwise unseen.

"It alters its aspect," Galileo told Fra Micanzio, "like one who shows to our eyes his full face, head on so to speak, and then goes changing this in all possible ways, that is, turning now a bit to the right and then a bit to the left, or else nodding up and down, or finally, tilting his left shoulder to right and left. All these variations are seen in the face of the Moon, and the large and ancient spots perceived in it make manifest and sensible what I say."

When the total darkness descended, Galileo tried to accept the loss of his sight gracefully, remarking how no son of Adam had seen farther than he. Still the irony overwhelmed him.

"This universe," he railed to Elia Diodati in 1638, "which I with my astonishing observations and clear demonstrations had enlarged a hundred, nay, a thousandfold beyond the limits commonly seen by wise men of all centuries past, is now for me so diminished and reduced, it has shrunk to the meager confines of my body."

Publishing *Two Sciences*

Antonio Favaro

Antonio Favaro charts the history of Galileo's work leading up to *Dialogues Concerning Two New Sciences* by citing letters in which Galileo described the progress of his ideas. Moreover, Favaro summarizes the steps Galileo took to find a book publisher without alerting the church authorities in Rome. Antonio Favaro is an authority on Galileo. He has edited many volumes of Galileo's works and letters and has published a biography entitled *Galileo Galilei a Padova.*

Writing to his faithful friend Elia Diodati, Galileo speaks of the "New Sciences" which he had in mind to print as being "superior to everything else of mine hitherto published"; elsewhere he says "they contain results which I consider the most important of all my studies"; and this opinion which he expressed concerning his own work has been confirmed by posterity: the "New Sciences" are, indeed, the masterpiece of Galileo who at the time when he made the above remarks had spent upon them more than thirty laborious years.

SUMMARY OF GALILEO'S THIRTY YEARS OF WORK

One who wishes to trace the history of this remarkable work will find that the great philosopher laid its foundations during the eighteen best years of his life—those which he spent at Padua. As we learn from his last scholar, Vincenzio Viviani, the numerous results at which Galileo had arrived while in this city, awakened intense admiration in the friends who had witnessed various experiments by means of which he was accustomed to investigate interesting questions in physics. [Mathematician and friend] Fra Paolo Sarpi exclaimed: To give us the Science of Motion, God and Nature have joined hands and created the intellect of Galileo. And when the "New Sciences" came from the press one of his foremost pupils, Paolo Aproino, wrote that the volume contained much which he had "already heard from his own

Reprinted from Antonio Favaro, Introduction, in *Dialogues Concerning Two New Sciences*, by Galileo Galilei, translated by Henry Crew and Alfonso de Salvio (New York: Macmillan, 1914).

lips" during student days at Padua.

Limiting ourselves to only the more important documents which might be cited in support of our statement, it will suffice to mention the letter, written to [scholar] Guidobaldo del Monte on the 29th of November, 1602, concerning the descent of heavy bodies along the arcs of circles and the chords subtended by them; that to Sarpi, dated 16th of October, 1604, dealing with the free fall of heavy bodies; the letter to Antonio de' Medici [of the ruling Florentine family] on the 11th of February, 1609, in which he states that he has "completed all the theorems and demonstrations pertaining to forces and resistances of beams of various lengths, thicknesses and shapes, proving that they are weaker at the middle than near the ends, that they can carry a greater load when that load is distributed throughout the length of the beam than when concentrated at one point, demonstrating also what shape should be given to a beam in order that it may have the same bending strength at every point," and that he was now engaged "upon some questions dealing with the motion of projectiles"; and finally in the letter to Belisario Vinta [secretary to the Grand Duke], dated 7th of May, 1610, concerning his return from Padua to Florence, he enumerates various pieces of work which were still to be completed, mentioning explicitly three books on an entirely new science dealing with the theory of motion. Although at various times after the return to his native state he devoted considerable thought to the work which, even at that date, he had in mind as is shown by certain fragments which clearly belong to different periods of his life and which have, for the first time, been published in the National Edition; and although these studies were always uppermost in his thought it does not appear that he gave himself seriously to them until after the publication of the *Dialogue* [*Concerning the Two Chief World Systems—Ptolemaic and Copernican*] and the completion of that trial which was rightly described as the disgrace of the century. In fact as late as October, 1630, he barely mentions to [mathematician Niccolò] Aggiunti his discoveries in the theory of motion, and only two years later, in a letter to [scientist Cesare] Marsili concerning the motion of projectiles, he hints at a book nearly ready for publication in which he will treat also of this subject; and only a year after this he writes to [mathematician Andrea] Arrighetti that he has in hand a treatise on the resistance of solids.

FINISHING THE WORK DURING HOUSE ARREST

But the work was given definite form by Galileo during his enforced residence at Siena: in these five months spent quietly with the Archbishop he himself writes that he has completed "a treatise on a new branch of mechanics full of interesting and useful ideas"; so that a few months later he was able to send word to [theologian Fulgenzio] Micanzio that the "work was ready"; as soon as his friends learned of this, they urged its publication. It was, however, no easy matter to print the work of a man already condemned by the Holy Office: and since Galileo could not hope to print it either in Florence or in Rome, he turned to the faithful Micanzio asking him to find out whether this would be possible in Venice, from whence he had received offers to print the *Dialogue on the Principal Systems,* as soon as the news had reached there that he was encountering difficulties. At first everything went smoothly; so that Galileo commenced sending to Micanzio some of the manuscript which was received by the latter with an enthusiasm in which he was second to none of the warmest admirers of the great philosopher. But when Micanzio consulted the Inquisitor, he received the answer that there was an express order prohibiting the printing or reprinting of any work of Galileo, either in Venice or in any other place, *nullo excepto* [without exception].

As soon as Galileo received this discouraging news he began to look with more favor upon offers which had come to him from Germany where his friend, and perhaps also his scholar, Giovanni Battista Pieroni, was in the service of the Emperor, as military engineer; consequently Galileo gave to Prince Mattia de' Medici who was just leaving for Germany the first two Dialogues to be handed to Pieroni who was undecided whether to publish them at Vienna or Prague or at some place in Moravia; in the meantime, however, he had obtained permission to print both at Vienna and at Olmütz. But Galileo recognized danger at every point within reach of the long arm of the Court of Rome; hence, availing himself of the opportunity offered by the arrival of Louis Elzevir in Italy in 1636, also of the friendship between the latter and Micanzio, not to mention a visit at Arcetri, he decided to abandon all other plans and entrust to the Dutch publisher the printing of his new work the manuscript of which, although not complete, Elzevir took with him on his return home.

THE FINAL DETAILS FOR PUBLICATION

In the course of the year 1637, the printing was finished, and at the beginning of the following year there was lacking only the index, the title-page and the dedication. This last had, through the good offices of Diodati, been offered to the Count of Noailles, a former scholar of Galileo at Padua, and since 1634 ambassador of France at Rome, a man who did much to alleviate the distressing consequences of the celebrated trial; and the offer was gratefully accepted. The phrasing of the dedication deserves brief comment. Since Galileo was aware, on the one hand, of the prohibition against the printing of his works and since, on the other hand, he did not wish to irritate the Court of Rome from whose hands he was always hoping for complete freedom, he pretends in the dedicatory letter (where, probably through excess of caution, he gives only main outlines) that he had nothing to do with the printing of his book, asserting that he will never again publish any of his researches, and will at most distribute here and there a manuscript copy. He even expresses great surprise that his new Dialogues have fallen into the hands of the Elzevirs and were soon to be published; so that, having been asked to write a dedication, he could think of no man more worthy who could also on this occasion defend him against his enemies.

As to the title which reads: *Discourses and Mathematical Demonstrations concerning Two New Sciences pertaining to Mechanics and Local Motions,* this only is known, namely, that the title is not the one which Galileo had devised and suggested; in fact he protested against the publishers taking the liberty of changing it and substituting "a low and common title for the noble and dignified one carried upon the title-page.". . .

In the Leyden Edition, the four Dialogues are followed by an *"Appendix containing some theorems and their proofs, dealing with centers of gravity of solid bodies, written by the same Author at an earlier date,"* which has no immediate connection with the subjects treated in the Dialogues; these theorems were found by Galileo, as he tells us, "at the age of twenty-two and after two years study of geometry" and were here inserted only to save them from oblivion.

But it was not the intention of Galileo that the *Dialogues on the New Sciences* should contain only the four Days and the above-mentioned appendix which constitute the Leyden Edition; while, on the one hand, the Elzevirs were hastening the printing and striving to complete it at the earliest possible date, Galileo, on the other hand, kept on speaking of another Day, besides the four, thus embarrassing and perplexing the printers. From the correspondence which went on between author and publisher, it appears that this Fifth Day was to have treated "of the force of percussion and the use of the catenary [a perfectly shaped curve]"; but as the typographical work approached completion, the printer became anxious for the book to issue from the press without further delay; and thus it came to pass that the *Discorsi e Dimostrazioni* appeared containing only the four Days and the Appendix, in spite of the fact that in April, 1638, Galileo had plunged more deeply than ever "into the profound question of percussion" and "had almost reached a complete solution."

CHAPTER 6

Evaluation of Galileo's Place in History

Galileo Symbolizes the Struggle for Intellectual Freedom

Gerald Holton

Gerald Holton argues that Galileo's persistent defense of the sun-centered solar system characterizes the battle common to scientists who have fought against enemies of new and revolutionary ideas. Holton reviews Galileo's arguments for the sun-centered system, the reasons why religious and traditional thinkers resisted it, and the tragic treatment Galileo experienced for his outspokenness. Holton cites modern instances exemplifying similar resistance and punishment. Gerald Holton, professor of physics and the history of science at Harvard University, is the author of *The Scientific Imagination* and *Thematic Origins of Scientific Thought, Kepler to Einstein.*

One of the few friends and fellow-scientists with whom [German astronomer Johannes] Kepler corresponded and exchanged news of the latest findings was Galileo Galilei. Although the Italian's *scientific* contribution to planetary theory is not so well developed as that of his friend across the Alps, he nevertheless was projected into history as a key figure in this subject. In a sense, Kepler and Galileo complemented each other in preparing the world for the eventual acceptance of the heliocentric theory—the one laying the scientific foundation with his astronomical work, the other fighting the dogmatic objections and, in his work on mechanics, helping to overturn the whole structure of scholastic[1] physics with which the old cosmology was entwined.

---

1. the dominant Western Christian theological and philosophical school of thought of the Middle Ages

Excerpted from *Introduction to Concepts and Theories in Physical Science*, by Gerald Holton (Reading, MA: Addison-Wesley, 1952). Reprinted by permission of the author.

GALILEO DIFFERED WITH HIS SCHOLASTIC CONTEMPORARIES

For it was Galileo more than any other man who, as we have already seen, challenged the fruitfulness of the ancient interpretation of experience, and focused the attention of physical science on the productive concepts—time and distance, velocity and acceleration, force and matter—and not on qualities or essences, ultimate causes or harmonies, which were still the motivation of a Copernicus and at times the ecstasy of a Kepler. Galileo's insistence, so clearly expressed in his work on freely falling bodies, on fitting the concepts and conclusions to observable facts, on expressing his results in the concise language of mathematics, are now accepted as central achievements, re-enforcing the same traits then emerging from the work of Kepler. But perhaps the greatest difference between the work of Galileo and that of his scholastic contemporaries was his orientation, his viewpoint, the kind of question he considered important. To most of his opponents, Galileo's specific problems were not general enough, since he excluded the orthodox philosophical problems. Then, too, his procedure for discovering truth seemed to them fantastic, his conclusions preposterous, haughty, often impious. There exists an almost perfectly parallel situation between these objections to Galileo's point of view and the outraged derision and even violence initially heaped on the discoverers of new ways of viewing the world in art, e.g., [French painter Edouard] Manet and his impressionists.

Like Kepler, Galileo was a Copernican in a Ptolemaic world.[2] His specific contributions to the development of heliocentric [sun-centered] theory are two: the invention in 1609 of a telescope for astronomical work, and the observations he made with its help. The same set of doctrines which then still generally upheld the geocentric [earth-centered] system as the only possible choice also required that the celestial objects be "perfect" (spherical and unblemished), yet he could now plainly see spots on the sun and mountains on the moon. Venus, sometimes fully illuminated by the sun and at other times not at all, was found to have moonlike phases. Saturn seemed to carry bulges around its equator. Most surprisingly, Jupiter showed him four (of its twelve now known) satellites or subplanets,

2. Copernicans believed that the earth and other heavenly bodies revolved around the sun. Followers of Ptolemy believed heavenly bodies revolved around the earth.

adding in a catastrophic manner to the seven scholastically acceptable members of the planetary system, and offering to plain view a miniature solar system with an "obvious" center of rotation far from the earth. The Milky Way resolved into aggregates of individual stars. The stars themselves, now visible in much greater numbers, appeared still as pinpoints of light, thus aiding the Copernican argument that they are extremely distant.

However, we must understand that these suggestive observations were to Galileo illustrations of a truth that seemed to him compelling even from a nonexperimental point of view. In his great work *The Dialogue on the Two Chief Systems of the World,* he stresses the one argument as much as the other. Observations alone, says Galileo, do not decide uniquely between a heliocentric and a geocentric hypothesis, "for the same phenomena would result from either hypothesis." This would be close to our modern view, but where we would make a choice between the two mainly on the basis of convenience in use, without regarding one as true and the other as false, Galileo understandably thinks of the earth's motion as "real," real just *because* it seems more reasonable and simplifies the picture. He then adduces several arguments, largely following Copernicus:

> "When we merely consider the immensity of the starry sphere in comparison with the smallness of the terrestrial ball . . . and then think of the rapidity of the motion which completes a whole rotation in one day and night, I cannot persuade myself how anyone can hold it to be more reasonable and credible that it is the heavenly sphere which rotates, while the earth stands still."

COMPARISON OF PTOLEMAIC ROTATIONS OF HEAVENLY BODIES WITH COPERNICAN

As a second point Galileo reminds his readers that in the geocentric model it is necessary to ascribe to the planets a motion opposite to that of the celestial sphere (why?), again an unreasonable, we might almost say unharmonious or unesthetic assumption. Third, Jupiter's four moons had shown him that there, too, existed the rule that the larger the orbit of the rotating body as reckoned from the center of rotation, the longer the period of rotation (qualitatively, Kepler's third law). This Copernicus had pointed out long before for the case of the planets themselves, and it held true even in the Ptolemaic system—but with this disharmony: in the Ptolemaic system the characteristic periods of revolution around the earth increase from the short one (27⅓ days) for the moon, to the very large one (30 years) for Saturn—and then suddenly drop back to 24 hours for the celestial sphere. In the Copernican system, however, "the rapidity of the periods is very well preserved; from the slowest sphere of Saturn we come to the wholly motionless fixed stars. We also escape thereby a fourth difficulty . . . I mean the great unevenness in the movement of these very stars [on the Ptolemaic hypothesis], some of which would have to revolve with extraordinary rapidity in immense circles, while others moved very slowly in small circles, since some of them are at a greater, others at a less distance from the pole." Fifth, owing to the slightly changing tilt of the earth's axis, the apparent paths of the stars on the celestial sphere change slowly over the centuries, again an improbable or at any rate an unreasonable feature of a geocentric theory that claimed to be based on the immutable, ideal, eternal characteristics of the heavenly bodies. Next, Galileo found it impossible to conceive in what manner the stars could be fixed in the celestial sphere to allow them rapid rotation and even motion as a group (*cf.* last point), while also having them preserve their relative distances so perfectly. "It seems to me much easier and more convenient to make them motionless instead of moving" and to ascribe the apparent motions to that of one "small insignificant body in comparison with the whole universe," the earth itself. Lastly Galileo points out "I could also not explain why the earth, a freely poised body, balancing itself about its center [on the geocentric scheme] and surrounded on all sides by a fluid medium [postulated at the time to provide means for communicating the "force and power" needed to keep up the celestial motions] should not be affected by the universal rotation." . . .

REASONS WHY SCHOLASTICS RESISTED GALILEO'S ARGUMENTS

In his characteristic enthusiasm, Galileo thought that through his telescopic discoveries everyone would see, *as with his own eyes,* the absurdity of the assumptions which prevented a general acceptance of the Copernican system. But man can believe only what he is ready to believe. In their fight against the new Copernicans the scholastics were convinced that they were surely "sticking to facts," that the heliocentric theory was obviously false and in contradiction with both sense-observation and common sense, not to speak of the theological heresies implied in the heliocentric view. They had made Aristotelian science their exclusive tool for understanding facts, just as today most laymen make their understanding of physical theory depend on their ability to visualize it in terms of simple mechanical models obeying Newtonian laws. But at the root of the tragic position of the Aristotelians was, in part, the fact that an acceptance of the Copernican theory as even a *possible* theory would have had to be preceded by a most far-reaching re-examination and re-evaluation of their personal beliefs. It would have required them to do the humanly almost impossible, to discard their common-sense ideas, to seek new bases for their old moral and theological doctrines, and to learn their science anew (which was of course what Galileo himself did to an amazing degree, for which his contemporaries called him fool, or worse, and for which we call him genius). Being satisfied with their system, the Aristotelians were, of course, unaware that history would soon prove their point of view to be far less effective in man's quest to understand nature.

Galileo's concrete observations meant little to them. The Florentine astronomer Francesco Sizzi (1611) argued in this manner why there could not, *must* not be any satellites around Jupiter:

"There are seven windows in the head, two nostrils, two ears, two eyes and a mouth; so in the heavens there are two favorable stars, two unpropitious, two luminaries, and Mercury alone undecided and indifferent. From which and many other similar phenomena of nature such as the seven metals, etc., which it were tedious to enumerate, we gather that the number of planets is necessarily seven . . . Besides, the Jews and other ancient nations, as well as modern Europeans, have adopted the division of the week into seven days, and have named them from the seven planets: now if we increase the number of planets, this whole system falls to the ground. . . . Moreover, the satellites are invisible to the naked eye and therefore can have no influence on the earth and therefore would be useless and therefore do not exist."

A year after his discoveries, Galileo had to write to Kepler:

"You are the first and almost the only person who, after a cursory investigation, has given entire credit to my statements. . . . What do you say of the leading philosophers here

to whom I have offered a thousand times of my own accord
to show my studies, but who, with the lazy obstinacy of a ser-
pent who has eaten his fill, have never consented to look at
the planets, or moon, or telescope?" . . .

THE TRAGEDY OF GALILEO'S TRIAL

The tragedy that descended on Galileo is described in many
places, and it is impossible to do justice to the whole story
without referring to the details. Briefly, he was warned in
1616 by the Inquisition[3] to cease teaching the Copernican theory, for it was now held "contrary to Holy Scripture." At the
same time Copernicus' book itself was placed on the Index
Expurgatorius [list of censored books], and was suspended
"until corrected." But Galileo could not suppress what he felt
deeply to be the truth. Whereas Copernicus had still invoked
Aristotelian doctrine to make his theory plausible, Galileo
had reached the new point of view where he urged acceptance of the heliocentric system on its own merits of simplicity and usefulness, and apart from such questions as those of
faith and salvation. This was the great break.

In 1623, Cardinal Barberini, formerly his dear friend, was
elevated to the Papal throne, and Galileo seems to have considered it safe enough to write again on the controversial
topic. In 1632, after making some required changes, Galileo
obtained the Inquisitor's necessary consent to publish the
work *Dialogue Concerning the Two Chief Systems of the
World* (from which the previous arguments for the Copernican theory were drawn), setting forth most persuasively the
Copernican view in a thinly disguised discussion of the relative merits of the Ptolemaic and Copernican systems. After
publication it was realized that he may have tried to circum-
vent the warning of 1616. Furthermore, Galileo's forthright
and tactless behavior and the Inquisition's need to demonstrate its power over suspected heretics conspired to mark
him for punishment.

Among the many other factors in this complex story a
prominent role is to be assigned to Galileo's religious attitude—which he himself believed to be devoutly faithful, but
which had come under suspicion by the Inquisition.
Galileo's letters of 1613 and 1615 showed he held that God's
mind contains all the natural laws, and that the occasional

---

3. a tribunal formerly held in the Roman Catholic Church which was directed to suppress heresy

glimpses of these laws which the human investigator may laboriously achieve are proofs and direct revelations of the Deity quite as valid and grandiose as those recorded in the Bible. "From the Divine Word, the Sacred Scripture and Nature did both alike proceed. . . . Nor does God less admirably discover himself to us in Nature's actions than in the Scripture's sacred dictions." These opinions—held, incidentally, by many present-day scientists—can, however, be taken for symptoms of pantheism,[4] one of the heresies for which Galileo's contemporary, Giordano Bruno, had been burned at the stake in 1600. Nor did Galileo help his case by such phrases as his quotation of Cardinal Baronius' saying: "The Holy Spirit intended to teach us in the Bible how to go to heaven, not how the heavens go."

The old, ailing man was called to Rome and confined for a few months. From the partly still secret proceedings we gather that he was tried (in absentia), threatened with torture, induced to making an elaborate formal renunciation of the Copernican theory, and finally sentenced to perpetual confinement. None of his friends in Italy dared to defend Galileo publicly. His book was placed on the Index (where it remained along with Copernicus' and one of Kepler's until 1835). In short, and this is the only point of interest to us here, he was set up as a warning for all men that the demand for spiritual obedience indisputably entails intellectual obedience also, that there can be no free science where there is no free conscience. His famous *Abjuration*,[5] later ordered to be read from the pulpits throughout Italy and posted as a warning, reveals an ominous modern sound.

SCIENTISTS FIGHT FOR INTELLECTUAL FREEDOM

But without freedom, science cannot flourish for long. It is perhaps not simply a coincidence that after Galileo, Italy, the mother of outstanding men till then, produced for the next 200 years hardly a single great scientist, while elsewhere in Europe they arose in great numbers. To scientists today this famous facet in the story of planetary theories is not just an episode in passing. Not a few teachers and scientists in our time have had to face powerful enemies of open-minded inquiry and of free teaching, and again must stand

---

4. a doctrine identifying the Deity with the universe and its phenomena   5. formal statement renouncing his Copernican beliefs

up before those men who rightly fear the strength of unindoctrinated intellect.

Even Plato knew that an authoritarian state is threatened by intellectual nonconformists, and he recommended for them the now time-honored treatment: "re-education," prison, or death. Today we find Russian geneticists and astronomers being expected to reject well-established theories, not on grounds of persuasive new *scientific* evidence, but because of doctrinal conflicts. This same struggle explains the banishment from Nazi Germany's textbooks of the discussion of relativity theory because by the obscure standards of racist metaphysics Einstein's Jewish faith invalidated his work for Germans. This, too, was in part the meaning behind the "Monkey Trial" in Tennessee, where the teaching of Darwin's theory was to be suppressed for conflicting with certain types of Bible interpretations.

The warfare of authoritarianism against science, like the warfare of ignorance against knowledge, has not diminished since Galileo's days. Scientists take what comfort they can from the verdict of history, for less than 50 years later, [British mathematician and physicist Isaac] Newton's great book, the *Principia*, had appeared, integrating the work of Copernicus, Kepler, and Galileo so brilliantly with the principles of mechanics that the long-delayed triumph of those pioneers of science was irrevocable, and more significant than they themselves might have hoped.

Galileo's Heroic Fight for a New Scientific System

Albert Einstein

Albert Einstein credits Galileo for heroically resisting the church-authorized view of the universe. He describes both the planetary system Galileo rejected and the one he advocated, pointing out flaws Galileo could not have overcome since he lacked a complete theory of mechanics. Einstein praises Galileo, despite his errors, for his determination to make experience and reflection a criteria for scientific truth. Albert Einstein was the German physicist who developed the theory of relativity. He wrote numerous papers on science, politics, education, pacifism, and the Jewish state.

Galileo's *Dialogue Concerning the Two Chief World Systems* is a mine of information for anyone interested in the cultural history of the Western world and its influence upon economic and political development.

A man is here revealed who possesses the passionate will, the intelligence, and the courage to stand up as the representative of rational thinking against the host of those who, relying on the ignorance of the people and the indolence of teachers in priest's and scholar's garb, maintain and defend their positions of authority. His unusual literary gift enables him to address the educated men of his age in such clear and impressive language as to overcome the anthropocentric and mythical thinking of his contemporaries and to lead them back to an objective and causal attitude toward the cosmos, an attitude which had become lost to humanity with the decline of Greek culture.

In speaking this way I notice that I, too, am falling in with the general weakness of those who, intoxicated with devo-

From Albert Einstein, Foreword, in *Dialogue Concerning the Two Chief World Systems: Ptolemaic and Copernican*, by Galileo Galilei, translated by Stillman Drake. Copyright © 1952, 1962, 1967 Regents of the University of California. Reprinted by permission of the University of California Press.

tion, exaggerate the stature of their heroes. It may well be that during the seventeenth century the paralysis of mind brought about by the rigid authoritarian tradition of the Dark Ages had already so far abated that the fetters of an obsolete intellectual tradition could not have held much longer—with or without Galileo.

Yet these doubts concern only a particular case of the general problem concerning the extent to which the course of history can be decisively influenced by single individuals whose qualities impress us as accidental and unique. As is understandable, our age takes a more sceptical view of the role of the individual than did the eighteenth and the first half of the nineteenth century. For the extensive specialization of the professions and of knowledge lets the individual appear "replaceable," as it were, like a part of a mass-produced machine.

GALILEO DESCRIBES THE PREVAILING VIEW OF THE UNIVERSE

Fortunately, our appreciation of the *Dialogue* as a historical document does not depend upon our attitude toward such precarious questions. To begin with, the *Dialogue* gives an extremely lively and persuasive exposition of the then prevailing views on the structure of the cosmos in the large. The naïve picture of the earth as a flat disc, combined with obscure ideas about star-filled space and the motions of the celestial bodies, prevalent in the early Middle Ages, represented a deterioration of the much earlier conceptions of the Greeks, and in particular of [Greek philosopher] Aristotle's ideas and of [Alexandrian philosopher and mathematician] Ptolemy's consistent spatial concept of the celestial bodies and their motions. The conception of the world still prevailing at Galileo's time may be described as follows:

There is space, and within it there is a preferred point, the center of the universe. Matter—at least its denser portion— tends to approach this point as closely as possible. Consequently, matter has assumed approximately spherical shape (earth). Owing to this formation of the earth the center of the terrestrial sphere practically coincides with that of the universe. Sun, moon, and stars are prevented from falling toward the center of the universe by being fastened onto rigid (transparent) spherical shells whose centers are identical with that of the universe (or space). These spherical shells revolve around the immovable globe (or center of the universe) with slightly differing angular velocities. The lunar shell has the smallest radius; it encloses everything "terrestrial." The outer shells with their heavenly bodies represent the "celestial sphere" whose objects are envisaged as eternal, indestructible, and inalterable, in contrast to the "lower, terrestrial sphere" which is enclosed by the lunar shell and contains everything that is transitory, perishable, and "corruptible."

Naturally, this naïve picture cannot be blamed on the Greek astronomers who, in representing the motions of the celestial bodies, used abstract geometrical constructions which grew more and more complicated with the increasing precision of astronomical observations. Lacking a theory of mechanics they tried to reduce all complicated (apparent) motions to the simplest motions they could conceive, namely, uniform circular motions and superpositions thereof. Attachment to the idea of circular motion as the truly natural one is still clearly discernible in Galileo; probably it is responsible for the fact that he did not *fully* recognize the law of inertia and its fundamental significance.

Thus, briefly, had the ideas of later Greece been crudely adapted to the barbarian, primitive mentality of the Europeans of that time. Though not causal, those Hellenistic ideas had nevertheless been objective and free from animistic views—a merit which, however, can be only conditionally conceded to Aristotelian cosmology.

GALILEO AIMED TO SUBSTITUTE OLD IDEAS WITH NEW

In advocating and fighting for the Copernican theory Galileo was not only motivated by a striving to simplify the representation of the celestial motions. His aim was to substitute for a petrified and barren system of ideas the unbiased and strenuous quest for a deeper and more consistent comprehension of the physical and astronomical facts.

The form of dialogue used in his work may be partly due to [Greek philosopher] Plato's shining example; it enabled Galileo to apply his extraordinary literary talent to the sharp and vivid confrontation of opinions. To be sure, he wanted to avoid an open commitment in these controversial questions that would have delivered him to destruction by the Inquisition. Galileo had, in fact, been expressly forbidden to advocate the Copernican theory. Apart from its revolutionary factual content the *Dialogue* represents a down-

GALILEO ERRS IN THE PENDULUM THEORY

In keeping with Einstein's observation that Galileo made errors, James Gleick points out in Chaos: Making a New Science *that Galileo made an error in his pendulum theory—small, but nonetheless measurable. Yet, his focus was on observation and measurement, a new method in his age.*

When Galileo looked at a pendulum, on the other hand, he saw a regularity that could be measured. To explain it required a revolutionary way of understanding objects in motion. Galileo's advantage over the ancient Greeks was not that he had better data. On the contrary, his idea of timing a pendulum precisely was to get some friends together to count the oscillations over a twenty-four-hour period—a labor-intensive experiment. Galileo saw the regularity because he already had a theory that predicted it. He understood what Aristotle could not: that a moving object tends to keep moving, that a change in speed or direction could only be explained by some external force, like friction.

In fact, so powerful was his theory that he saw a regularity

right roguish attempt to comply with this order in appearance and yet in fact to disregard it. Unfortunately, it turned out that the Holy Inquisition was unable to appreciate adequately such subtle humor.

The theory of the immovable earth was based on the hypothesis that an abstract center of the universe exists. Supposedly, this center causes the fall of heavy bodies at the earth's surface, since material bodies have the tendency to approach the center of the universe as far as the earth's impenetrability permits. This leads to the approximately spherical shape of the earth.

Galileo opposes the introduction of this "nothing" (center of the universe) that is yet supposed to act on material bodies; he considers this quite unsatisfactory.

But he also draws attention to the fact that this unsatisfactory hypothesis accomplishes too little. Although it accounts for the spherical shape of the earth it does not explain the spherical shape of the other heavenly bodies. However, the lunar phases and the phases of Venus, which latter he had discovered with the newly invented telescope, proved the spherical shape of these two celestial bodies; and the detailed observation of the sunspots proved the same for the sun. Actually, at Galileo's time there was hardly any doubt that did *not* exist. He contended that a pendulum of a given length not only keeps precise time but keeps the same time no matter how wide or narrow the angle of its swing. A wide-swinging pendulum has farther to travel, but it happens to travel just that much faster. In other words, its period remains independent of its amplitude. "If two friends shall set themselves to count the oscillations, one counting the wide ones and the other the narrow, they will see that they may count not just tens, but even hundreds, without disagreeing by even one, or part of one." Galileo phrased his claim in terms of experimentation, but the theory made it convincing——so much so that it is still taught as gospel in most high school physics courses. But it is wrong. The regularity Galileo saw is only an approximation. The changing angle of the bob's motion creates a slight nonlinearity in the equations. At low amplitudes, the error is almost nonexistent. But it is there, and it is measurable even in an experiment as crude as the one Galileo describes.

James Gleick, *Chaos: Making a New Science.* New York: Penguin, 1987.

left as to the spherical shape of the planets and stars.

Therefore, the hypothesis of the "center of the universe" had to be replaced by one which would explain the spherical shape of the stars, and not only that of the earth. Galileo says quite clearly that there must exist some kind of interaction (tendency to mutual approach) of the matter constituting a star. The same cause has to be responsible (after relinquishing the "center of the universe") for the free fall of heavy bodies at the earth's surface. . . .

GALILEO'S IDEAS REGARDING GRAVITY AND MOTION

Galileo also recognized that the effect of gravity on freely falling bodies manifests itself in a vertical acceleration of constant value; likewise that an unaccelerated horizontal motion can be superposed on this vertical accelerated motion.

These discoveries contain essentially—at least qualitatively —the basis of the theory later formulated by Newton. But first of all the general formulation of the principle of inertia is lacking, although this would have been easy to obtain from Galileo's law of falling bodies by a limiting process. (Transition to vanishing vertical acceleration.) Lacking also is the idea that the same matter which causes a vertical acceleration at the surface of a heavenly body can also accel-

erate another heavenly body; and that such accelerations together with inertia can produce revolving motions. There
was achieved, however, the knowledge that the presence of
matter (earth) causes an acceleration of free bodies (at the
surface of the earth).

It is difficult for us today to appreciate the imaginative
power made manifest in the precise formulation of the
concept of acceleration and in the recognition of its physical significance.

Once the conception of the center of the universe had,
with good reason, been rejected, the idea of the immovable
earth, and, generally, of an exceptional role of the earth, was
deprived of its justification. The question of what, in describing the motion of heavenly bodies, should be considered "at rest" became thus a question of convenience. Following Aristarchus[1] and Copernicus, the advantages of
assuming the sun to be at rest are set forth (according to
Galileo not a pure convention but a hypothesis which is either "true" or "false"). Naturally, it is argued that it is sim-
pler to assume a rotation of the earth around its axis than a
common revolution of all fixed stars around the earth. Furthermore, the assumption of a revolution of the earth around
the sun makes the motions of the inner and outer planets appear similar and does away with the troublesome retrograde
motions of the outer planets, or rather explains them by the
motion of the earth around the sun.

GALILEO STRUGGLED WITH THE PROBLEM
OF ROTATIONS AND REVOLUTIONS

Convincing as these arguments may be—in particular coupled with the circumstance, detected by Galileo, that Jupiter
with its moons represents so to speak a Copernican system
in miniature—they still are only of a qualitative nature. For
since we human beings are tied to the earth, our observations will never directly reveal to us the "true" planetary
motions, but only the intersections of the lines of sight
(earth–planet) with the "fixed-star sphere." A support of the
Copernican system over and above qualitative arguments
was possible only by determining the "true orbits" of the
planets—a problem of almost insurmountable difficulty,

---

1. Aristarchus was a Greek astronomer who was among the first to propose that the
sun is the center of the universe and that the earth moves around the sun. Copernicus
proposed the same ideas.

which, however, was solved by Kepler (during Galileo's lifetime) in a truly ingenious fashion. But this decisive progress did not leave any traces in Galileo's life work—a grotesque illustration of the fact that creative individuals are often not receptive.

Galileo takes great pains to demonstrate that the hypothesis of the rotation and revolution of the earth is not refuted by the fact that we do not observe any mechanical effects of these motions. Strictly speaking, such a demonstration was impossible because a complete theory of mechanics was lacking. I think it is just in the struggle with this problem that Galileo's originality is demonstrated with particular force. Galileo is, of course, also concerned to show that the fixed stars are too remote for parallaxes produced by the yearly motion of the earth to be detectable with the measuring instruments of his time. This investigation also is ingenious, notwithstanding its primitiveness.

It was Galileo's longing for a mechanical proof of the motion of the earth which misled him into formulating a wrong theory of the tides. The fascinating arguments in the last conversation would hardly have been accepted as proofs by Galileo, had his temperament not got the better of him. It is hard for me to resist the temptation to deal with this subject more fully.

GALILEO ACCEPTED ONLY EXPERIENCE AND REFLECTION IN SEEKING TRUTH

The *leitmotif* [dominant and recurring theme] which I recognize in Galileo's work is the passionate fight against any kind of dogma based on authority. Only experience and careful reflection are accepted by him as criteria of truth. Nowadays it is hard for us to grasp how sinister and revolutionary such an attitude appeared at Galileo's time, when merely to doubt the truth of opinions which had no basis but authority was considered a capital crime and punished accordingly. Actually we are by no means so far removed from such a situation even today as many of us would like to flatter ourselves; but in theory, at least, the principle of unbiased thought has won out, and most people are willing to pay lip service to this principle.

It has often been maintained that Galileo became the father of modern science by replacing the speculative, deductive method with the empirical, experimental method. I believe, however, that this interpretation would not stand close scrutiny. There is no empirical method without speculative concepts and systems; and there is no speculative thinking whose concepts do not reveal, on closer investigation, the empirical material from which they stem. To put into sharp contrast the empirical and the deductive attitude is misleading, and was entirely foreign to Galileo. Actually it was not until the nineteenth century that logical (mathematical) systems whose structures were completely independent of any empirical content had been cleanly extracted. Moreover, the experimental methods at Galileo's disposal were so imperfect that only the boldest speculation could possibly bridge the gaps between the empirical data. (For example, there existed no means to measure times shorter than a second.) The antithesis Empiricism *vs.* Rationalism does not appear as a controversial point in Galileo's work. Galileo opposes the deductive methods of Aristotle and his adherents only when he considers their premises arbitrary or untenable, and he does not rebuke his opponents for the mere fact of using deductive methods. In the first dialogue, he emphasizes in several passages that according to Aristotle, too, even the most plausible deduction must be put aside if it is incompatible with empirical findings. And on the other hand, Galileo himself makes considerable use of logical deduction. His endeavors are not so much directed at "factual knowledge" as at "comprehension." But to comprehend is essentially to draw conclusions from an already accepted logical system.

Galileo's Influence in Modern Society

Gilberto Bernardini

Speaking at a conference honoring Galileo, Gilberto Bernardini identifies three ways Galileo has influenced modern society. As "the father of physics," Galileo laid groundwork on which later scientists built. As "the first physicist," he established methods of observation and experimentation scientists have used ever since. As "the first man of the enlightenment," he struggled for the principles of reason and freedom and promoted the idea that science benefits all people. Unfortunately, according to Bernardini, the greatest message of Galileo—the dignity of rationality and freedom—has been lost in the nineteenth and twentieth centuries. Gilberto Bernardini was the director of the Scuola Normale Superiore in Pisa, Italy. He is the author, with Laura Fermi, of *Galileo and the Scientific Revolution.*

Galileo is often called the "Father of Physics"; less frequently, the "first modern physicist."

One may notice the subtle difference between these two designations. I think, however, that they are not quite appropriate in characterizing Galileo's historical significance. He was the "Father of Physics" for the revolutionary trends of his natural philosophy. He is the "first modern physicist" because he first went from a commonsense consideration of natural phenomena—the slow swinging of the pendant lamp or the too-quickly-falling body—to *quantitative* experiments made by constructed pendula or the tilted plane, where respectively the length of the lamp or the acceleration of the body was made large or small at will. He is the "first physicist," not because his name is bound to discoveries

Excerpted from *Homage to Galileo: Papers Presented at the Galileo Quadricentennial, University of Rochester, October 8 and 9, 1964,* edited by Morton F. Kaplon. Copyright © 1965 by The Massachusetts Institute of Technology. Reprinted by permission of the publisher, The M.I.T. Press.

comparable to the gravitation law or Maxwell's equations,[1] but because he first expressed the results of systematic observations in mathematical terms and stated that one should try the simplest assumptions in guessing how to describe a new phenomenon in mathematical language. He was the "Father of Physics" because with concrete wisdom and conscious intellectual humility he approached the immensity of nature with these words: "It always seems to me extreme rashness on the part of some when they want to make human abilities the measure of what nature can do. On the contrary, there is not a single effect in nature, even the least that exists, such that the most ingenious theorists can arrive at a complete understanding of it. This vain presumption of understanding everything can have no other basis than never understanding anything."

Let me give evidence for what I have said with a few classical examples. The principle of inertia and mechanical relativity uphold him as the "Father of Physics"; the measurement of time and of the velocity of light recognize him as the "first physicist."

GALILEO'S ROLE AS "FATHER OF PHYSICS"

With regard to the principle of inertia, modern scientific thinking is so closely linked to it that it is often hard to realize that it embodies one of the greatest discoveries of science. As so frequently happened with other discoveries, it was formulated over and over again, and [French mathematician and philosopher René] Descartes, [Dutch physicist and astronomer Christiaan] Huygens, and [British mathematician Isaac] Newton expressed it in more precise and general terms. But Galileo's discovery differs from most of the others because it was reached by a solitary thinker, who—gradually building for himself a new philosophical approach—found at last the solution to a problem which had been haunting his unique mind for more than forty years.

When a young teacher at Pisa and still almost completely permeated with Aristotelian Natural Philosophy, he posed these questions in his lectures on motion. Two kinds of motion are allowed to a heavy body: a "natural" one when it falls and a "violent" one when it goes against gravity. What happens when it lies on a horizontal plane and an infinitely small

1. James Clerk Maxwell (1831–1879) was a British physicist who made fundamental contributions to electromagnetic theory and the kinetic theory of gases.

impulsion suffices to move it? What is its motion?

The answer is formulated with increasing clarity in his last and greatest work: *Dialogues Concerning Two New Sciences.* At the beginning of the fourth day [of dialogue], one finds the celebrated statement, "mobile quodam super planum orizontale, omni secluso impedimento, etc. . . . ," which synthesizes previous discussions on the problem. Going from Latin to English, the statement is read as follows: "Imagine any particle projected along a horizontal plane without friction; then this particle will move along this

Galileo Galilei

same plane with a motion which is uniform and perpetual, provided the plane has no limits. But if the plane is limited, then the moving particle . . . in addition to its previous motion, *which will be uniform and perpetual,* will acquire a downward propensity due to its own weight; so that the resulting motion . . ." Then the answer came to him through the synthesis of two thoughts: first, *imagining* out of the results of a series of experiments what the *reality* would be if the imperfection of instruments and subjective sensations could be surpassed and the phenomenon occur in a world *without friction;* then, figuring out rationally what the motion of a *free body* would be in this world.

Today the motion of a free body is represented by a plane wave, the solution of the free-particle wave equation. One arrives here by starting from the principle of inertia formulated in terms of the relativistic invariance of the energy momentum vector, and then imposing the wave-particle dualism. It is a long way; the two steps in between are Einstein relativity and quantum mechanics, but the philosophical pattern is always the same.

LATER SCIENTISTS BUILT ON GALILEO'S EXPERIMENTS

As another example of the extension of this way of thinking in modern physics, let me consider the concept of *antimat-*

ter.[2] Also in this case we are essentially overriding our more anthropological sensations. For the principle of inertia, it is necessary to imagine a world with no friction—a world where our hands will not be capable of catching anything, where it would be impossible to move around with our legs, to slow down any motion with brakes, etc. In conceiving the antimatter world, the main step, as shown by [American physicist Richard Phillips] Feynman, is the *inversion of time.* This is a very hard concept for us to grasp, animals as we are. Life means irreversible time, and while for an animal used to walking back and forth the conception of inverting motion and space is quite easy, the idea of growing younger again is completely beyond our perception.

On the principle of relativity there is no need to insist. These are Galileo's words:

> Closet yourself with some friends in the largest quarters that can be found under the hatches of some big ship and see that you have . . . small winged animals, etc. . . . : let there be also a small bucket suspended high above another vase with a small opening so that water may drip slowly from the higher into the lower basin and, as the boat *stands still,* observe attentively how the winged animals dart to and fro within the room in all directions . . . the drops fall into the basin underneath. . . .
>
> Have then *the ship move* as fast as you will and (*so long as the motion is uniform* and not rocking this way and that) you will not notice the slightest alteration in all the above de-scribed effects, nor will you be able to understand through any of them whether the ship moves or stands still.

I chose these examples for their peculiar significance, but in the lectures of these past two days . . . you have heard already that there are many examples, all characterized by the same type of understanding of natural phenomena. What this "understanding" means can be summed up as follows: *Scientific reality, the only one scientifically accept-able,* is made up of rational schemes which represent the results of all the experiments and observations that could be made, *assuming* that there exist no impediments—"*omni secluso impedimento*"—due to the imperfection of our senses and instruments. . . .

We focus our attention on some of Galileo's many pas-sages concerning the meaning and value of "experiments." In these passages, we clearly see the transition from a first

2. matter made of particles with identical mass and spin as those of ordinary matter, but with opposite charge

experiment, with all its inherent errors and misleading appearances, to the interpretation of it; and *then* the *return* to the new experiments to see whether the guess that has been made was right or wrong, whether the presumption of the human mind—wanting to give a rational interpretation to facts—was well justified or not. We know that this procedure simply means to build, fragment after fragment, the Edifice of Science.

GALILEO'S ROLE AS THE "FIRST PHYSICIST"

Let us now try to view Galileo, the "first physicist," through examples of the measurement of time and the velocity of light. I use again a few fragments of the *Dialogues Concerning Two New Sciences,* quite significant in many other respects. "The experiment made to ascertain whether two bodies differing in weight will fall from a given height with the same speed, offers some difficulty; because . . . the retarding effect of the medium. If the height be small, one may well doubt whether there is any difference, and if there be a difference, it will be unappreciable. It occurred to me therefore to repeat many times the fall through a small height in such a way that I might accumulate all those small intervals of time that elapse between the arrival of the heavy and light bodies respectively, so that summing up, one gets an interval of time which is not only observable, but measurable." Ten pages after, he introduces the pendulum. In another section of the book, while describing experiments on the motion along inclined planes, he says, "For the measurement of time, we employed a large vessel of water placed in an elevated position; to the bottom of this vessel was soldered a pipe of small diameter giving a thin jet of water, which we collected in a small glass . . . the water thus collected was weighed, after each descent, on a very accurate balance. . . ."

There is something more: Galileo introduced time as a normal coordinate. In his diagrams he drew a straight line as the time axis on which he marked time intervals from a zero point chosen at will. Today everybody carries a watch, reads time-space diagrams, etc.; but three centuries ago, time was only the correlation between the cyclic conception of day and night, of moons and years, and the unresting evolution that brings everything but human souls to an end.

Let us now see how he used this concept of measurable

short times in one experiment concerning the velocity of light. The experiment is described on the first day of the two sciences. *Salviati*[3] *speaks:* "Let each of two persons take . . . a lantern . . . such that by interposition of the hand, the one can shut off or admit the light to the vision of the other. Next, let them stand opposite each other at a distance of a few feet and practice until they reach such skill . . . that the instant one sees the light of his companion, he will uncover his own. . . . Having acquired skill at this short distance, let the two experimenters, equipped as before, take up positions separated by a distance of two or three miles, and let them perform the same experiment at night. . . . If the experiment is to be made at still greater distances, say eight or ten miles, telescopes may be employed." *Sagredo remarks:* "This experiment strikes me as a clever and reliable invention; but tell us what you concluded from the result." *Salviati answers:* ". . . I have not been able to ascertain with certainty whether the appearance of the opposite light was instantaneous or not; but if not instantaneous, it is extraordinarily rapid." In this example one finds everything that is desirable in a physicist: imagination in inventing experiments, skill, objective reporting of results, correct estimate of experimental errors.

THE VALUE OF SCIENCE FOR ORDINARY PEOPLE

Besides physics, there is another aspect of Galilean philosophy which goes beyond the limits of any branch of science and which, if we so wished, we could call to mind every day of our lives. But this aspect has often been confused with the problem of the character of Galileo and has been for three centuries the subject of a debate going far beyond the controversy on his philosophical approach. This debate is centered on the value of scientific culture in terms of moral and religious principles. In this respect, it is worth remarking that a drama (intentionally written with all the artistic imagination required to synthesize the greatness and the misery of our scientific and technical society) succeeded in stirring a new polemic about the deeper human roots of that very debate.

It is my opinion that, when looking at these roots, it is of very limited interest to know whether or not Galileo bought his first telescope from a Dutch merchant. But it seems to

---

3. Galileo presents his scientific information in the form of dialogues among three characters: Salviati, Sagredo, and Simplicio.

me essential to know that, having a telescope in his hands, after weeks of observations repeated over and over again to check the power and reliability of the instrument in magnifying terrestrial objects far away, he raised it toward the sky with absolute faith in the keenness of his senses mediated and enhanced by an instrument contrived by man. The point that seems essential to me is that he proved through his eager pursuit of knowledge and the unprejudiced use of his intellect—by discovering mountains on the moon, spots on the sun, the satellites of Jupiter, and many new stars never seen before—that he had more faith in his instruments than in the mystical perfection of the sky.

Before Galileo, instruments and machines were used only to increase the efficiency of human and animal labor, while after him, machines and instruments became the means to hew down the fence that kept within extremely narrow limits man's perception of the world.

Today, thanks to optical or radar telescopes, we "see" things that are extremely far away from us: electronic devices and instruments allow us to "see" a virus or to follow the track of an electron; we "hear" sound signals emitted by a bee or a bat; we measure time with electronic or atomic clocks; we know when and where a single photon has been absorbed.

At this point, one may argue that this "technical" development was more or less on the way and that in this sense Galileo was only the most eminent man of his time. This is certainly true; however, there is one thing which distinguishes him from all the others and which is unrelated to any scientific achievement. The *Sidereus Nuncius*—the booklet of thirty-five pages in which his main astronomical discoveries are condensed—is practically his last work written in Latin, the language of the scholars of his time. Thereafter, he intentionally wrote in the vulgar tongue so as to include in his audience not only scholars but all people able to think for themselves.

This is the last point I would like to consider. The *Sidereus Nuncius* was published on March 12, 1610. In September, he moved from Padua to Florence and became "Matematico primario dello Studio di Pisa e filosofo del Serenissimo Granduca senza obbligo di leggere e di risiedere nè nello Studio nè nella citta di Pisa etc., . . ." [Mathematics chair of the University of Pisa and philosopher to the Serene Grand Duke without obligation to read or teach in the University of

Pisa] which means, in addition to a salary comparable with the salary of an American Nobel Prize winner and the elegant title, that he had no obligations whatever with respect to teaching and residence.

But the *Sidereus Nuncius,* in less than one year, stirred a violent and large debate which involved the highest authorities of the Catholic Church and of science, such as Cardinal Bellarmino and Kepler, as well as thousands of laymen. Considering the content of this booklet, this appears today rather predictable. However, Galileo was shocked, and from that time—from 1611 to July 6, 1633, the day on which he left Rome, the theater of his ignominy—he conceived a vast and ambitious program: a project to diffuse over all intelligent men the great assets of the new scientific culture.

GALILEO, THE FIRST MAN OF THE ENLIGHTENMENT

Free from all duties, finally well settled economically, instead of writing the long-conceived book on mechanics, instead of extending his explorations of the sky, he started what we may call a political campaign in defense of a new society potentially free from prejudice and oriented toward irreversible progress.

This statement is not arbitrary or overdone, and well-qualified historians agree with it. We may refer here to the many letters written by him; for instance, that to Benedetto Castelli (1613) and that to the Principessa Cristina di Lorena (1615) where, with his basically catholic spirit, he tries to demonstrate the possible coexistence (not the consistency) of Catholic dogma and Copernican doctrine. But to demonstrate the statement, it suffices to read the *Dialogue Concerning the Two Great World Systems,* appreciating its general frame and presentation as an open debate. According to his words, "the true philosophers, the lovers of the true, should not be irritated, but knowing to have erroneously thought would thank who showed to them the very true." Listen to his language, the language of the people, written in a splendid style, but elucidating the essentials of the problems. With this language, conscious of the significance and value of what he and the scholars of the sixteenth century had discovered, he wanted to raise from ignorance and prejudice the generations to come. In this respect, the battle to defend the Copernican system goes far beyond the struggle for an idea thought to be right. It is the expression of a faith, the faith that a free human being has the right and the power to fight perennially against fictitious dogma, intellectual and moral idleness. This seems to me the greatest legacy of Galileo. In this sense, he is also the first man of the "enlightenment."

As stated clearly quite a few times in the penetrating and very gratifying discussions of these two days, certainly in scientific revolution he is at one of the highest peaks, though not alone. However, precursor and prophet at the same time, he is the Socrates of this revolution and the only one. This statement is not a personal fantasy. The new religious trends have condemned Copernicus and those who supported his ideas. To consider some significant examples, Kepler and Descartes, in private letters written to friends, strongly criticized Galileo's attitude, stating that his behavior was bold and imprudent.

I would thus conclude that in modern times, from the Renaissance on, there has been no philosopher nor philosophy which has exerted a deeper influence on history than the influence exerted by the works and troubled life of Galileo. In many ways, although for widely varying reasons, we may be tempted to compare him to Aristotle.

Aristotle's thought and, even more, his ideals of perfection, found in [Italian theologian] Thomas Aquinas and in Christianity the robust walls that defended, for over a thousand years, their integrity and immense prestige. Galileo's thought found in the essential rationality and simplicity which pertain to science the power to hand itself down, from one generation to the next, in an irreversible progress that knows no setbacks. However, one has to admit that Galileo is not the Aristotle of modern times: his presence is not at all equivalent to the lasting influence of Thomas' doctrine in defending moral and intellectual principles during the Middle Ages.

GALILEO'S INFLUENCE DIMINISHED AFTER THE EIGHTEENTH CENTURY

Galileo's influence was determinant in the eighteenth century. This was the century of the triumph of human reason; the century in which the discovery of Newton's laws was a source of light along the intellectual and moral road of the future, not limited to the circle of scholars, but also including many of the alert bourgeois, profoundly affected by their reading of the encyclopedia. It was the century in which science was a determining force in provoking the most enlightened social revolutions, the American and the French. But since the first decades of the nineteenth century, a great divorce has occurred between science and technique. The new trend, which has changed many essential features of human society, was technical development. With the industrial revolution, the feedback reaction between science and technique, between discovery and invention, becomes more and more rapid; but, at the same time, the scientist increasingly returns to the position of the scholar intellectually bound only to other scholars. The scientific value of the discoveries of Volta, Ampère, Faraday, Fresnel, Gibbs, Maxwell, and Hertz[4] reached the crowd of *honnêtes hommes* [honest, upright people] through the inventions of Watt, a watchmaker, and Pacinotti and Gramme, one a rather modest physicist, the other a brilliant, aggressive engineer, etc., . . ., up to Marconi,[5] a very ingenious fellow, whose intellectual limitations were comparable with his moral ones.

Nowadays, with respect to the nineteenth century, the only noticeable difference is that the scale of time is extremely contracted. The feedback between pure and applied science is so rapid that the feeling of scientific evolution penetrates daily into most men, innocently, but brutally, through the offer of an increasingly leisured life.

At the same time, the comprehension of the more general value of science is more and more confused. One meets daily strangely biased and distorted ideas even in gifted persons whose approach to scientific culture goes from lasting memories of the horrors of the last war to a superficial, almost ridiculous, exaltation of technical development as the highest mark of the human mind. This seems to me the reason why we have lost the greatest message of Galileo. In the years which followed the 22nd of June 1633, the day of abjuration [his public renunciation of Copernican theory], Galileo returned to pure science. Only four years later, the *Dialogues Concerning Two New Sciences* was published in Holland. But the return to pure science was not an abjuration of his faith in the general moral and intellectual value

---

4. Volta: first electric battery; Ampère: magnetic field; Faraday: electromagnetic induction; Fresnel: compound lens for use in lighthouses; Gibbs: vector analysis; Maxwell: electromagnetic theory; Hertz: impact of electrons upon atoms   5. transmitted long-range radio signals across the Atlantic Ocean

of science. This last work of Galileo is actually his greatest contribution to modern civilization. Here he no longer speaks polemically for or against the Copernican system; he speaks calmly and serenely of the first discoveries in physics; he uses this means to convey to all men the high dignity of rationality and freedom. How many modern scientists and new scholars contribute consciously to the increase of this human dignity?

The Church Acknowledges Injustice Done to Galileo

John Paul II

Speaking to scientists gathered to commemorate the centenary of Albert Einstein's birth, Pope John Paul II, acknowledging that Galileo had suffered much at the hands of men in the Roman Catholic Church, called for a thorough examination of the Galileo case. The Pope declared that today the church supports fundamental scientific research and a scientist's freedom to pursue the truth. He quoted Galileo, whose ideas written nearly four hundred years ago ironically resemble the church's position today. Pope John Paul II, the first Polish-born pope, has served in that capacity since 1978. He has traveled widely promoting human rights and his moral values.

I feel myself to be fully one with my predecessor Pius XI, and with the two who followed him in the Chair of Peter, in inviting the members of the Academy of the Sciences and all scientists with them, to bring about "the ever more noble and intense progress of the sciences, without asking any more from them; and this is because in this excellent proposal and this noble work there consists that mission of serving truth with which we charge them."

The search for truth is the fundamental task of science. The researcher who moves on this plane of science feels all the fascination of St. Augustine's words, *Intellectum valde ama,* "love intelligence greatly," and its proper function, which is to know the truth. Pure science is a good in itself which deserves to be greatly loved, for it is knowledge, the perfection of human beings in their intelligence. Even before its technical applications, it should be loved for itself, as an integral part of human culture. Fundamental science is a universal boon, which every nation should cultivate in full freedom from all forms of international servitude or intellectual colonialism.

THE FREEDOM AND RESPONSIBILITY OF FUNDAMENTAL RESEARCH

Fundamental research should be free vis-à-vis political and economic powers, which should cooperate in its development, without fettering its creativity or enslaving it to their own ends. As with all other truth, scientific truth has, in fact, to render an account only to itself and to the supreme truth that is God, the creator of humankind and of all that is.

On its second plane, science turns toward practical applications, which find their full development in various technologies. In the phase of its concrete applications, science is necessary for humanity in order to satisfy the just requirements of life, and to conquer the various evils that threaten it. There is no doubt that applied science has rendered and will render humankind immense services, especially if it is inspired by love, regulated by wisdom, and accompanied by the courage that defends it against the undue interference of all tyrannical powers. Applied science should be allied with conscience, so that, in the triad, science–technology– conscience, it may be the cause of the true good of humankind, whom it should serve.

Unhappily, as I have had occasion to say in my encyclical[1] *Redemptor hominis,* "Humankind today seems constantly to be menaced by what it constructs. . . . In this there seems to consist the principal chapter of the drama of human existence today." Humankind should emerge victorious from this drama, which threatens to degenerate into tragedy, and should once more find its authentic sovereignty over the world and its full mastery of the things it has made. At this present hour, as I wrote in the same encyclical, "the fundamental significance of this "sovereignty" and this 'mastery' of humankind over the visible world, assigned to it as a task by the Creator, consists in the priority of ethics over technology, in the primacy of person over things, and in the superiority of spirit over matter."

This threefold superiority is maintained to the extent that there is conserved the sense of human transcendence over the world and God's transcendence over humankind. Exer-

1. a papal letter addressed to the bishops of the Roman Catholic Church

cising its mission as guardian and defender of both these transcendences, the church desires to assist science to conserve its ideal purity on the plane of fundamental research, and to help it fulfill its service to humankind on the plane of practical applications.

The church freely recognizes, on the other hand, that it has benefited from science. It is to science, among other things, that there must be attributed that which Vatican II has said with regard to certain aspects of modern culture:

> New conditions in the end affect the religious life itself. . . . The soaring of the critical spirit purifies that life from a magical conception of the world and from superstitious survivals, and demands a more and more personal and active adhesion to faith; many are the souls who in this way have come to a more living sense of God.

THE ADVANTAGE OF COLLABORATION BETWEEN SCIENCE AND RELIGION

Collaboration between religion and modern science is to the advantage of both, and in no way violates the autonomy of either. Just as religion requires religious freedom, so science legitimately requires freedom of research. The Second Vatican Council, after having affirmed, together with Vatican I, the just freedom of the arts and human disciplines in the domain of their proper principles and method, solemnly recognized "the legitimate autonomy of culture and particularly that of the sciences."

On this occasion of the solemn commemoration of Einstein, I wish to confirm anew the declarations of Vatican II on the autonomy of science in its function of research into the truth inscribed in nature by the hand of God. Filled with admiration for the genius of the great scientist, a genius in which there is revealed the imprint of the Creator Spirit, the Church, without in any way passing a judgment on the doctrine concerning the great systems of the universe, since that is not its area of competence, nevertheless proposes this doctrine to the reflection of theologians in order to discover the harmony existing between scientific and revealed truth.

Mr. President, in your address you have rightly said that Galileo and Einstein have characterized an epoch. *The greatness of Galileo is known to all,* as is that of Einstein; but with this difference, that by comparison with the one whom we are today honoring before the College of Cardinals in the Apostolic Palace, the first had much to suffer—we cannot conceal it—at the hands of men and departments within the church. The Second Vatican Council has recognized and deplored, certain undue interventions: "May we be permitted to deplore"—it is written in § 36 of the Conciliar Constitution *Gaudium et Spes* [Joy and Hope]—"certain attitudes that have existed among Christians themselves, insufficiently informed as to the legitimate autonomy of science. Sources of tension and conflict, they have led many to consider that science and faith are opposed." The reference to Galileo is clearly expressed in the note appended to this text, which cites the volume *Vita e opere di Galileo Galilei* [The Life and Work of Galileo Galilei] by Pio Paschini, published by the Pontifical Academy of Sciences.

In order to go beyond this position adopted by the Council, I desire that theologians, scientists, and historians, animated by a spirit of sincere collaboration, deepen their examination of the Galileo case, and, in a loyal recognition of errors, from whatever side they come. I also desire that they bring about the disappearance of the mistrust that, in many souls, this affair still arouses in opposition to a fruitful concord between science and faith, between the church and the world. I give my full support to this task, which can honor the truth of faith and of science, and open the door to future collaboration.

THE CASE OF THE SCIENTIST GALILEO GALILEI

May I be permitted, gentlemen, to submit to your attention and your reflection, some points that seem to me important for placing the Galileo affair in its true light, in which agreements between religion and science are more important than those misunderstandings from which there has arisen the bitter and grievous conflict that has dragged itself out in the course of the following centuries.

He who is justly entitled the founder of modern physics, has explicitly declared that the truths of faith and of science can never contradict each other: "Holy Scripture and nature equally proceed from the divine Word, the first as dictated by the Holy Spirit, the second as the very faithful executor of God's commands," as he wrote in his letter to Fr. Benedetto Castelli on December 21, 1613. The Second Vatican Council does not differ in its mode of expression; it even adopts similar expressions when it teaches: "Methodical research, in all domains of knowledge, if it follows moral norms, will never really be opposed to faith; both the realities of this world and of the faith find their origin in the same God."

In scientific research Galileo perceived the presence of the Creator who stimulates it, anticipates and assists its intuitions, by acting in the very depths of its spirit. In connection with the telescope, he wrote at the commencement of the *Sidereus Nuntius,* ("the starry messenger"), recalling some of his astronomical discoveries: *Quae omnia ope perspicilli a me excogitavi divina prius illuminante gratia, paucis abhinc diebus reperta, atque observata fuerunt,* "I worked all these things out with the help of the telescope and under the prior illumination of divine grace they were discovered and observed by me a few days ago."

The Galilean recognition of divine illumination in the spirit of the scientist finds an echo in the already quoted text of the Conciliar Constitution on the church in the modern world: "One who strives, with perseverance and humility, to penetrate the secret of things, is as if led by the hand of God, even if not aware of it." The humility insisted on by the conciliar text is a spiritual virtue equally necessary for scientific research as for adhesion to the faith. Humility creates a climate favorable to dialogue between the believer and the scientist, it is a call for illumination by God, already known or still unknown but loved, in one case as in the other, on the part of the one who is searching for truth.

Galileo has formulated important norms of an epistemological character, which are confirmed as indispensable for placing Holy Scripture and science in agreement. In his letter to the grand duchess of Tuscany, Christine of Lorraine, he reaffirms the truth of Scripture:

> Holy Scripture can never propose an untruth, always on condition that one penetrates to its true meaning, which—I think nobody can deny—is often hidden and very different from that which the simple signification of the words seems to indicate.

Galileo introduced the principle of an interpretation of the sacred books that goes beyond the literal meaning but is in conformity with the intention and type of exposition proper to each one of them. As he affirms, it is necessary that "the wise who expound it show its true meaning."

The ecclesiastical magisterium admits the plurality of rules of interpretation of Holy Scripture. It expressly teaches, in fact, with the encyclical *Divino Afflante Spiritu* [abundant divine spirit] of Pius XII, the presence of different genres in the sacred books and hence the necessity of interpretations conforming to the character of each of them.

AN HONEST AND LOYAL SOLUTION OF LONG-STANDING OPPOSITIONS

The various agreements that I have recalled do not by themselves solve all the problems of the Galileo affair, but they help to create a point of departure favorable to their honorable solution, a frame of mind propitious for an honest and loyal resolving of long-standing oppositions.

The existence of this Pontifical Academy of Science, with which Galileo was to some extent associated through the venerable institution that preceded the academy of today, in which eminent scientists participate, is a visible sign that demonstrates to all, with no racial or religious discrimination, the profound harmony that can exist between the truths of science and the truths of faith.

Discussion Questions

Chapter 1

1. Many writers credit Galileo with a fine writing style. According to Leonardo Olschki, how did Galileo's education prepare him to be a writer?

2. According to George Spini, Galileo came from a family with several generations belonging to the ruling class in Florence. What were the expectations of someone from this class? What changes in the traditional way of life occurred in Galileo's youth and how did they affect Galileo?

3. Galileo quit the university to study mathematics for two years. How did Greek mathematician Archimedes influence Galileo? Did Galileo make a good decision in leaving the university?

Chapter 2

1. Allen Debus explains that Galileo developed a method to show how, not why, events happen in nature. What were the steps in Galileo's method and why was this approach important?

2. According to Lynn Thorndike, what form did Galileo use to communicate his research? Provide examples to show that Galileo had a broad range of interest in scientific questions?

3. Try to imagine the world without clocks that Bronowski and Mazlish describe. What elements of daily living would have been affected by not having clocks? What did Galileo contribute to the measurement of time?

Chapter 3

1. Thomas S. Kuhn maintains that Galileo really did not prove that Copernicus's theory is correct. What were Galileo's arguments? How were Galileo's findings valuable even if they were not proof?

2. Timothy Ferris and Arthur Koestler each reveal elements of Galileo's personality. What qualities did each reveal? How did the qualities relate to Galileo's character and success?

CHAPTER 4

1. According to Hermann Kesten, how did Galileo's enthusiasm for and confidence in his beliefs lead him into greater involvement and, later, trouble with church authorities?

2. Galileo's conflict with church authorities escalates from a warning to a trial and punishment. How does each side, the church and Galileo, contribute to this escalation?

3. Rivka Feldhay suggests that Galileo's trial has traditionally been portrayed in opposing viewpoints. What does she see wrong in this approach? What does she recommend instead?

CHAPTER 5

1. In light of his crime, was Galileo's punishment severe or mild? Cite evidence from Ludovico Geymonat's viewpoint to explain how Galileo capitalized on his situation?

2. In light of Dava Sobel's essay, why do you think church authorities were so determined to keep Galileo away from contact with the public?

3. According to Antonio Favaro, what was Galileo's strategy for publishing *Dialogue Concerning Two New Sciences*? Was Galileo morally wrong to violate the church's orders not to publish?

CHAPTER 6

1. Compare Gerald Holton's and Albert Einstein's opinions regarding Galileo's importance. Point out the similarities and differences in their views.

2. According to Gilberto Bernardini, in what three ways has Galileo influenced modern society? Are these ways equally significant?

3. Does Pope John Paul II apologize for the church's treatment of Galileo? What is ironic about the quotation from Galileo and the statement of the church's current position on science?

GENERAL QUESTIONS

1. Why did Galileo succeed in advancing the notion of a sun-centered universe when others with the same viewpoint had little influence?

2. Which was more important, Galileo's contribution to physics or his contribution to astronomy?

3. How do you evaluate Galileo's personality? How did it affect his work and importance in history?

APPENDIX OF DOCUMENTS

DOCUMENT 1: COPERNICUS ARGUES FOR THE EARTH'S MOTION

After centuries of belief that the earth is the stationary center of the universe and that the sun revolves around it, Copernicus, with great diplomacy, refuted the system in De Revolutionibus. *In these excerpts, he states that the universe is spherical, as is the earth; motion is circular; the earth is not the center of the universe; and the earth is a planet that rotates. The ideas Copernicus set down in this book are the ones Galileo defended with great vigor.*

In the first place we must observe that the Universe is spherical. This is either because that figure is the most perfect, as not being articulated but whole and complete in itself; or because it is the most capacious and therefore best suited for that which is to contain and preserve all things [of all solids with a given surface the sphere has the greatest volume]; or again because all the perfect parts of it, namely, Sun, Moon and Stars, are so formed; or because all things tend to assume this shape, as is seen in the case of drops of water and liquid bodies in general if freely formed. No one doubts that such a shape has been assigned to the heavenly bodies.

The Earth also is spherical, since on all sides it inclines [or falls] toward the center. . . . As we pass from any point northward, the North Pole of the daily rotation gradually rises, while the other pole sinks correspondingly and more stars near the North Pole cease to set, while certain stars in the South do not rise. . . . Further, the change in altitude of the pole is always proportional to the distance traversed on the Earth, which could not be save on a spherical figure. Hence the Earth must be finite and spherical. . . .

We now note that the motion of heavenly bodies is circular. Rotation is natural to a sphere and by that very act is its shape expressed. For here we deal with the simplest kind of body, wherein neither beginning nor end may be discerned nor, if it rotate ever in the same place, may the one be distinguished from the other.

Because there are a multitude of spheres, many motions occur. Most evident to sense is the diurnal rotation . . . marking day and night. By this motion the whole Universe, save Earth alone, is thought to glide from East to West. This is the common measure of all motions, since Time itself is numbered in days. Next we see other revolutions in contest, as it were, with this daily motion and opposing it from West to East. Such opposing motions are those of Sun and Moon and the five planets. . . .

It is then generally agreed that the motions of Sun, Moon, and Planets do but seem irregular either by reason of the divers directions of their axes of revolution, or else by reason that Earth is not the center of the circles in which they revolve, so that to us on Earth the displacements of these bodies [along their orbits] seem greater when they are near [the earth] than when they are more remote (as is demonstrated in optics [or in everyday observation—boats or carriages always seem to move by more quickly when they are closer]). Thus, equal [angular] motions of a sphere, viewed from different distances, will seem to cover different distances in equal times. It is therefore above all needful to observe carefully the relation of the Earth toward the Heavens, lest, searching out the things on high, we should pass by those nearer at hand, and mistakenly ascribe earthly qualities to heavenly bodies. . . .

If this [possibility of the earth's motion] is admitted, then a problem no less grave arises about the Earth's position, even though almost everyone has hitherto held that the Earth is at the center of the Universe. [Indeed, if the earth can move at all, it may have more than a simple axial motion about the center of the Universe. It may move away from the center altogether, and there are some good astronomical reasons for supposing that it does.] For grant that Earth is not at the exact center but at a distance from it which, while small compared [with the distance] to the starry sphere, is yet considerable compared with [the distances to] the spheres of the Sun and the other planets. Then calculate the consequent variations in their seeming motions, assuming these [motions] to be really uniform and about some center other than the Earth's. One may then perhaps adduce a reasonable cause for the irregularity of these variable motions. And indeed since the Planets are seen at varying distances from the Earth, the center of Earth is surely not the center of their circles. Nor is it certain whether the Planets move toward and away from Earth, or Earth toward and away from them. It is therefore justifiable to hold that the Earth has another motion in addition to the diurnal rotation. That the Earth, besides rotating, wanders with several motions and is indeed a Planet, is a view attributed to Philolaus the Pythagorean, no mean mathematician, and one whom Plato is said to have sought out in Italy.

Thomas S. Kuhn, *The Copernican Revolution: Planetary Astronomy in the Development of Western Thought*. Cambridge, MA: Harvard University Press, 1957.

DOCUMENT 2: GALILEO ARGUES THAT FORCE EXISTS

In On Motion, *Galileo ridicules Aristotle's notion that objects are projected by air once they leave the source that moved them. Galileo demolishes the notion with examples that make his opponent's idea seem foolish and that make his idea of force look logical.*

Aristotle, as in practically everything that he wrote about locomotion, wrote the opposite of the truth on this question too. And surely this is not strange. For who can arrive at true conclusions from false assumptions? Aristotle could not maintain his view that the mover must be in contact with the moving body, unless he said that projectiles are moved by the air. And he gave testimony of this opinion of his in many passages. And since we must refute this view, we shall first state it, but only in a summary way, for it is explained at considerable length by the commentators.

Aristotle holds that the mover, e.g., one who throws a stone, before he lets go of the stone, sets the contiguous parts of the air in motion; that these parts, similarly, move other parts, and these still others, and so on in succession; that the stone, after being released by the projector, is then moved along by those portions of air; and that thus the motion of the stone becomes, as it were, discontinuous, and is not a single motion but several. Aristotle and his followers, who could not persuade themselves that a body could be moved by a force impressed upon it, or recognize what that force was, tried to take refuge in this view. But in order that the other view, the true one, may be made clear, we shall first seek to demolish completely this view of Aristotle. Then we shall, so far as we can, explain and illustrate with examples the other view, which concerns the impressed force. . . .

And so, against Aristotle I argue as follows: Suppose the parts of air which move the body are A, B, C, D, and E, and suppose A is in contact with the mover. Now either all of these parts are moved at the same time, or one part is moved after another. If A, B, C, D, and E are all moved at the same time, then I ask by what they are moved when the mover comes to rest; and in that case one must come to the notion of an impressed force. If, however, A is moved before B, then again I ask by what B is moved when A comes to rest. Furthermore, again according to Aristotle, forced motion is swifter in the middle of the motion than at the beginning. Therefore part C of the air under the impulse of B, is moved more swiftly than is B. Hence C will likewise move D more swiftly than A, B, C, D, and E have themselves been moved by B. Hence D will also move E more swiftly than it [D] was moved by C: and so on in succession. Therefore forced motion will always be accelerated. . . .

Do you wonder what it is that passes from the hand of the projector and is impressed upon the projectile? Yet you do not wonder what passes from the hammer and is transferred to the bell of the clock, and how it happens that so loud a sound is carried over from the silent hammer to the silent bell, and is preserved in the bell when the hammer which struck it is no longer in contact. The bell is struck by the striking object; the stone is moved by the mover. The bell is deprived of its silence; the stone of its state of rest. A sonorous quality is imparted to the bell contrary to its natural silence; a motive quality is imparted to the stone contrary to its state of rest. The sound is preserved in the bell, when the striking object is no longer in contact; motion is preserved in the stone when the mover is no longer in contact. The sonorous quality gradually diminishes in the bell; the motive quality gradually diminishes in the stone. But who of sound mind will say that it is the air that continues to strike the bell? For, in the first place, only one small portion of air is moved by the hammer. But if someone puts his hand on the bell, even on the side opposite the hammer, he will immediately feel a sharp, stinging, and numbing action that runs through all the metal. Secondly, if it is the air that strikes the bell and causes the sound in it, why is the bell silent even if the strongest wind is blowing? Can it be that the strong south wind, which churns up the whole sea and topples towers and walls, strikes [the bell] more gently than does the hammer, which hardly moves. In the third place, if it were the air that caused the sound in the bronze, rather than the bronze that caused the sound in the air, all bells of the same shape would emit the same sound; indeed, even a wooden bell, or at least a leaden or marble one, would produce as much sound as a bronze one. But, finally, let those be still who keep saying that it is the air which causes the sound or carries the sound [to the bell]. For the bell vibrates as it emits the sound, and the vibration and sound remain in it and are preserved even when the striking agent is no longer in contact. But to ascribe to the air the setting in motion of such a great mass [i.e., the bell], when it [the air] has scarcely been moved itself by the hammer, exceeds all reason. To return, then, to our point, why are they puzzled that a motive quality can be impressed in a body by a mover, but not that a sound and a certain motion of vibration can be impressed in a bell by a hammer?

Galileo Galilei, *On Motion and On Mechanics: Comprising De Motu (ca. 1590)*. Trans. with Intro. and Notes by I.E. Drabkin. Madison: The University of Wisconsin Press, 1960.

DOCUMENT 3: LITERAL AND INTERPRETATIVE MEANING OF THE SCRIPTURE

In these excerpts from Galileo's letter to Don Benedetto Castelli, Galileo explains his thoughts regarding close reading of the scripture. He argues that some passages should be taken literally and others should be interpreted with further elaboration. The occasion of the letter arose because Castelli had reported in a letter to Galileo, dated December 14, 1613, on a breakfast he attended with members of the ruling Medici family and a few philosophers. After those in attendance praised Galileo for his work with the telescope, Her Ladyship (wife of Cosimo Medice II) argued against them and referred to the scripture to discount the notion of a sun-centered universe. This letter and the one following in Document 5 aroused the attention of authorities and marked the beginning of Galileo's conflict with the church.

The seal of my pleasure was to hear him [Mr. Niccolò Arrighetti] re-late the arguments which, through the great kindness of their Most Serene Highnesses, you had the occasion of advancing at their table and then of continuing in the chambers of the Most Serene Lady-ship, in the presence also of the Grand Duke and the Most Serene Archduchess, the Most Illustrious and Excellent Don Antonio and Don Paolo Giordano, and some of the very excellent philosophers there. What greater fortune can you wish than to see their High-nesses themselves enjoying discussing with you, putting forth doubts, listening to your solutions, and finally remaining satisfied with your answers?

After Mr. Arrighetti related the details you had mentioned, they gave me the occasion to go back to examine some general ques-tions about the use of the Holy Scripture in disputes involving phys-ical conclusions and some particular other ones about Joshua's passage,[1] which was presented in opposition to the earth's motion and sun's stability by the Grand Duchess Dowager with some sup-port by the Most Serene Archduchess.

In regard to the first general point of the Most Serene Ladyship, it seems to me very prudent of her to propose and of you to concede and to agree that the Holy Scripture can never lie or err, and that its declarations are absolutely and inviolably true. I should have added only that, though the Scripture cannot err, nevertheless some of its interpreters and expositors can sometimes err in vari-ous ways. One of these would be very serious and very frequent, namely to want to limit oneself always to the literal meaning of the words; for there would thus emerge not only various contradictions but also serious heresies and blasphemies, and it would be neces-sary to attribute to God feet, hands, and eyes, as well as bodily and human feelings like anger, regret, hate, and sometimes even for-getfulness of things past and ignorance of future ones. Thus in the Scripture one finds many propositions which look different from the truth if one goes by the literal meaning of the words, but which are expressed in this manner to accommodate the incapacity of common people; likewise, for the few who deserve to be separated from the masses, it is necessary that wise interpreters produce their true meaning and indicate the particular reasons why they have been expressed by means of such words.

Thus, given that in many places the Scripture is not only capable but necessarily in need of interpretations different from the appar-ent meaning of the words, it seems to me that in disputes about nat-ural phenomena it should be reserved to the last place. For the Holy Scripture and nature both equally derive from the divine Word, the former as the dictation of the Holy Spirit, the latter as the most obe-

---

1. The Joshua passage was used to prove that the sun moves around the earth. "Then spake Joshua to the Lord . . . Sun, stand still. . . . So the sun stood still in the midst of the heaven, and hasted not to go down about a whole day." Joshua 10:12–13.

dient executrix [one who carries out the will of another] of God's commands; moreover, in order to adapt itself to the understanding of all people, it was appropriate for the Scripture to say many things which are different from absolute truth, in appearance and in regard to the meaning of the words; on the other hand, nature is inexorable and immutable, and she does not care at all whether or not her recondite reasons and modes of operations are revealed to human understanding, and so she never transgresses the terms of the laws imposed on her; therefore, whatever sensory experience places before our eyes or necessary demonstrations prove to us concerning natural effects should not in any way be called into question on account of scriptural passages whose words appear to have a different meaning, since not every statement of the Scripture is bound to obligations as severely as each effect of nature. . . .

I should believe that the authority of the Holy Writ has merely the aim of persuading men of those articles and propositions which are necessary for their salvation and surpass all human reason, and so could not become credible through some other science or any other means except the mouth of the Holy Spirit itself. However, I do not think it necessary to believe that the same God who has furnished us with senses, language, and intellect would want to bypass their use and give us by other means the information we can obtain with them. This applies especially to those sciences about which one can read only very small phrases and scattered conclusions in the Scripture, as is particularly the case for astronomy, of which it contains such a small portion that one does not even find in it the names of all the planets; but if the first sacred writers had been thinking of persuading the people about the arrangement and the movements of the heavenly bodies, they would not have treated of them so sparsely, which is to say almost nothing in comparison to the infinity of very lofty and admirable conclusions contained in such a science. . . .

For I have discovered and conclusively demonstrated that the solar globe turns on itself, completing an entire rotation in about one lunar month, in exactly the same direction as all the other heavenly revolutions; moreover, it is very probable and reasonable that, as the chief instrument and minister of nature and almost the heart of the world, the sun gives not only light (as it obviously does) but also motion to all the planets that revolve around it; hence, if in conformity with Copernicus's position the diurnal motion is attributed to the earth, anyone can see that it sufficed stopping the sun to stop the whole system, and thus to lengthen the period of the diurnal illumination without altering in any way the rest of the mutual relationships of the planets; and that is exactly how the words of the sacred text sound. Here then is the manner in which by stopping the sun one can lengthen the day on the earth, without introducing any confusion among the parts of the world and without altering the words of the Scripture.

I have written much more than is appropriate in view of my slight illness. So I end by reminding you that I am at your service, and I kiss your hands and pray the Lord to give you happy holidays and all you desire.

Florence, 21 December 1613.

To Your Very Reverend Paternity.

> Your Most Affectionate Servant,
> Galileo Galilei.

Maurice A. Finocchiaro, ed., *The Galileo Affair: A Documentary History.* Berkeley: University of California Press, 1989.

DOCUMENT 4: THE DIFFERENT PURPOSES OF THE SCRIPTURES AND SCIENCE

Galileo followed his letter to Castelli with a letter in 1615 to the Grand Duchess Christina, who also attended the breakfast discussion with Castelli and others. In this letter Galileo mounts an elaborate defense against those who had begun circulating criticism of his views concerning Copernicanism and Scripture. Moreover, he further clarifies his views on the kind of information on which the Scripture is an authority and on which science is the better authority. These distinctions are quoted here in the excerpts from his letter to the Grand Duchess.

To the Most Serene Ladyship the Grand Duchess Dowager [mother of Grand Duke Cósimo Medici II]:

As Your Most Serene Highness knows very well, a few years ago I discovered in the heavens many particulars which had been invisible until our time. Because of their novelty, and because of some consequences deriving from them which contradict certain physical propositions commonly accepted in philosophical schools, they roused against me no small number of such professors, as if I had placed these things in heaven with my hands in order to confound nature and the sciences. These people seemed to forget that a multitude of truths contribute to inquiry and to the growth and strength of disciplines rather than to their diminution or destruction, and at the same time they showed greater affection for their own opinions than for the true ones; thus they proceeded to deny and to try to nullify those novelties, about which the senses themselves could have rendered them certain, if they had wanted to look at those novelties carefully. To this end they produced various matters, and they published some writings full of useless discussions and sprinkled with quotations from the Holy Scripture, taken from passages which they do not properly understand and which they inappropriately adduce. This was a very serious error, and they might not have fallen into it had they paid attention to St. Augustine's very useful advice concerning how to proceed with care in reaching definite decisions about matters which are obscure and difficult to understand by means of reason alone. . . .

Therefore, I think that in disputes about natural phenomena one must begin not with the authority of scriptural passages but with sensory experience and necessary demonstrations. For the Holy Scripture and nature derive equally from the Godhead, the former as the dictation of the Holy Spirit and the latter as the most obedient executrix [one who carries out the will] of God's orders; moreover, to accommodate the understanding of the common people it is appropriate for Scripture to say many things that are different (in appearance and in regard to the literal meaning of the words) from the absolute truth; on the other hand, nature is inexorable and immutable, never violates the terms of the laws imposed upon her, and does not care whether or not her recondite reasons and ways of operating are disclosed to human understanding; but not every scriptural assertion is bound to obligations as severe as every natural phenomenon; finally, God reveals Himself to us no less excellently in the effects of nature than in the sacred words of Scripture, as [theologian Quintus] Tertullian perhaps meant when he said, "We postulate that God ought first to be known by nature, and afterward further known by doctrine—by nature through His works, by doctrine through official teaching" (*Against Marcion,* 1.18); and so it seems that a natural phenomenon which is placed before our eyes by sensory experience or proved by necessary demonstrations should not be called into question, let alone condemned, on account of scriptural passages whose words appear to have a different meaning.

However, by this I do not wish to imply that one should not have the highest regard for passages of Holy Scripture; indeed, after becoming certain of some physical conclusions, we should use these as very appropriate aids to the correct interpretation of Scripture and to the investigation of the truths they must contain, for they are most true and agree with demonstrated truths. That is, I would say that the authority of Holy Scripture aims chiefly at persuading men about those articles and propositions which, surpassing all human reason, could not be discovered by scientific research or by any other means than through the mouth of the Holy Spirit himself. Moreover, even in regard to those propositions which are not articles of faith, the authority of the same Holy Writ should have priority over the authority of any human writings containing pure narration or even probable reasons, but no demonstrative proofs; this principle should be considered appropriate and necessary inasmuch as divine wisdom surpasses all human judgment and speculation. . . .

Let us now come down from these matters to our particular point. We have seen that the Holy Spirit did not want to teach us whether heaven moves or stands still, nor whether its shape is spherical or like a discus or extended along a plane, nor whether the earth is located at its center or on one side. So it follows as a necessary consequence that the Holy Spirit also did not intend to teach us about other questions of the same kind and connected to those just mentioned in such a way that without knowing the truth about the former one cannot decide the latter, such as the question of the motion or rest of the earth or sun. But if the Holy Spirit deliberately avoided teaching us such propositions, inasmuch as they are of no relevance to His intention (that is, to our salvation), how can one now say that to hold this rather than that proposition on this topic is so important that one is a principle of faith and the other erroneous? Thus, can an opinion be both heretical and irrelevant to the salvation of souls? Or can one say that the Holy Spirit chose not to teach us something relevant to our salvation? Here I would say what I heard from an ecclesiastical person in a very eminent position (Cardinal Baronio), namely that the intention of the Holy Spirit is to teach us how one goes to heaven and not how heaven goes.

Maurice A. Finocciaro, ed., *The Galileo Affair: A Documentary History.* Berkeley: University of California Press, 1989.

DOCUMENT 5: PROCEEDINGS OF GALILEO'S FIRST TRIAL

Vatican manuscripts record the proceedings of Galileo's trial in 1616. On February 25, 1616, the Pope ordered Galileo to abandon his Copernican beliefs or be imprisoned. That order was given to Galileo at a meeting on February 26, but Galileo did not receive a copy of the minutes of that meeting. The minutes of the meeting on March 3, 1616, report that Galileo had complied with the Pope's order, and they also review the index of prohibited books (including Copernicus's book). When Galileo requested a written report of the February 26 proceeding, Cardinal Bellarmine wrote the report dated May 26, 1616, in which he omitted the sentence ordering Galileo "not to hold, teach, or defend" his Copernican ideas. He was told only that his Copernican ideas were wrong. Galileo tried to use the discrepancy between the two reports in his defense during the second trial in 1633.

Inquisition Minutes (25 February 1616)
    Thursday, 25 February 1616.
    The Most Illustrious Lord Cardinal Millini [secretary of the Holy Office] notified the Reverend Fathers Lord Assessor and Lord Commissary of the Holy Office that, after the reporting of the judgment by the Father Theologians against the propositions of the mathematician Galileo (to the effect that the sun stands still at the center of the world and the earth moves even with the diurnal motion), His Holiness ordered the Most Illustrious Lord Cardinal Bellarmine to call Galileo before himself and warn him to abandon these opinions; and if he should refuse to obey, the Father Commissary, in the presence of a notary and witnesses, is to issue him an injunction to abstain completely from teaching or defending this doctrine and opinion or from discussing it; and further, if he should not acquiesce, he is to be imprisoned.

Special Injunction (26 February 1616)

Friday, the 26th of the same month.

At the palace of the usual residence of the said Most Illustrious Lord Cardinal Bellarmine and in the chambers of His Most Illustrious Lordship, and fully in the presence of the Reverend Father Michelangelo Segizzi of Lodi, O.P. and Commissary General of the Holy Office, having summoned the above-mentioned Galileo before himself, the same Most Illustrious Lord Cardinal warned Galileo that the abovementioned opinion was erroneous and that he should abandon it; and thereafter, indeed immediately, before me and witnesses, the Most Illustrious Lord Cardinal himself being also present still, the aforesaid Father Commissary, in the name of His Holiness the Pope and the whole Congregation of the Holy Office, ordered and enjoined the said Galileo, who was himself still present, to abandon completely the abovementioned opinion that the sun stands still at the center of the world and the earth moves, and henceforth not to hold, teach, or defend it in any way whatever, either orally or in writing; otherwise the Holy Office would start proceedings against him. The same Galileo acquiesced in this injunction and promised to obey.

Done in Rome at the place mentioned above, in the presence, as witnesses, of the Reverend Badino Nores of Nicosia in the kingdom of Cyprus and Agostino Mongardo from the Abbey of Rose in the diocese of Montepulciano, both belonging to the household of the said Most Illustrious Lord Cardinal.

Inquisition Minutes (3 March 1616)

The Most Illustrious Lord Cardinal Bellarmine having given the report that the mathematician Galileo Galilei had acquiesced when warned of the order by the Holy Congregation to abandon the opinion which he held till then, to the effect that the sun stands still at the center of the spheres but the earth is in motion, and the Decree of the Congregation of the Index [of prohibited books] having been presented, in which were prohibited and suspended, respectively, the writings of Nicolaus Copernicus *On the Revolutions of the Heavenly Spheres*, of Diego Zuñiga *On Job*, and of the Carmelite Father Paolo Antonio Foscarini, His Holiness ordered that the edict of this suspension and prohibition, respectively, be published by the Master of the Sacred Palace.

Cardinal Bellarmine's Certificate (26 May 1616)

We, Robert Cardinal Bellarmine, have heard that Mr. Galileo Galilei is being slandered or alleged to have abjured in our hands and also to have been given salutary penances for this. Having been sought about the truth of the matter, we say that the abovementioned Galileo has not abjured in our hands, or in the hands of others here in Rome, or anywhere else that we know, any opinion or doctrine of his; nor has he received any penances, salutary or otherwise. On the contrary, he has only been notified of the declaration made by the Holy Father and published by the Sacred Congregation of the Index, whose content is that the doctrine attributed to Copernicus (that the earth moves around the sun and the sun stands at the center of the world without moving from east to west) is contrary to Holy Scripture and therefore cannot be defended or held. In witness whereof we have written and signed this with our own hands, on this 26th day of May 1616.

The same mentioned above,
Robert Cardinal Bellarmine.

Maurice A. Finocchiaro, ed., *The Galileo Affair: A Documentary History*. Berkeley: University of California Press, 1989.

DOCUMENT 6: GALILEO CONCLUDES HIS *DIALOGUE* IN A MOCKING TONE

At the conclusion of Dialogue Concerning the Two Chief World Systems, *Galileo restates his major points. Then, in a tone of mockery, Galileo feigns—through the words of his character Salviati—his limitations and his doubts about the validity of his ideas. And from the mouth of his simpleton character, Simplicio, who defends the earth-centered universe, he mimics the Pope's argument. Needless to say, church authorities were unhappy with Galileo, both because of his views and because of his insults.*

In the conversations of these four days we have, then, strong evidences in favor of the Copernican system, among which three have been shown to be very convincing—those taken from the stoppings and retrograde motions of the planets, and their approaches toward and recessions from the earth; second, from the revolution of the sun upon itself, and from what is to be observed in the sunspots; and third, from the ebbing and flowing of the ocean tides.

Salviati. To these there may perhaps be added a fourth, and maybe even a fifth. The fourth, I mean, may come from the fixed stars, since by extremely accurate observations of these there may be discovered those minimal changes that Copernicus took to be imperceptible. And at present there is transpiring a fifth novelty from which the mobility of the earth might be argued. This is being revealed most perspicuously by the illustrious Caesar Marsili, of a most noble family at Bologna, and a Lincean Academician. He explains in a very learned manuscript that he has observed a continual change, though a very slow one, in the meridian line. I have recently seen this treatise, and it has much astonished me. I hope that he will make it available to all students of the marvels of nature.

Sagredo. This is not the first time that I have heard mention of the subtle learning of this gentleman, who has shown himself to be the zealous protector of all men of science and letters. If this or any other of his works is made public, we may be sure in advance that it will become famous.

Salviati. Now, since it is time to put an end to our discourses, it remains for me to beg you that if later, in going over the things that I have brought out, you should meet with any difficulty or any question not completely resolved, you will excuse my deficiency because of the novelty of the concept and the limitations of my abilities; then because of the magnitude of the subject; and finally because I do not claim and have not claimed from others that assent which I myself do not give to this invention, which may very easily turn out to be a most foolish hallucination and a majestic paradox.

To you, Sagredo, though during my arguments you have shown yourself satisfied with some of my ideas and have approved them highly, I say that I take this to have arisen partly from their novelty rather than from their certainty, and even more from your courteous wish to afford me by your assent that pleasure which one naturally feels at the approbation and praise of what is one's own. And as you have obligated me to you by your urbanity, so Simplicio has pleased me by his ingenuity. Indeed, I have become very fond of him for his constancy in sustaining so forcibly and so undauntedly the doctrines of his master. And I thank you, Sagredo, for your most courteous motivation, just as I ask pardon of Simplicio if I have offended him sometimes with my too heated and opinionated speech. Be sure that in this I have not been moved by any ulterior purpose, but only by that of giving you every opportunity to introduce lofty thoughts, that I might be the better informed.

Simplicio. You need not make any excuses; they are superfluous, and especially so to me, who, being accustomed to public debates, have heard disputants countless times not merely grow angry and get excited at each other, but even break out into insulting speech and sometimes come very close to blows.

As to the discourses we have held, and especially this last one concerning the reasons for the ebbing and flowing of the ocean, I am really not entirely convinced; but from such feeble ideas of the matter as I have formed, I admit that your thoughts seem to me more ingenious than many others I have heard. I do not therefore consider them true and conclusive; indeed, keeping always before my mind's eye a most solid doctrine[1] that I once heard from a most eminent and learned person, and before which one must fall silent, I know that if asked whether God in His infinite power and wisdom could have conferred upon the watery element its observed reciprocating motion using some other means than moving its containing vessels, both of you would reply that He could have, and that He would have known how to do this in many ways which are unthinkable to our minds. From this I forthwith conclude that, this being so, it would be excessive boldness for anyone to limit and restrict the Divine power and wisdom to some particular fancy of his own.

Salviati. An admirable and angelic doctrine, and well in accord

---

1. This is the famous passage setting forth the favorite argument of Pope Urban VIII against the conclusiveness of this "proof" of the motion of the earth.

with another one, also Divine, which, while it grants to us the right to argue about the constitution of the universe (perhaps in order that the working of the human mind shall not be curtailed or made lazy) adds that we cannot discover the work of His hands. Let us, then, exercise these activities permitted to us and ordained by God, that we may recognize and thereby so much the more admire His greatness, however much less fit we may find ourselves to penetrate the profound depths of His infinite wisdom.

Sagredo. And let this be the final conclusion of our four days' arguments, after which if Salviati should desire to take some interval of rest, our continuing curiosity must grant that much to him. But this is on condition that when it is more convenient for him, he will return and satisfy our desires—mine in particular—regarding the problems set aside and noted down by me to submit to him, at one or two further sessions, in accordance with our agreement. Above all, I shall be waiting impatiently to hear the elements of our Academician's new science of natural and constrained local motions.

Meanwhile, according to our custom, let us go and enjoy an hour of refreshment in the gondola that awaits us.

Galileo Galilei, *Dialogue Concerning the Two Chief World Systems—Ptolemaic & Copernican.* Trans. by Stillman Drake, foreword by Albert Einstein. Berkeley: University of California Press, 1953.

DOCUMENT 7: GALILEO'S *DIALOGUE* VIOLATES 1616 INJUNCTION

The Vatican clerk reviewing Galileo's 1632 Dialogue *concludes that in this book Galileo transgressed the words "teach and defend." These words were originally stated in the injunction of February 26, 1616, the document Galileo never saw.*

Pasqualigo's Report on the Dialogue
(17 April 1633)

I, Zaccaria Pasqualigo, Clerk Regular, Professor of Sacred Theology, in the presence of the Most Eminent and Most Reverend Cardinal Ginetti, Vicar of His Holiness Pope Urban VIII, have been asked whether Galileo Galilei, by the publication of his *Dialogue* where he deals with the Copernican system, has transgressed the injunction by which the Holy Office prohibits him to hold, teach, or defend in any way whatever, orally or in writing, this opinion of the earth's motion and sun's immobility at the center of the world. Having diligently inspected his book, I am of the opinion that he transgressed it as regards the words "teach or defend," since indeed he tries as best he can to support the earth's motion and the sun's immobility, and also that he is strongly suspected of holding such an opinion. And so for the formal declaration of these things I sign with my own hand.

Zaccaria Pasqualigo, Clerk Regular,
Professor of Sacred Theology.

Maurice A. Finocchiaro, ed., *The Galileo Affair: A Documentary History.* Berkeley: University of California Press, 1989.

DOCUMENT 8: GALILEO'S SENTENCING

After four sessions of questioning, the Inquisition sentenced Galileo on June 22, 1633. The excerpt from the Inquisition's sentence states the reason he was found guilty and the punishment imposed. Of the ten Cardinals, seven signed the sentence.

Because we did not think you had said the whole truth about your intention, we deemed it necessary to proceed against you by a rigorous examination. Here you answered in a Catholic manner, though without prejudice to the above-mentioned matters confessed by you and deduced against you about your intention.

Therefore, having seen and seriously considered the merits of your case, together with the above-mentioned confessions and excuses and with any other reasonable matter worth seeing and considering, we have come to the final sentence against you given below.

Therefore, invoking the Most Holy name of Our Lord Jesus Christ and his most glorious Mother, ever Virgin Mary; and sitting as a tribunal, with the advice and counsel of the Reverend Masters of Sacred Theology and the Doctors of both laws, our consultants; in this written opinion we pronounce final judgment on the case pending before us between the Magnificent Carlo Sinceri, Doctor of both laws, and Prosecuting Attorney of this Holy Office, on one side, and you the above-mentioned Galileo Galilei, the culprit here present, examined, tried, and confessed as above, on the other side:

We say, pronounce, sentence, and declare that you, the above-mentioned Galileo, because of the things deduced in the trial and confessed by you as above, have rendered yourself according to this Holy Office vehemently suspected of heresy,[1] namely of having held and believed a doctrine which is false and contrary to the divine and Holy Scripture: that the sun is the center of the world and does not move from east to west, and the earth moves and is not the center of the world, and that one may hold and defend as probable an opinion after it has been declared and defined contrary to Holy Scripture. Consequently you have incurred all the censures and penalties imposed and promulgated by the sacred canons and all particular and general laws against such delinquents. We are willing to absolve you from them provided that first, with a sincere heart and unfeigned faith, in front of us you abjure, curse, and detest the above-mentioned errors and heresies, and every other error and heresy contrary to the Catholic and Apostolic Church, in the manner and form we will prescribe to you.

Furthermore, so that this serious and pernicious error and transgression of yours does not remain completely unpunished, and so that you will be more cautious in the future and an example for others to abstain from similar crimes, we order that the book *Dialogue* by Galileo Galilei be prohibited by public edict.

---

1. "Vehement suspicion of heresy" was a technical term designating a specific category of crime, second in seriousness only to formal heresy.

We condemn you to formal imprisonment in this Holy Office at our pleasure. As a salutary penance we impose on you to recite the seven penitential Psalms once a week for the next three years. And we reserve the authority to moderate, change, or condone wholly or in part the above-mentioned penalties and penances.

This we say, pronounce, sentence, declare, order, and reserve by this or any other better manner or form that we reasonably can or shall think of.

So we the undersigned Cardinals pronounce:

> Felice Cardinal d' Ascoli.
> Guido Cardinal Bentivoglio.
> Fra Desiderio Cardinal di Cremona.
> Fra Antonio Cardinal di Sant' Onofrio.
> Berlinghiero Cardinal Gessi.
> Fabrizio Cardinal Verospi.
> Marzio Cardinal Ginetti.

Maurice A. Finocchiaro, ed., *The Galileo Affair: A Documentary History.* Berkeley: University of California Press, 1989.

DOCUMENT 9: GALILEO'S ABJURATION

At the sentencing session on June 22, 1633, Galileo, dressed in the white robe of the penitent, knelt and read aloud this abjuration, a text which had been prepared by the Holy Tribunal. Because Galileo had been threatened with torture and perhaps death, he complied with the Tribunal's words and conclusions; a story prevails, however, that as Galileo rose from his knees, he muttered under his breath, "Eppur si muove" (But still it moves).

I, Galileo, son of the late Vincenzio Galilei of Florence, seventy years of age, arraigned personally for judgment, kneeling before you Most Eminent and Most Reverend Cardinals Inquisitors-General against heretical depravity in all of Christendom, having before my eyes and touching with my hands the Holy Gospels, swear that I have always believed, I believe now, and with God's help I will believe in the future all that the Holy Catholic and Apostolic Church holds, preaches, and teaches. However, whereas, after having been judicially instructed with injunction by the Holy Office to abandon completely the false opinion that the sun is the center of the world and does not move and the earth is not the center of the world and moves, and not to hold, defend, or teach this false doctrine in any way whatever, orally or in writing; and after having been notified that this doctrine is contrary to Holy Scripture; I wrote and published a book in which I treat of this already condemned doctrine and adduce very effective reasons in its favor, without refuting them in any way; therefore, I have been judged vehemently suspected of heresy, namely of having held and believed that the sun is the center of the world and motionless and the earth is not the center and moves.

Therefore, desiring to remove from the minds of Your Eminences and every faithful Christian this vehement suspicion, rightly conceived against me, with a sincere heart and unfeigned faith I abjure, curse, and detest the above-mentioned errors and heresies, and in general each and every other error, heresy, and sect contrary to the Holy Church; and I swear that in the future I will never again say or assert, orally or in writing, anything which might cause a similar suspicion about me; on the contrary, if I should come to know any heretic or anyone suspected of heresy, I will denounce him to this Holy Office, or to the Inquisitor or Ordinary of the place where I happen to be.

Furthermore, I swear and promise to comply with and observe completely all the penances which have been or will be imposed upon me by this Holy Office; and should I fall to keep any of these promises and oaths, which God forbid, I submit myself to all the penalties and punishments imposed and promulgated by the sacred canons and other particular and general laws against similar delinquents. So help me God and these Holy Gospels of His, which I touch with my hands.

I, the above-mentioned Galileo Galilei, have abjured, sworn, promised, and obliged myself as above; and in witness of the truth I have signed with my own hand the present document of abjuration and have recited it word for word in Rome, at the convent of the Minerva, this twenty-second day of June 1633.

I, Galileo Galilei, have abjured as above, by my own hand.

Maurice A. Finocchiaro, ed., *The Galileo Affair: A Documentary History.* Berkeley: University of California Press, 1989.

Document 10: Galileo Comforted by His Daughter

Galileo's oldest daughter, the nun Suor Maria Celeste, kept a regular correspondence with her father and supported him during years of work and turmoil. In the first letter quoted here, Maria Celeste responds to the news of her father's sentencing; in the second she offers to take over his required recitation of Psalms; and in the third she awaits his return home.

Most Illustrious and Beloved Lord Father

Just as suddenly and unexpectedly as word of your new torment reached me, Sire, so intensely did it pierce my soul with pain to hear the judgment that has finally been passed, denouncing your person as harshly as your book. I learned all this by importuning Signor Geri, because, not having any letters from you this week, I could not calm myself, as though I already knew all that had happened.

My dearest lord father, now is the time to avail yourself more than ever of that prudence which the Lord God has granted you, bearing these blows with that strength of spirit which your religion, your profession, and your age require. And since you, by virtue of your vast experience, can lay claim to full cognizance of the fallacy and instability of everything in this miserable world, you must not make too much of these storms, but rather take hope that they will soon subside and transform themselves from troubles into as many satisfactions.

In saying all that I am speaking what my own desires dictate, and also what seems a promise of leniency demonstrated toward you, Sire, by His Holiness, who has destined for your prison a place so delightful, whereby it appears we may anticipate another commutation of your sentence conforming even more closely with all your and our wishes; may it please God to see things turn out that way, if it be for the best. Meanwhile I pray you not to leave me without the consolation of your letters, giving me reports of your condition, physically and especially spiritually: though I conclude my writing here, I never cease to accompany you with my thoughts and prayers, calling on His Divine Majesty to grant you true peace and consolation.

From San Matteo, the 2nd day of July 1633.

Most affectionate daughter,

S.M. Celeste

Most Beloved Lord Father

Saturday I wrote to you, Sire, and Sunday, thanks to Signor [Niccolò] Gherardini [a young admirer, and later biographer, of Galileo, who was related to Suor Elisabetta], your letter was delivered to me, through which, learning of the hope you hold out for your return, I am consoled, as every hour seems a thousand years to me while I await that promised day when I shall see you again; and hearing that you continue to enjoy your well-being only doubles my desire to experience the manifold happiness and satisfaction that will come from watching you return to your own home and moreover in good health.

I would surely not want you to doubt my devotion, for at no time do I ever leave off commending you with all my soul to blessed God, because you fill my heart, Sire, and nothing matters more to me than your spiritual and physical well-being. And to give you some tangible proof of this concern, I tell you that I succeeded in obtaining permission to view your sentence, the reading of which, though on the one hand it grieved me wretchedly, on the other hand it thrilled me to have seen it and found in it a means of being able to do you good, Sire, in some very small way; that is by taking upon myself the obligation you have to recite one time each week the seven psalms, and I have already begun to fulfill this requirement and to do so with great zest, first because I believe that prayer accompanied by the claim of obedience to Holy Church is effective, and then, too, to relieve you of this care. Therefore had I been able to substitute myself in the rest of your punishment, most willingly would I elect a prison even straiter than this one in which I dwell, if by so doing I could set you at liberty. Now we have come this far, and the many favors we have already received give us hope of having still others bestowed on us, provided that our faith is accompanied by good works, for, as you know better than I, Sire, *fides sine operibus mortua est* [faith without works is lifeless].

My dear Suor Luisa continues to fare badly, and because of the pains and spasm that afflict her right side, from the shoulder to the hip, she can hardly bear to stay in bed, but sits up on a chair day and night: the doctor told me the last time he came to visit her that he suspected she had an ulcer in her kidney, and that if this were her problem it would be incurable; the worst thing of all for me is to see her suffer without being able to help her at all, because my remedies bring her no relief.

Yesterday they put the funnels in the six barrels of rose wine, and all that remains now is to refill the cask. Signor Rondinelli was there, just as he also attended the harvesting of the grapes, and told me that the must was fermenting vigorously so that he hoped it would turn out well, though there is not a lot of it; I do not yet know exactly how much. This is all that for now in great haste I am able to tell you. I send you loving regards on behalf of our usual friends, and pray the Lord to bless you.

From San Matteo, the 3rd day of October 1633.

Most affectionate daughter,

S.M. Celeste

Most Beloved Lord Father

Only a moment before the news of your dispatch reached me, Sire, I had taken my pen in hand to write to Her Ladyship the Ambassadress to beg her once more to intercede in this affair; for having watched it wear on so long, I feared that it might not be resolved even by the end of this year, and thus my sudden joy was as great as it was unexpected: nor are your daughters alone in our rejoicing, but all these nuns, by their grace, give signs of true happiness, just as so many of them have sympathized with me in my suffering.

We are awaiting your arrival with great longing, and we cheer ourselves to see how the weather has cleared for your journey.

Signor Geri was leaving this morning with the Court [for the annual winter session at Pisa], and I made sure to have him notified before daybreak of your return, Sire; seeing as he had already learned something of the decision, and came here last evening to tell me what he knew.

I also explained to him the reason you have not written to him, Sire, and I bemoaned the fact that he will not be here when you arrive to share in our celebration, since he is truly a perfect gentleman, honest and loyal.

I set aside the container of verdea wine, which Signor Francesco could not bring along because his litter was too overloaded. You will be able to send it to the Archbishop later, when the litter makes a return trip: the citron candy morsels I have already consigned to him. The casks for the white wine are all in order.

More I cannot say for the dearth of time, except that all of us send you our loving regards.

From San Matteo, the 10th day of December 1633.

Your most affectionate daughter,

S.M. Celeste

Dava Sobel, *Galileo's Daughter.* New York: Walker, 1999.

DOCUMENT 11: PHYSICS TAUGHT BY DIALOGUE

In his last and greatest work, Dialogues Concerning Two New Sciences, *Galileo refines his work on mechanics and motion, but presents it in his usual form of dialogues involving three characters: Salviati (Galileo), Sagredo, and Simplicio. The excerpt from the fourth day of conversations about physics illustrates the dialogue form.*

Salviati. Once more, Simplicio is here on time; so let us without delay take up the question of motion. The text of our Author is as follows:

The Motion of Projectiles

In the preceding pages we have discussed the properties of uniform motion and of motion naturally accelerated along planes of all inclinations. I now propose to set forth those properties which belong to a body whose motion is compounded of two other motions, namely, one uniform and one naturally accelerated; these properties, well worth knowing, I propose to demonstrate in a rigid manner. This is the kind of motion seen in a moving projectile; its origin I conceive to be as follows:

Imagine any particle projected along a horizontal plane without friction; then we know, from what has been more fully explained in the preceding pages, that this particle will move along this same plane with a motion which is uniform and perpetual, provided the plane has no limits. But if the plane is limited and elevated, then the moving particle, which we imagine to be a heavy one, will on passing over the edge of the plane acquire, in addition to its previous uniform and perpetual motion, a downward propensity due to its own weight; so that the resulting motion, which I call projection [*projectio*], is compounded of one which is uniform and horizontal and of another which is vertical and naturally accelerated. We now proceed to demonstrate some of its properties, the first of which is as follows:

Theorem I, Proposition I

A projectile which is carried by a uniform horizontal motion compounded with a naturally accelerated vertical motion describes a path which is a semi-parabola.

Sagredo. Here, Salviati, it will be necessary to stop a little while for my sake and, I believe, also for the benefit of Simplicio; for it so happens that I have not gone very far in my study of Apollonius and am merely aware of the fact that he treats of the parabola and other conic sections, without an understanding of which I hardly think one will be able to follow the proof of other propositions depending upon them. Since even in this first beautiful theorem the author finds it necessary to prove that the path of a projectile is a parabola, and since, as I imagine, we shall have to deal with only this kind of curves, it will be absolutely necessary to have a thorough acquaintance, if not with all the properties which Apollonius has demonstrated for these figures, at least with those which are needed for the present treatment.

Salviati. You are quite too modest, pretending ignorance of facts which not long ago you acknowledged as well known—I mean at the time when we were discussing the strength of materials and needed to use a certain theorem of Apollonius which gave you no trouble.

Sagredo. I may have chanced to know it or may possibly have assumed it, so long as needed, for that discussion; but now when we have to follow all these demonstrations about such curves we ought not, as they say, to swallow it whole, and thus waste time and energy.

Simplicio. Now even though Sagredo is, as I believe, well equipped for all his needs, I do not understand even the elementary terms; for although our philosophers have treated the motion of projectiles, I do not recall their having described the path of a projectile except to state in a general way that it is always a curved line, unless the projection be vertically upwards. But if the little Euclid [geometry] which I have learned since our previous discussion does not enable me to understand the demonstrations which are to follow, then I shall be obliged to accept the theorems on faith without fully comprehending them.

Salviati. On the contrary, I desire that you should understand them from the Author himself, who, when he allowed me to see this work of his, was good enough to prove for me two of the principal properties of the parabola because I did not happen to have at hand the books of Apollonius. These properties, which are the only ones we shall need in the present discussion, he proved in such a way that no prerequisite knowledge was required.

Galileo Galilei, *Dialogues Concerning Two New Sciences.* Trans. by Henry Crew and Alfonso de Salvio. Intro. by Antonio Favaro. New York: Dover, 1954.

Chronology

1543

Nicolaus Copernicus publishes *On the Revolutions of the Heavenly Spheres.*

1559

First Index of Prohibited Books compiled by the Roman Inquisition.

1564

Galileo Galilei is born in Pisa on February 15; Michelangelo Buonarroti dies in Florence on February 18; William Shakespeare is born in England on April 23.

1569

Cosimo I, duke of Florence, is named grand duke of Tuscany by Pope Pius V.

1571

German astronomer Johannes Kepler is born.

1572

Danish astronomer Tycho Brahe observes a new star.

1581

Galileo enrolls at the University of Pisa.

1585

Galileo leaves the University of Pisa without a degree.

1589

Galileo begins teaching at the University of Pisa and begins to study falling bodies.

1591

Vincenzio Galilei (father) dies.

1592

Galileo begins teaching at the University of Padua.

1600

Virginia Galilei (daughter) is born in Padua.

1601

Livia Galilei (daughter) is born in Padua.

1604

A new star appears in the heavens; Galileo gives three lectures on it.

1605

Prince Cosimo de' Medici becomes Galileo's pupil.

1606

Galileo publishes a treatise on his geometric and military compass; Vincenzio Galilei (son) is born in Padua.

1609

Kepler publishes his *New Astronomy;* Galileo builds a strong telescope and observes the moon's surface.

1610

Galileo discovers the moons of Jupiter; *Starry Messenger* is published in Venice; Galileo is appointed court mathematician and philosopher to the grand duke of Tuscany, Cosimo II.

1611

Galileo visits Rome and is appointed to membership in the Lyncean Academy.

1612

Bodies That Stay Atop Water or Move Within It is published in Florence.

1613

Letters on the Solar Spots is published in Rome; Virginia and Livia Galilei enter the Convent of San Matteo in Arcetri; Galileo writes *Letter to Castelli.*

1614

Dominican Tommaso Caccini preaches a sermon against Galileo and all mathematicians.

1615

Dominican Niccolò Lorini files a complaint against Galileo with the Inquisition; Caccini gives a deposition to the Inquisition charging Galileo with heresy; Galileo writes *Letter to*

Christina and goes to Rome to clear his name and prevent condemnation of Copernicanism.

1616

Galileo writes "Theory of the Tides"; theologians decide that Copernicanism is opposed to Scripture; the pope orders Cardinal Bellarmine to warn Galileo to abandon Copernicanism; Bellarmine warns Galileo and writes a declaration on Galileo's behalf; the Congregation of the Index bans all books teaching Copernicanism; Galileo returns to Florence; Virginia Galilei takes vows as Suor Maria Celeste; William Shakespeare dies.

1617

Livia Galilei takes vows as Suor Arcangela.

1618

Three comets appear; the Thirty Years' War begins.

1619

Galileo's mate Marina Gamba dies; Vincenzio Galilei is legitimized.

1623

Galileo's sister Virginia dies; Cardinal Maffeo Barberini becomes Pope Urban VIII; *Assayer*, dedicated to Pope Urban, is published in Rome.

1624

Galileo travels to Rome for an audience with the pope; writes "Reply to Ingoli," and begins *Dialogue*.

1629

The bubonic plague enters Italy from Germany.

1630

Galileo finishes *Dialogue* and travels to Rome to obtain the printing license for it; publisher Cesi dies.

1631

Michelangelo Galilei (brother) dies from the plague in Germany; Galileo requests that *Dialogue* be reviewed and published in Florence.

1632

Dialogue Concerning the Two Chief World Systems: Ptolemaic and Copernican is published in Florence; a special papal commission reviews *Dialogue* and forwards the case to the Inquisition; Galileo is summoned to Rome but protests that he is too sick; the pope threatens to arrest Galileo.

1633

Galileo is tried for heresy by the Holy Office of the Inquisition and found guilty; *Dialogue* is prohibited; Galileo recites a public abjuration at the Convent of the Minerva and is allowed to stay with the archbishop of Siena; he begins *Two New Sciences* and is allowed to return to Arcetri under house arrest.

1634

Suor Maria Celeste Galilei dies in Arcetri.

1637

Galileo loses his eyesight.

1638

Louis Elzevir publishes *Two New Sciences* in Leiden, Holland.

1642

Galileo dies in Arcetri on January 8; Isaac Newton is born in England on December 25.

1835

Galileo's *Dialogue* is dropped from the Index of Prohibited Books.

1979

Pope John Paul II admits that Galileo suffered unjustly at the hands of the church.

FOR FURTHER RESEARCH

WORKS BY GALILEO

Maurice A. Finocchiaro, ed. and trans., *The Galileo Affair: A Documentary History.* Berkeley and Los Angeles: University of California Press, 1989. (This volume is a collection of Galileo's correspondence and miscellaneous documents.)

Galileo Galilei, *Dialogue Concerning the Two Chief World Systems: Ptolemaic and Copernican.* Trans. Stillman Drake. Berkeley and Los Angeles: University of California Press, 1953.

———, *Dialogues Concerning Two New Sciences.* Trans. Henry Crew and Alfonso de Salvio. New York: Dover, 1954.

———, *On Motion and On Mechanics: Comprising De Motu* (ca. 1590). Trans. and Intro. I.E. Drabkin. Madison: University of Wisconsin Press, 1960.

BIOGRAPHIES OF GALILEO

Stillman Drake, *Galileo.* Oxford, England: Oxford University Press, 1980.

Leonard Everett Fisher, *Galileo.* New York: Macmillan, 1992.

Ludovico Geymonat, *Galileo Galilei: A Biography and Inquiry into His Philosophy of Science.* New York: McGraw-Hill, 1957.

Institute and Museum of the History Science of Florence, Italy. www.imss.fi.it/museo/4/index.html. This virtual museum provides a biography of Galileo and pages devoted to each of his inventions. An interactive look at his manuscript pages is available at www.imss.fi.it/ms72.

Ernan McMullin, ed., *Galileo: Man of Science.* New York: Basic Books, 1967.

James Reston Jr., *Galileo: A Life*. New York: HarperCollins, 1994.

Dava Sobel, *Galileo's Daughter*. New York: Walker, 1999.

SCIENTIFIC AND HISTORICAL BACKGROUND

Sarah K. Bolton, *Famous Men of Science*. New York: Dodd, Mead, 1960.

Bertolt Brecht, *Galileo*. 1952. Trans. Charles Laughton. Ed. and Intro. Eric Bentley. New York: Grove Press, 1966.

J. Bronowski and Bruce Mazlish, *The Western Intellectual Tradition: From Leonardo to Hegel*. New York: Harper and Row, 1960.

Fritjof Capra, *The Turning Point: Science, Society, and the Rising Culture*. New York: Bantam, 1983.

A.C. Crombie, *Augustine to Galileo: The History of Science A.D. 400–1650*. London: Falcon Press, 1952.

H.G. Crowthers, *Six Great Scientists: Copernicus, Galileo, Newton, Darwin, Marie Curie, Einstein*. London: H. Hamilton, 1961.

Will and Ariel Durant, *The Age of Reason Begins: A History of European Civilization in the Period of Shakespeare, Bacon, Montaigne, Rembrandt, Galileo, and Descartes: 1558–1648*. New York: Simon and Schuster, 1961.

Donald Goldsmith, *The Astronomers*. New York: St. Martin's Press, 1991.

Hal Hellman, *Great Feuds in Science: Ten of the Liveliest Disputes Ever*. New York: John Wiley, 1998.

Rocky Kolb, *Blind Watchers of the Sky: The People and Ideas That Shaped Our View of the Universe*. New York: Addison-Wesley, 1996.

Steve Parker, *Galileo and the Universe*. New York: Harper-Collins, 1992.

Lynn and Gray Poole, *Scientists Who Changed the World*. New York: Dodd, Mead, 1960.

Frank and James M. Siedel, *Pioneers in Science*. Boston: Houghton Mifflin, 1968.

William Oliver Stevens, *Famous Scientists*. New York: Dodd, Mead, 1967.

INDEX